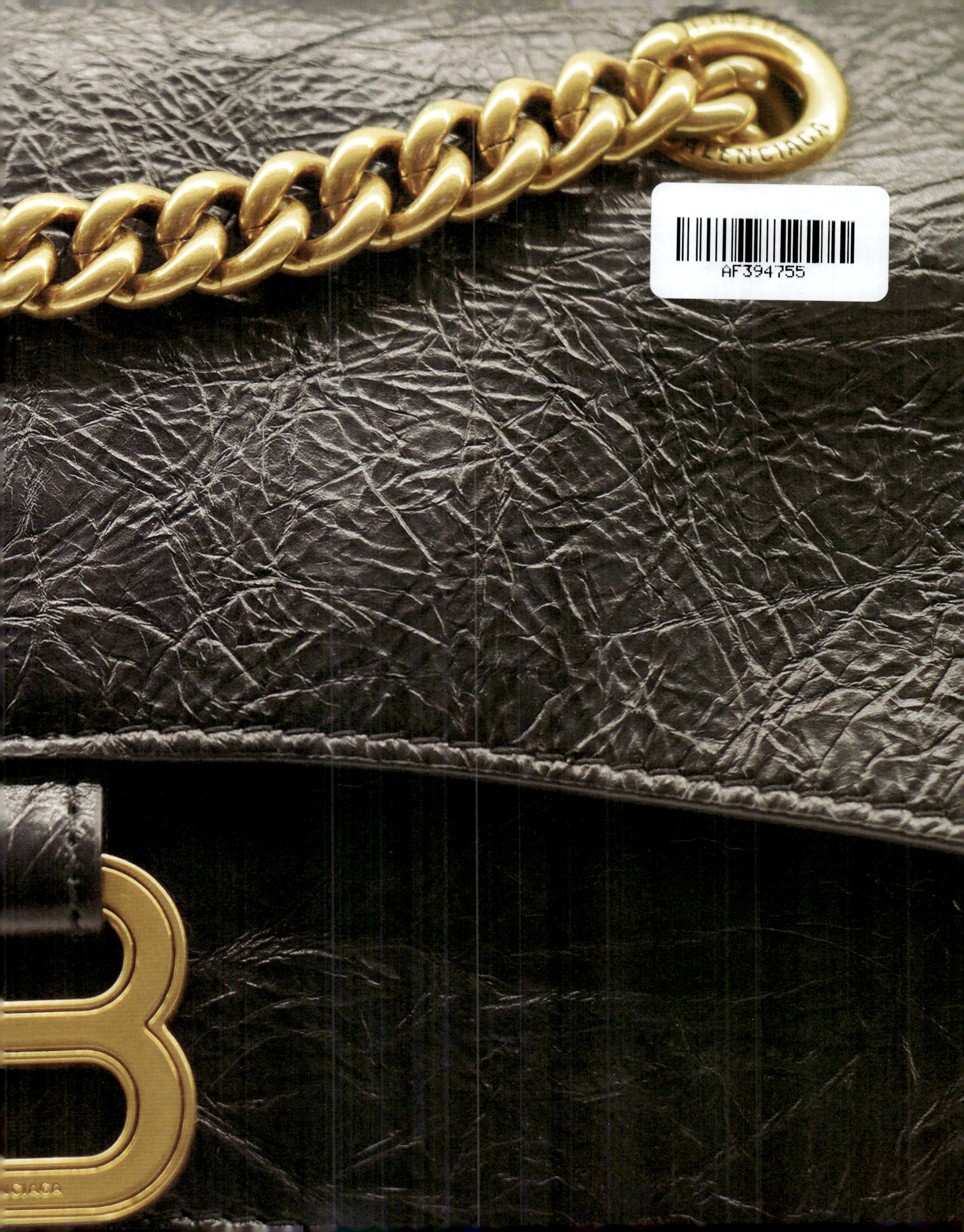

AF394755

THE FASHION ICONS

BALENCIAGA

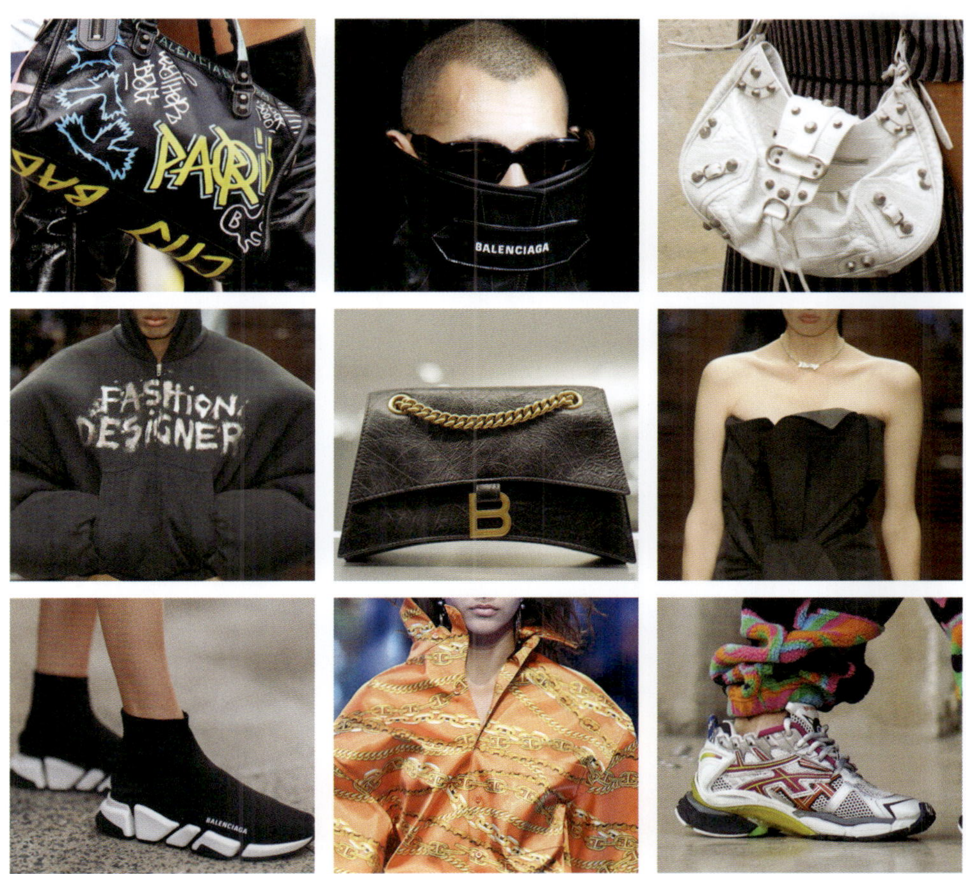

Alison James

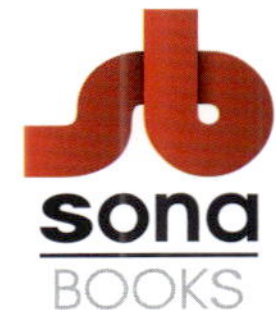

sona
BOOKS

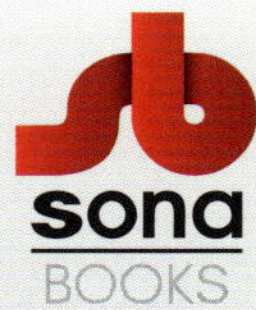

sona
BOOKS

CONTENTS

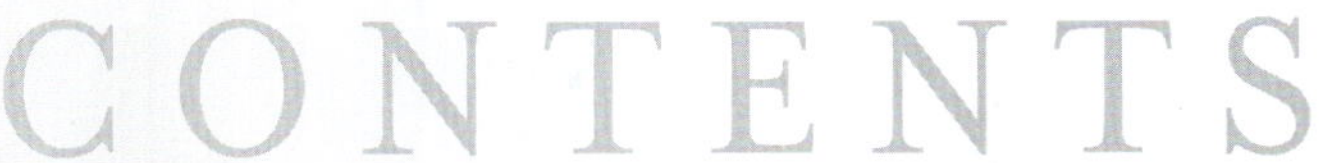

INTRODUCTION
BALENCIAGA - A LEGACY REIMAGINED

Balenciaga is not just a name – it is an almost mythical force in fashion. Born from the quiet genius of Spanish designer Cristóbal Balenciaga in 1917, the house has long stood at the crossroads of tradition and innovation. From its beginnings in the Basque Country to its reinvention in the ateliers of Paris, Balenciaga has shaped the language of sartorial style for more than a century.

Cristóbal Balenciaga was often called *'the master of us all'* by his contemporaries, including Christian Dior. Known for architectural silhouettes, pure lines and a sense of volume that defied convention, he redefined what haute couture could be. His designs weren't just worn - they were constructed, sculpted and revered. Even after his retirement in 1968, the legacy of his precision continued to influence designers worldwide.

Over the decades, Balenciaga has undergone several creative evolutions. Nicolas Ghesquière brought a futuristic edge in the early 2000s. From 2012, Demna, with his streetwise rebellion and sharp social commentary, steered the brand into bold, often controversial, territory. Each chapter has pushed boundaries while keeping the brand's DNA intact - experimental, unexpected and always ahead of its time.

Now, a new chapter begins. In 2025, Balenciaga announced the appointment of Pierpaolo Piccioli as Creative Director - a decision that both stunned and thrilled the fashion world. Known for his romantic, deeply humanistic work at Valentino, Piccioli arrives with a rare ability to blend emotion with elegance. His designs celebrate inclusivity, individuality and timeless beauty. With Piccioli at the helm, the future of Balenciaga promises an intriguing future. How will his poetic sensibility interact with Balenciaga's more radical past? Will the silhouettes soften? Will the runway, long a platform for provocation, now become a canvas of beauty, restrained elegance and quiet empathy, harking back to Cristóbal Balenciaga's 'Golden Age' of the 1950s and early '60s?

OPP PAGE: Cristóbal Balenciaga, 1927

This book invites you to explore the rich story of Balenciaga. From Cristóbal's sculptural gowns to Ghesquière's revival and Demna's streetwear revolution through to now - the advent of Piccioli's artistic journey at the label. Through archival photographs, rare sketches, runway moments and candid glimpses behind the scenes, you'll witness the evolution of one of fashion's most iconic houses.

Balenciaga has always been more than clothing. It is a study in contrasts. Structure and fluidity, classicism and rebellion, restraint and flamboyance. Under Piccioli's guidance, we may see yet another layer unfold - one rooted in humanity, artistry and quiet strength.

As you turn these pages, consider not only what fashion looks like but what it feels like. Because at its best, fashion doesn't just reflect the world - it reshapes it.

Welcome to Balenciaga.

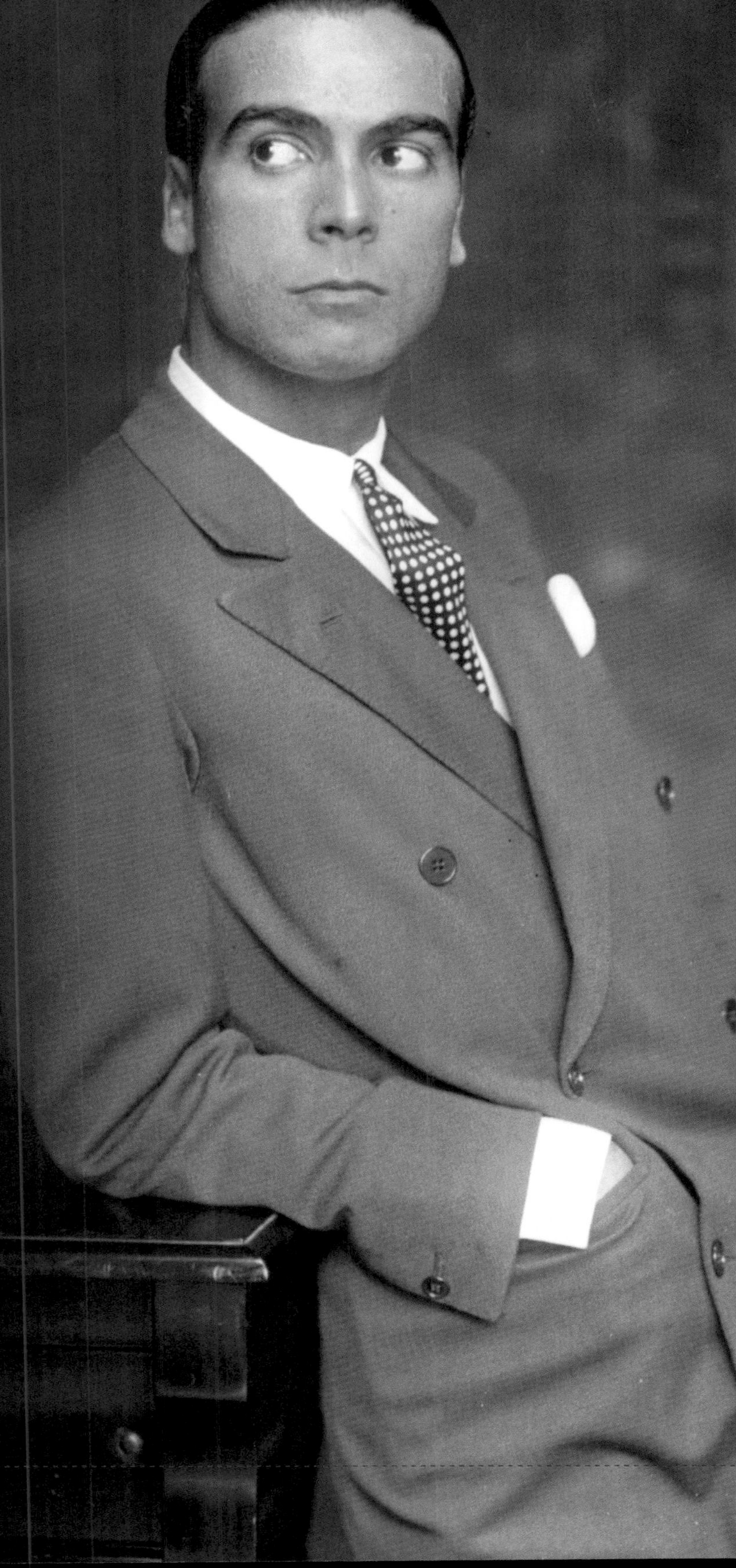

BEFORE PARIS

"I am not a tailor, I am not a dressmaker, I am a craftsman"
Cristóbal Balenciaga

It is the early 1900s in Getaria, a small fishing town situated along the rugged Basque coast of northern Spain. The young Cristóbal Balenciaga sits at the kitchen table of his modest home, watching his widowed mother sew – her needle swiftly and skilfully darting in and out of sumptuous fabric. She is a seamstress for the wealthy families of the town. It is her work that will introduce Cristóbal to the world of high society and, ultimately, see her son go on to become a fashion legend.

Thanks to his beloved mother, Balenciaga learned how to sew and developed an early respect for the craft of clothing - the weight of wool, the luxury of silks and satins, the line of a hem, the way a garment could command presence without excess. . . However, the place of his birth - the Basque region with its austere churches, bull-rings and sharply contoured landscape – also made a lasting visual impression on the young Christobal. The religious processions, traditional mantillas and flamenco costumes fed into a visual vocabulary that would reappear in his lexicon of iconic designs decades later.

Balenciaga's first break came around the age of

12. Fascinated by a Parisian ensemble worn by the Marquesa de Casa Torres, one of his mother's clients, he sketched a version of the look from memory. When asked to recreate it, he succeeded. With the Marquesa's backing, he started to study tailoring and relocated to nearby San Sebastián, a fashionable seaside retreat for Spain's aristocracy and royals, often referred to as the 'Biarritz of Spain'. He was employed at 'Casa Gomez', a well-known tailor's

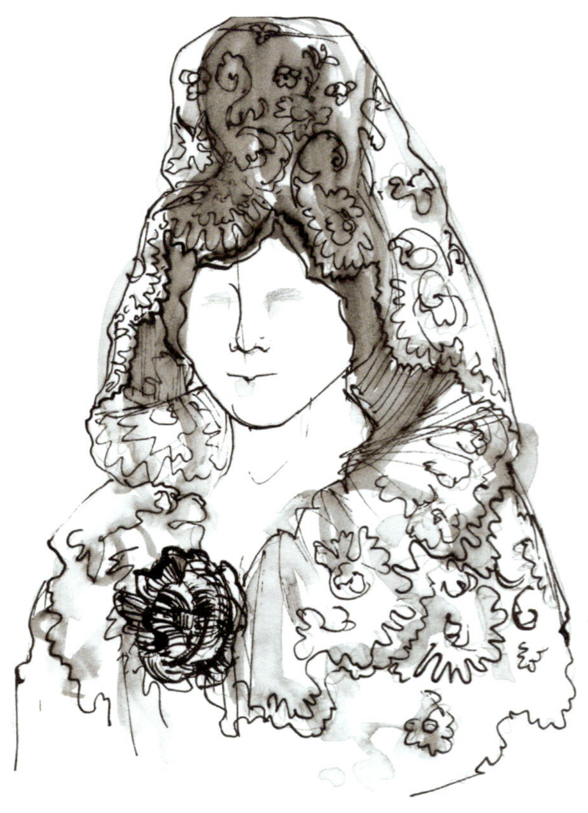

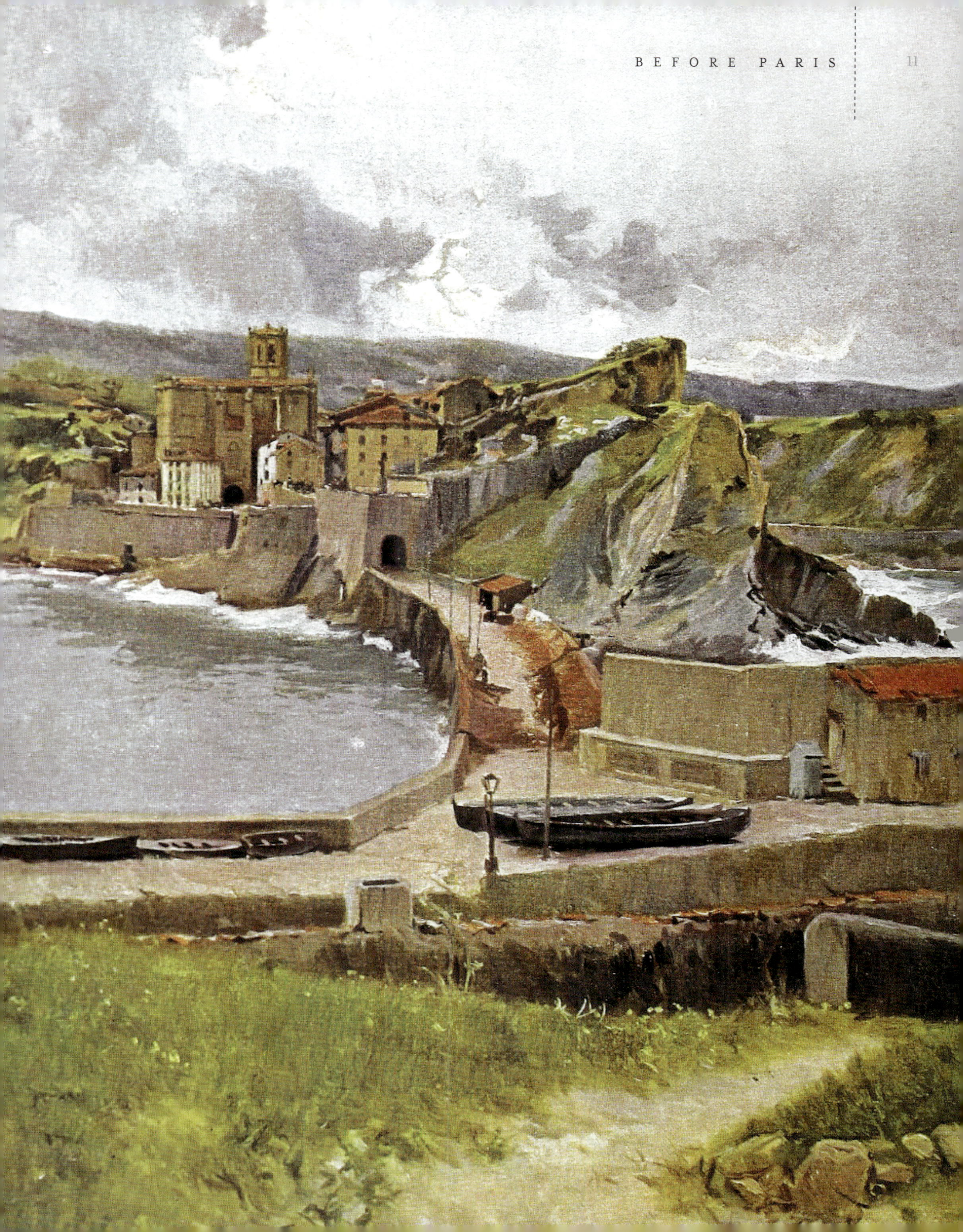

shop, where he was trained in traditional tailoring techniques, including pattern making and garment construction - skills that would form the foundations of his later precision and craftsmanship. Impressed by Balenciaga's early designs and his instinct for form and fabric, the Marquesa commissioned a number of garments from him. As a member of the Spanish nobility, her endorsement carried significant weight and her support gave him credibility and visibility in the most elite circles. Her patronage attracted other wealthy and fashionable clients, helping Balenciaga build a strong client base among the Spanish aristocracy and upper classes. Such was his success that in 1917, he opened his first fashion boutique 'Eisa Costura', named in honour of his mother's surname. The timing could not have been better. World War I had made it difficult for the Spanish elite to travel to Paris for their wardrobes and a new class of domestic designers was emerging. However, Balenciaga quickly stood out from his contemporaries. His designs combined precise tailoring with Spanish cultural elements such as bolero jackets, matador-inspired embellishments and high-waisted gowns echoing the Infanta portraits of Velázquez.

His success in San Sebastián was swift. By the early 1920s, Balenciaga had expanded to Madrid and Barcelona, creating salons that catered to the most elite women of Spanish society. His clientele included Queen Ena of Spain and other members of the aristocracy who valued discretion, luxury and impeccable craftsmanship. His 'Eisa' salons offered both custom couture and ready-to-wear options - but always

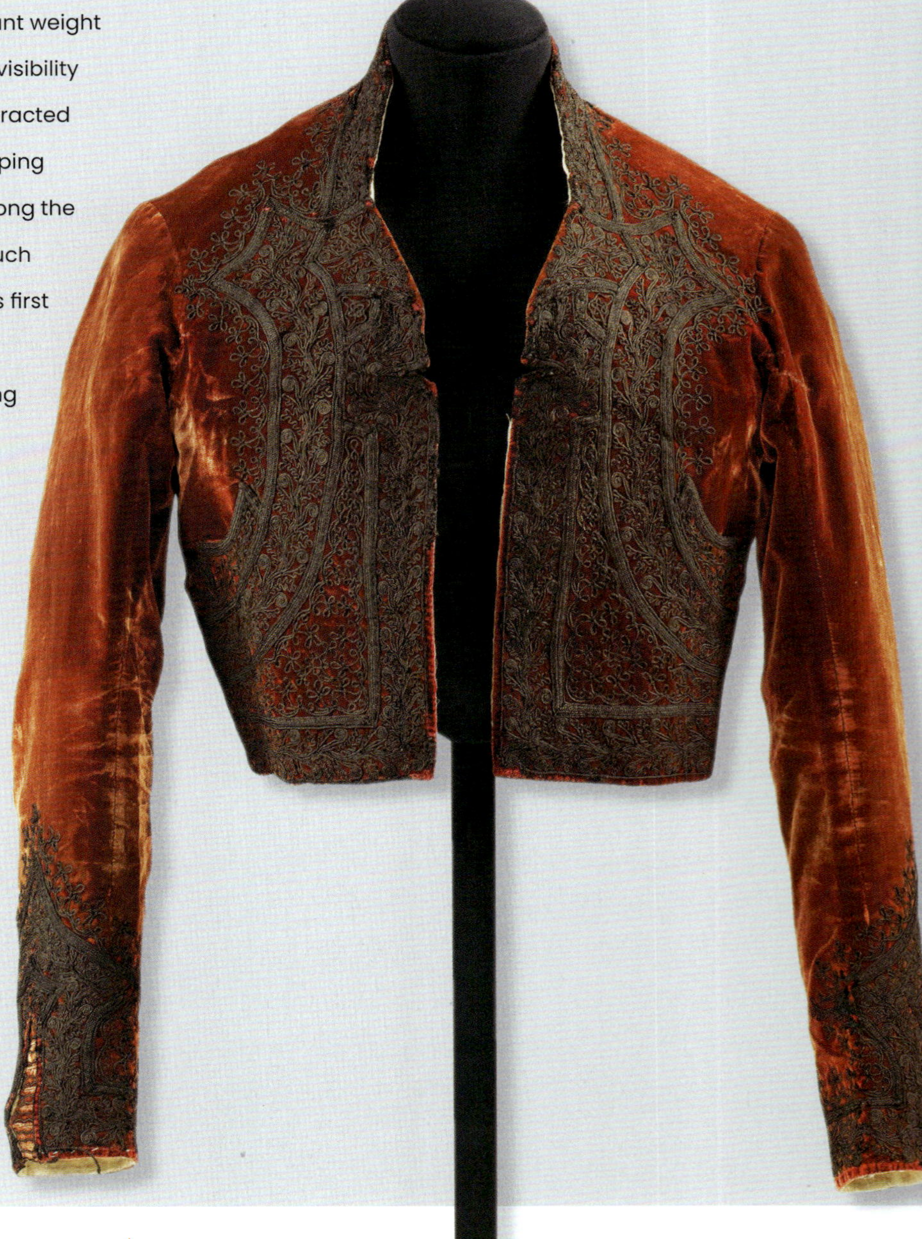

refined, always serious. From the outset, Balenciaga distanced himself from the frivolity often associated with fashion. His garments were studies in elegant restraint with his colour palette favouring blacks, ivories, deep reds and solemn greys – the hues of both Spanish ecclesiastical dress and royal portraiture.

Balenciaga's success continued throughout the 1920s and early '30s. He drew inspiration from Spanish paintings, especially those by Goya, Zurbarán and, of course, Velázquez. The silhouettes of his gowns echoed the stately proportions of baroque portraiture. Many featured stiff bodices and expansive skirts but were always tempered by his exquisite eye for modernity. He simplified the lines, reduced ornamental detail and elevated the garment through construction alone. Balenciaga's early designs weren't radical in appearance yet they were quietly subversive in method. He was obsessed with structure. Every pleat, every seam was exact. Each garment was an exercise in geometry. He took an almost architectural approach to fashion, one grounded in three-dimensional thinking. He designed not for illustration, but for the moving body. He insisted on excellence from his seamstresses and demanded complete control of the creative process. He was even known to cancel collections if he wasn't satisfied. Clients respected – and feared – his standards. He created not for trend but for permanence. Unlike other Spanish designers who sought to mimic French fashion, Balenciaga fused Iberian tradition with innovation. His embroidery often

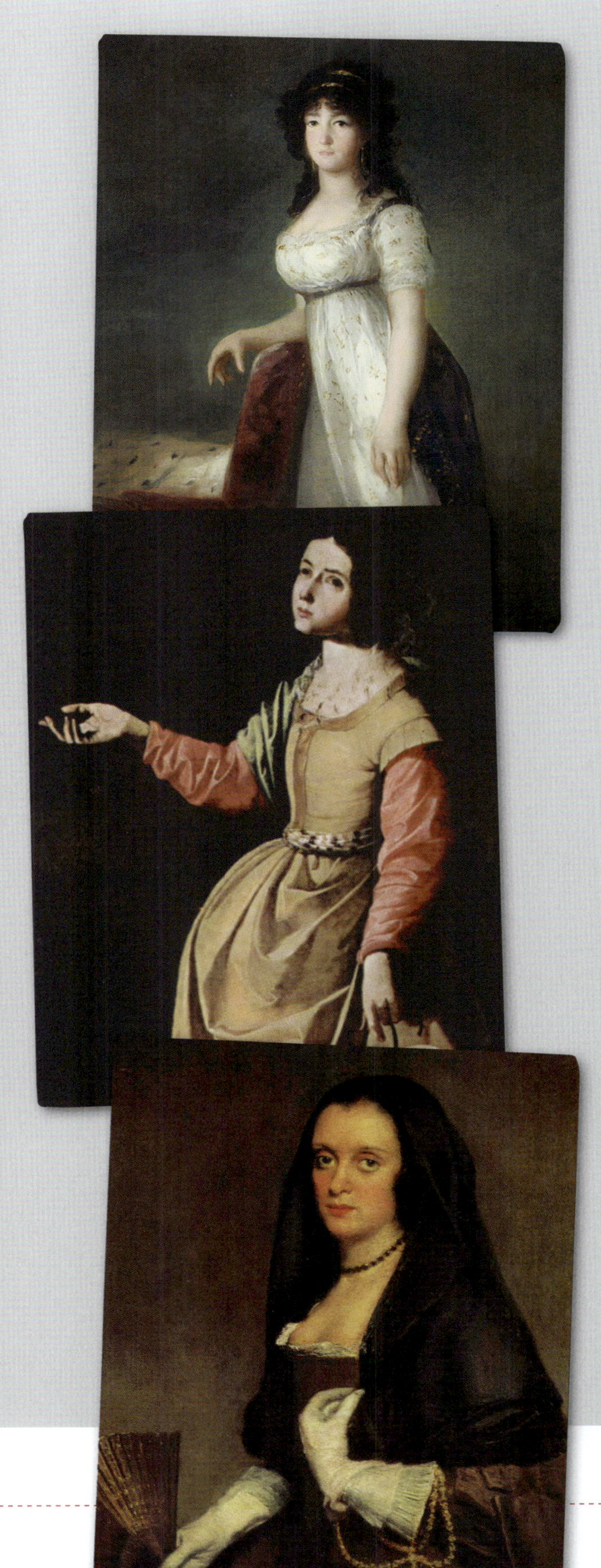

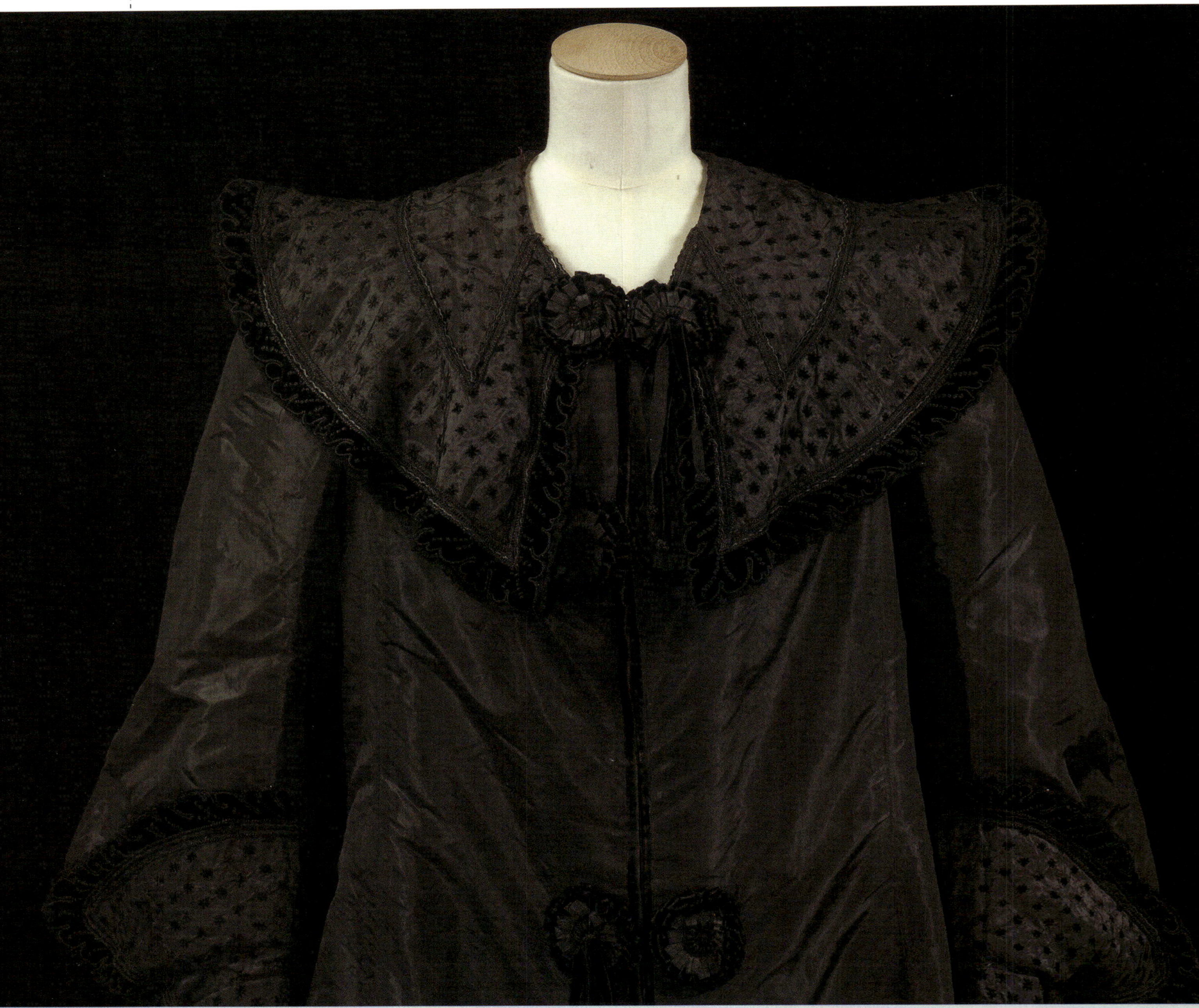

referenced Spanish folk motifs which were applied with minimalist precision. A single appliqué, a bold sleeve, a sharp collar. . . Balance and discipline were his trademarks. He also began experimenting with fabric manipulation - folding, cutting and draping material with increasing confidence. These years were like his laboratory - what he learned about volume and movement in his Madrid and Barcelona workrooms would form the bedrock of his later Parisian masterpieces.

ABOVE: An early 20th century Taffeta coat that was part of Balenciaga's personal collection donated to the Fashion Museum, Paris along with around 100 items in 1979

Balenciaga's Spanish ateliers were not opulent, in fact they operated more like sacred spaces. Privacy was paramount. Fittings were a quiet, intense, almost religious experience. When women walked out in a Balenciaga dress, she did so not merely to be seen but to also be understood. This aesthetic clarity and emotional restraint would become the designer's calling card - forged by the sombre elegance of Spanish heritage, the rigour of royal and elite expectation and his own uncompromising vision.

By 1936, Spain was engulfed in a civil war between the Nationalists and the Republicans. The monarchy fell and was replaced by the fragile Second Republic. Political unrest and violence destabilised the very society that had supported Balenciaga's rise with the result that the aristocratic clientele fled and the salons emptied. Like many artists and intellectuals, Balenciaga faced a decision - adapt, resist or escape. He chose the latter, closing his Spanish operations and leaving for Paris. It was a decision borne out of necessity rather than ambition, and was his only option in order to continue creating.

When he crossed the border into France in 1937, he was already a master tailor, an acclaimed couturier and a cultural conduit between Spanish tradition and European modernism. He was 42 years old - seasoned, respected but largely unknown outside Spain. That would soon change. . .

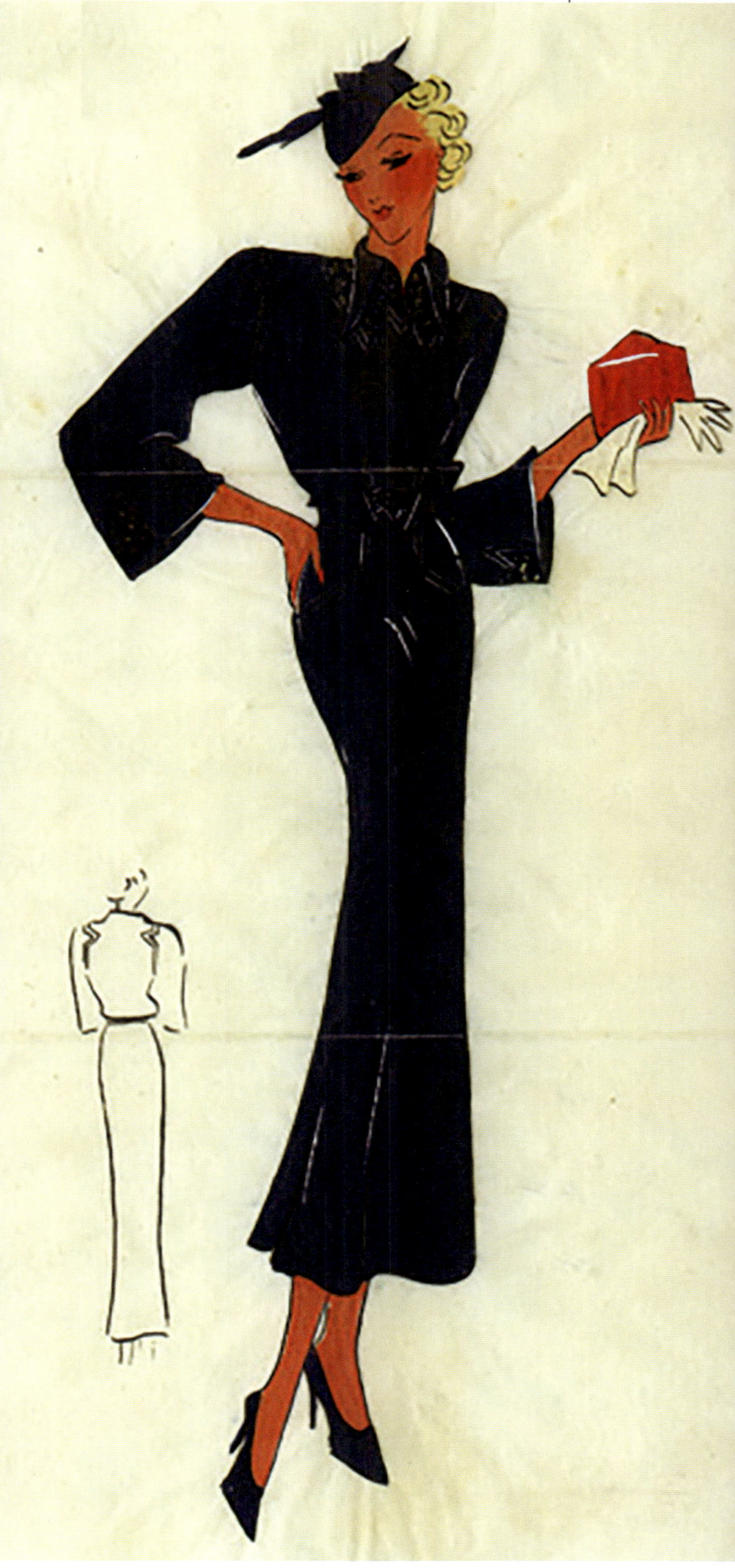

ABOVE: Parisian influence in Spain – this fashion sketch of a Madeleine Vionnet dress is from an embroidery factory in Barcelona, circa 1932-1934

MASTER OF COUTURE

"For the first time, a couturier had not only dared but succeeded in showing something new"

Fashion writer Carmel Snow after Balenciaga's inaugural show in Paris

Cristóbal Balenciaga launched his first Parisian collection under the name 'Maison Balenciaga' from his new HQ – 10 Avenue George V – in August 1937. This primary outing featured lace gowns inspired by flamenco dresses, structured coats that channelled ecclesiastical robes and minimalist daywear that went against the flamboyantly decorative norms of the day. Fashion editors, buyers and society clients alike were deeply impressed by the collection's refinement, craftsmanship and innovative reinterpretation of Spanish styles. Balenciaga had left Spain in exile but he carried it with him in every sleeve, every silhouette and every seam of every garment he created. *Vogue* and other publications approved of the architectural quality of his creations - a level of construction that set him apart from other couturiers

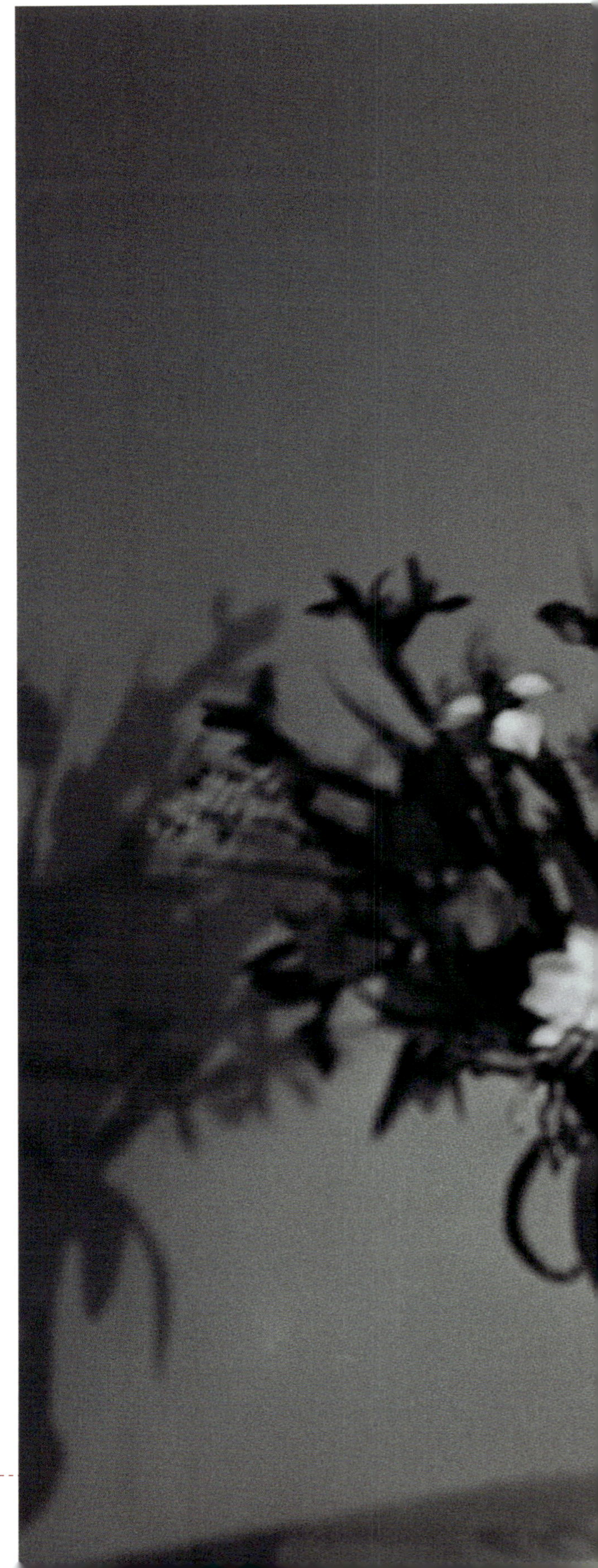

RIGHT: A woman models a polka dot evening dress by Balenciaga, 1946

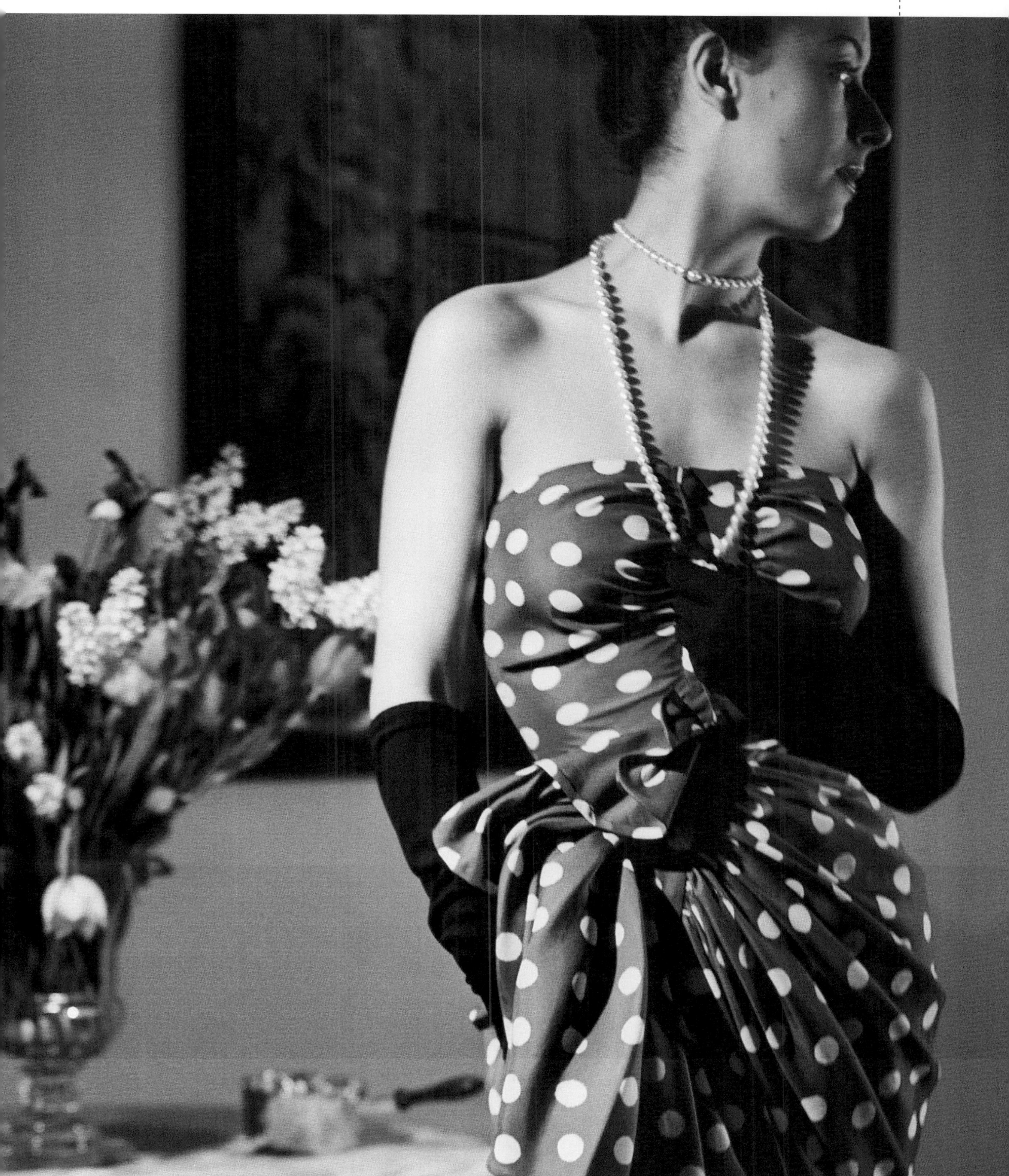

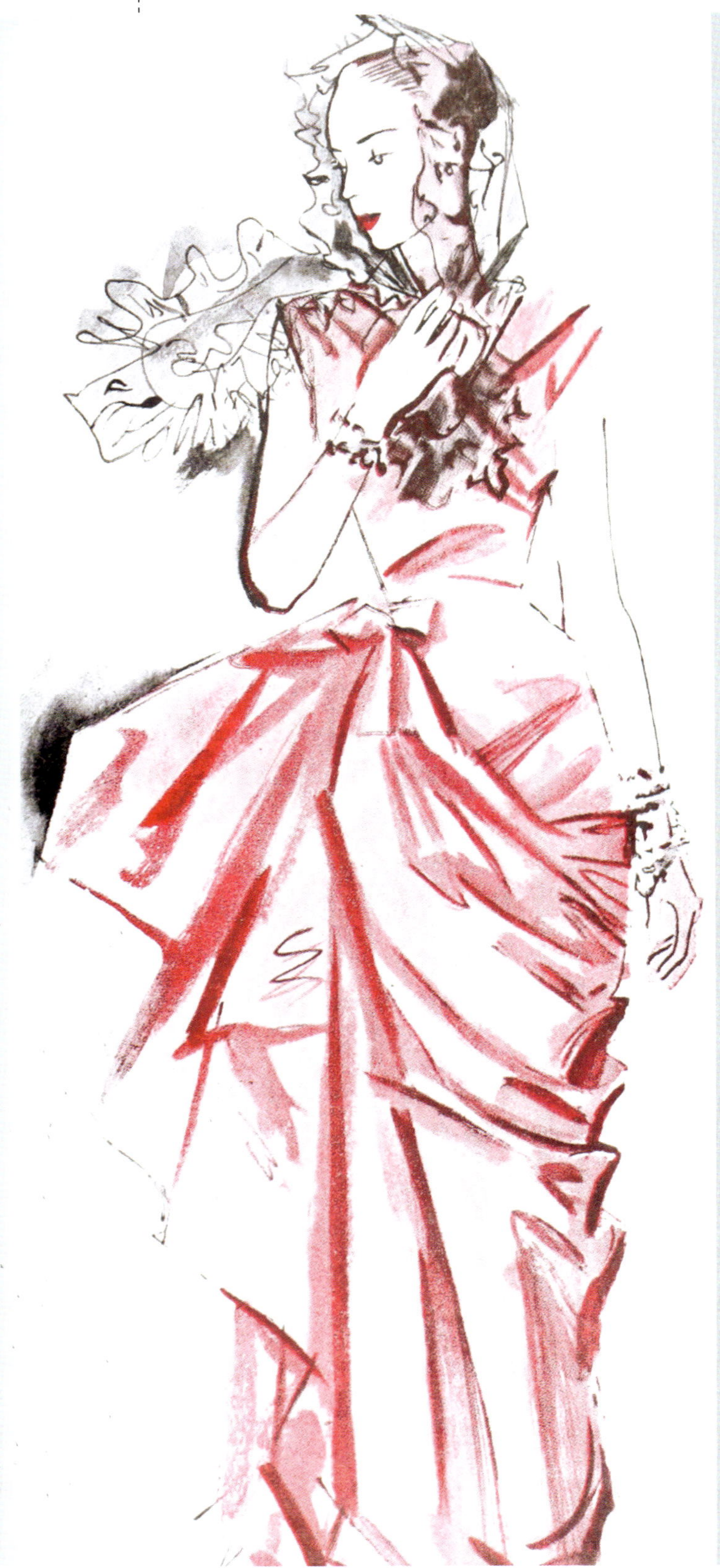

ABOVE: Enchantment in pink taffeta, divinely draped at the sides and paired with a black lace scarf by Balenciaga. Featured in *The Ladies' Home Journal*, 1947

even at his debut. Aristocrats and wealthy women, including Countess Mona Bismarck and Wallis Simpson, the Duchess of Windsor, quickly became clients, drawn to the elegance and originality of his designs. Within a few short seasons, Balenciaga had firmly established himself among the top Parisian couturiers.

During World War II, Balenciaga managed to not only survive the turmoil but actually strengthen his reputation as one of Paris's premier couturiers — a remarkable feat given the wartime challenges. He kept his Paris atelier open throughout the German occupation (1940–1944) while many fashion houses struggled or shut down. This was possible in part due to the Nazis' interest in maintaining Paris as the fashion capital which allowed select designers like Balenciaga, Chanel and Dior to continue operating. As an individual from neutral Spain, Cristóbal Balenciaga was also in a unique position. He could travel between Spain and France more easily than designers from the Allied nations and so he was able to continue sourcing materials from his home country. He also maintained his Spanish clients, helping him stay financially afloat. During the war, Balenciaga's designs were more austere due to fabric rationing but he adapted by emphasizing inventive tailoring, unusual cuts, draping and sophisticated minimalism. He often worked with black and dark fabrics, creating clothes with a dramatic yet elegant and subdued

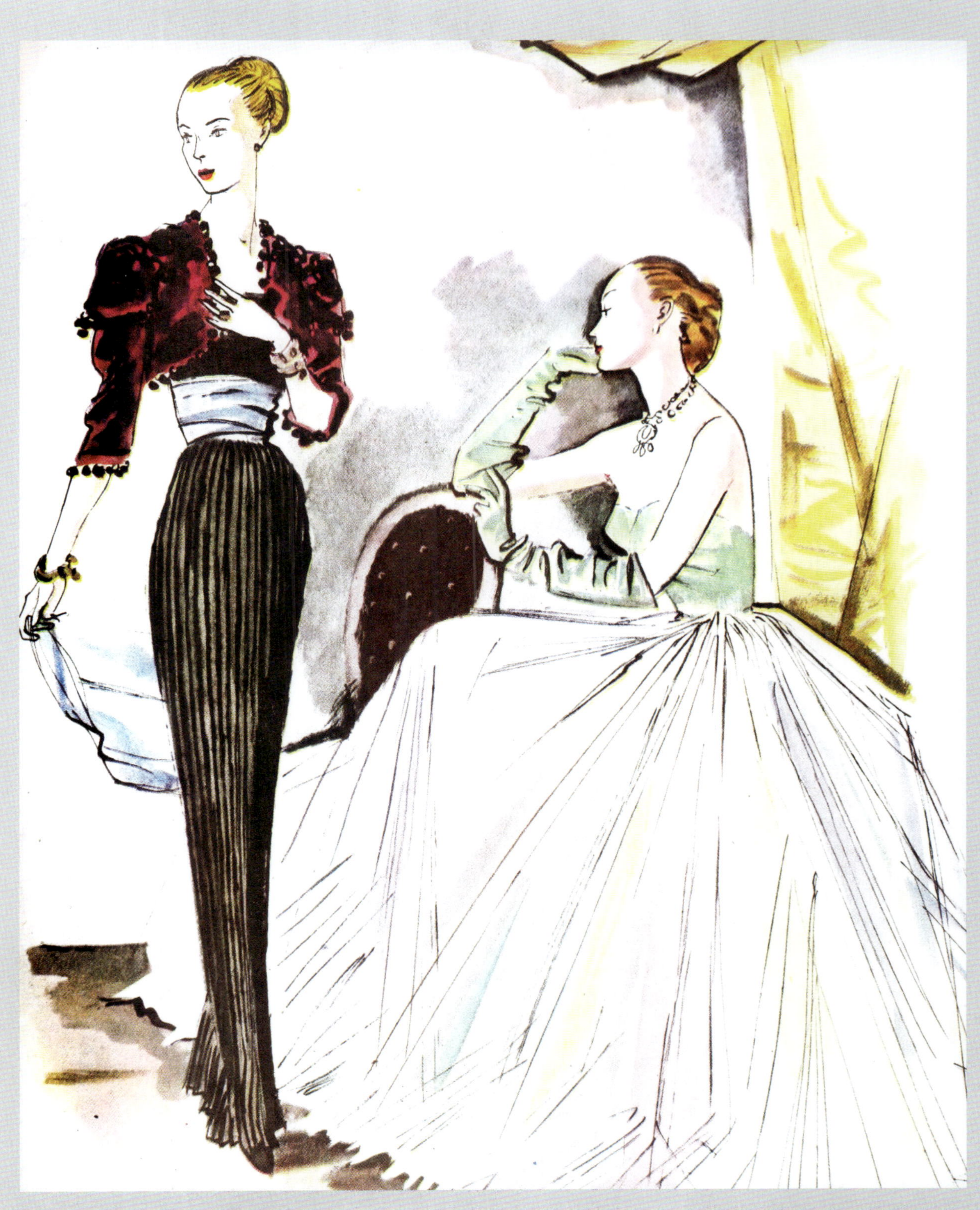

ABOVE: Burgundy velvet ribbed bolero with cummerbund sash and ankle-slim pleated skirt by Balenciaga (left), shown beside an evening dress by Jacques Fath (right). Featured in *The Ladies' Home Journal*, 1947

silhouette that echoed both Spanish mourning attire and the atmosphere of the times.

Post-war saw Balenciaga ascending to near-mythical status in the world of couture. Unlike other designers who eagerly engaged with the press, Balenciaga shunned publicity. He refused interviews, banned photographers from his shows and even declined to take a bow at the end of presentations. His clothes, he insisted, should speak for themselves. His most devoted clients would sit in reverent silence during private showings as each model slowly glided into the room, allowing the full weight and subtlety of the garment to be appreciated. This silence was not affectation - it was part of the ritual. While other designers adapted to post-war optimism with lavish decoration and overt femininity, Balenciaga refined a vision that was purist, sculptural and modern. He was less interested in trend than in timelessness. Every seam, every fold, every curve of fabric was calculated but for balance rather than attention.

Balenciaga did not design in the traditional sense. He rarely sketched. Instead, he worked directly with fabric on a mannequin, letting the material guide the shape. This hands-on method gave his garments an organic, architectural quality - as though they were born rather than made. His philosophy was that fashion was a discipline - requiring control, harmony and profound respect for form.

'A woman has no need to be perfect or beautiful to wear my dresses. The dress will do all that for her,' he would say.

True enough. By transforming rather than emphasising a woman's curves, Balenciaga redefined her shape. Where other designers celebrated femininity through embellishment, Balenciaga sculpted it through volume and silhouette.

In the early 1950s, Balenciaga began to collaborate with the Swiss textile firm Abraham in order to develop 'silk gazar' - a crisp, weightless fabric that allowed for the creation of dramatic shapes without the need for heavy under-structure. This innovation meant he could push silhouettes beyond what had previously been possible in haute couture. It was during this decade that he produced some of his most iconic designs.

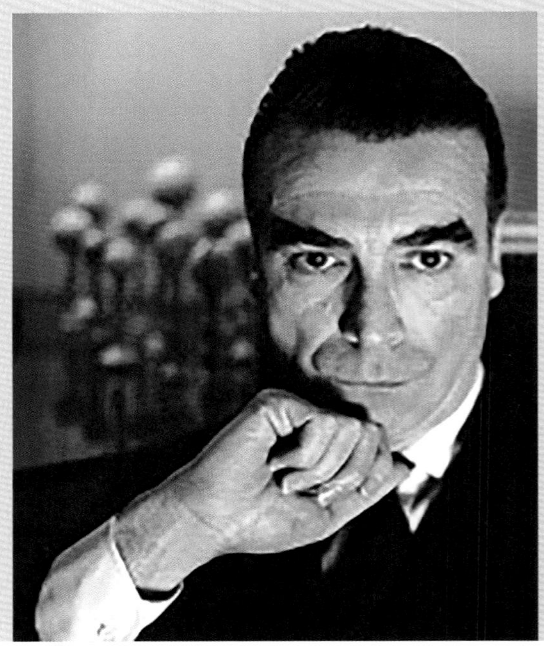

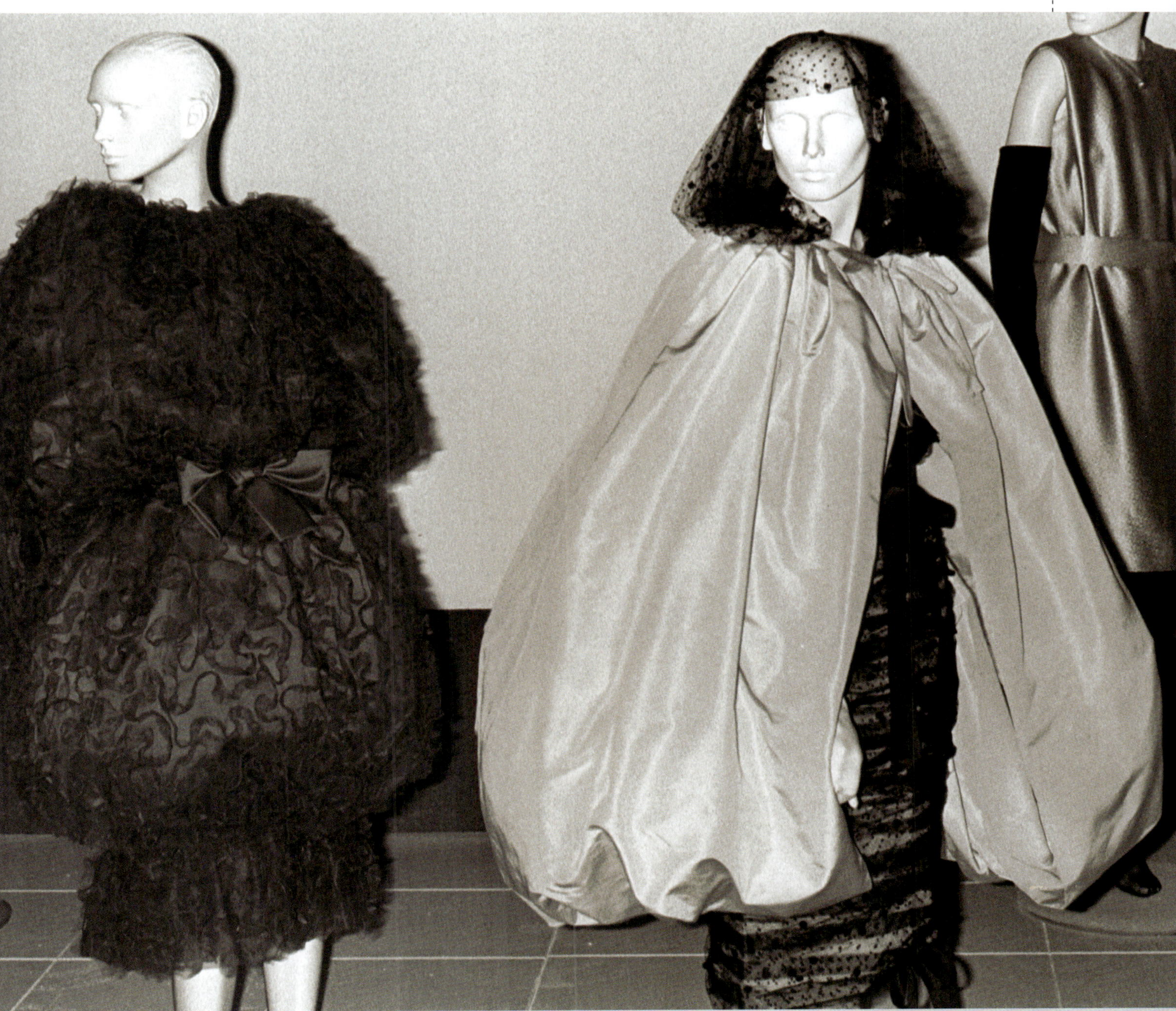

THE BALLOON JACKET, 1953

This voluminous, oval-shaped jacket - often with no discernible seam or fastening - was a masterclass in form and construction. Perfectly balanced, perfectly light, it seemed to almost hover off the shoulders. The balloon jacket exemplified Balenciaga's ability to defy gravity and logic with nothing but fabric and skill.

THE EMPIRE DRESS, 1954

Drawing from the Empire silhouette popularised in the early 19th century, the dress featured a high waistline just below the bust and a flowing, elongated skirt. Balenciaga reimagined this classic shape with minimal seams, luxurious fabrics and impeccable draping – thus creating volume without bulk. The result was a modern, sculptural form that moved effortlessly with the body.

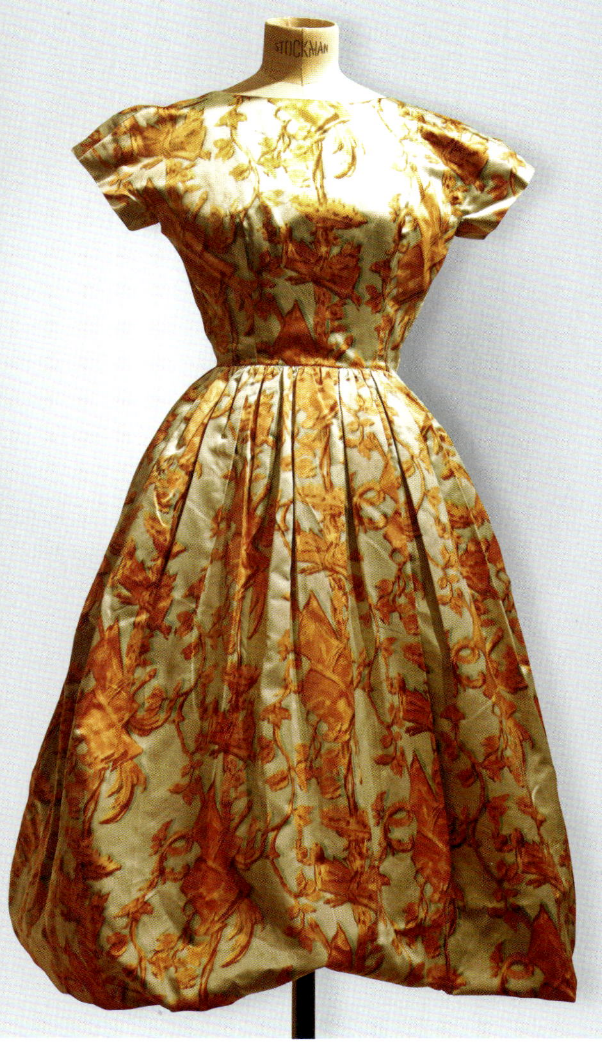

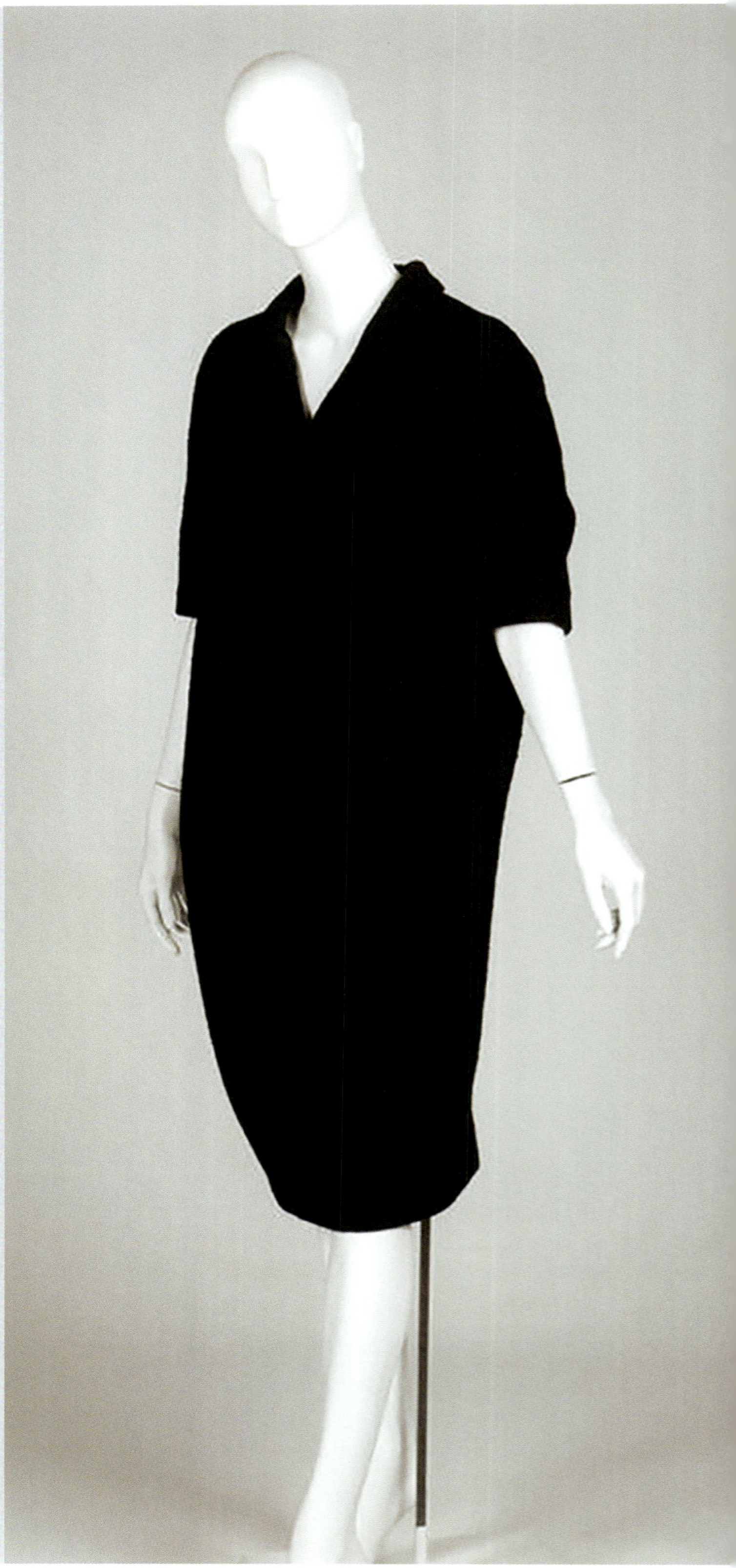

ABOVE: A creation by designer Cristóbal Balenciaga, Haute Couture collection, Fall/Winter, 1957
RIGHT: 1957 Sack Dress
OPP PAGE: Examples of Balenciaga Tunic Dress and Cocoon Coat, Metropolitan Museum of Art

THE TUNIC DRESS, 1955

This design featured a straight, unfitted shape that draped gracefully over the body, emphasizing purity of line and form. It laid the groundwork for future minimalist fashion movements.

THE SACK DRESS, 1957

A radical departure from the cinched waists of the post-war 'New Look', the sack dress was loose, straight and devoid of any defined waistline. Some thought it unflattering but fashion insiders recognized it as a bold reimagining of silhouette. The sack dress liberated the body from corsetry and constraint - an idea that would ripple through the fashion world for decades.

THE COCOON COAT, 1957

With its seamless, rounded back and minimalistic front, the cocoon coat exemplified Balenciaga's skill in creating sculptural garments that combined comfort with elegance.

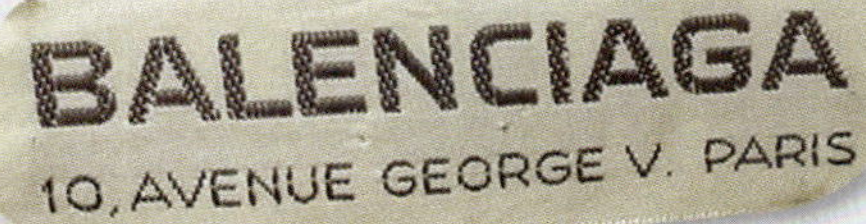

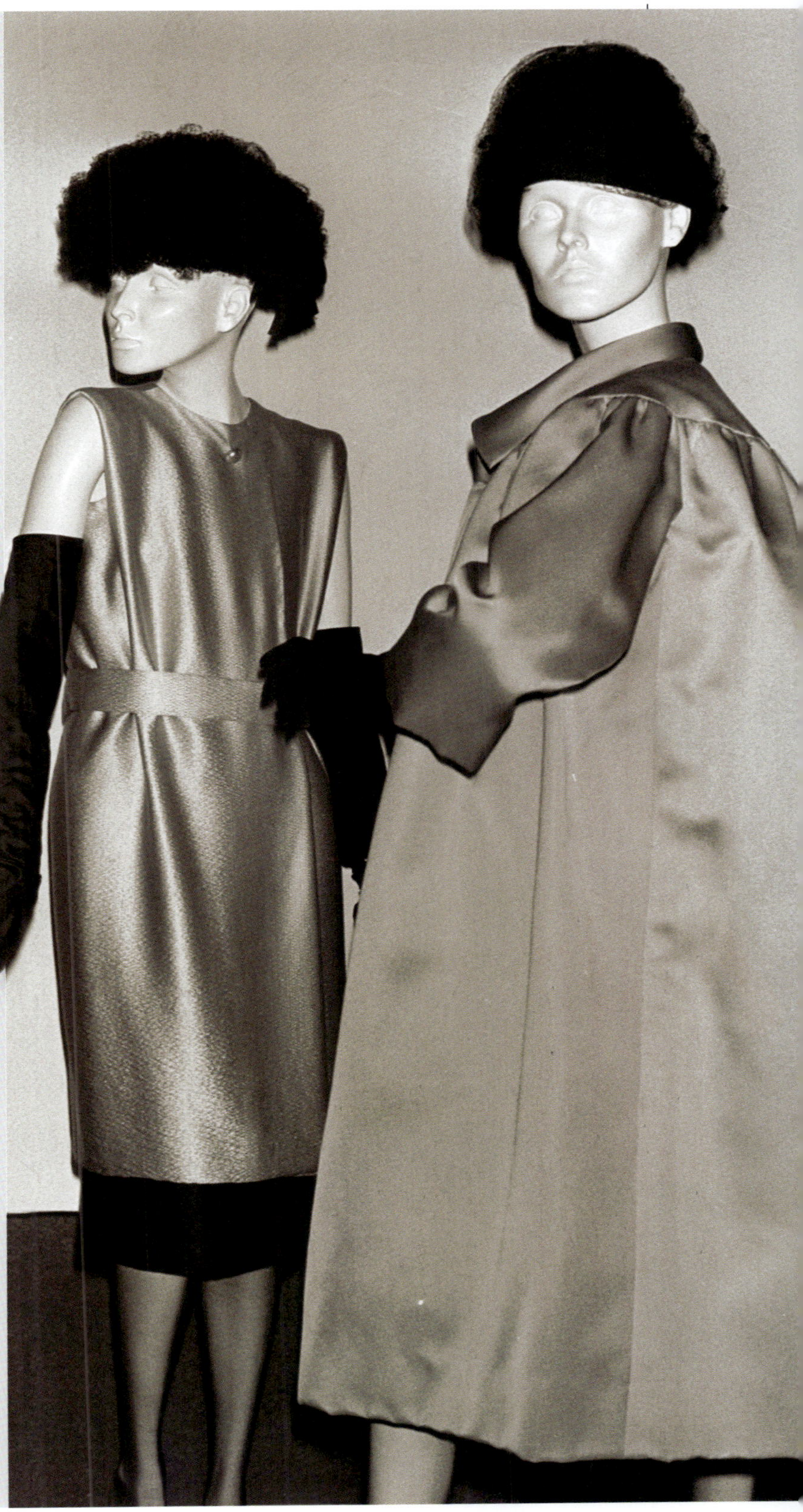

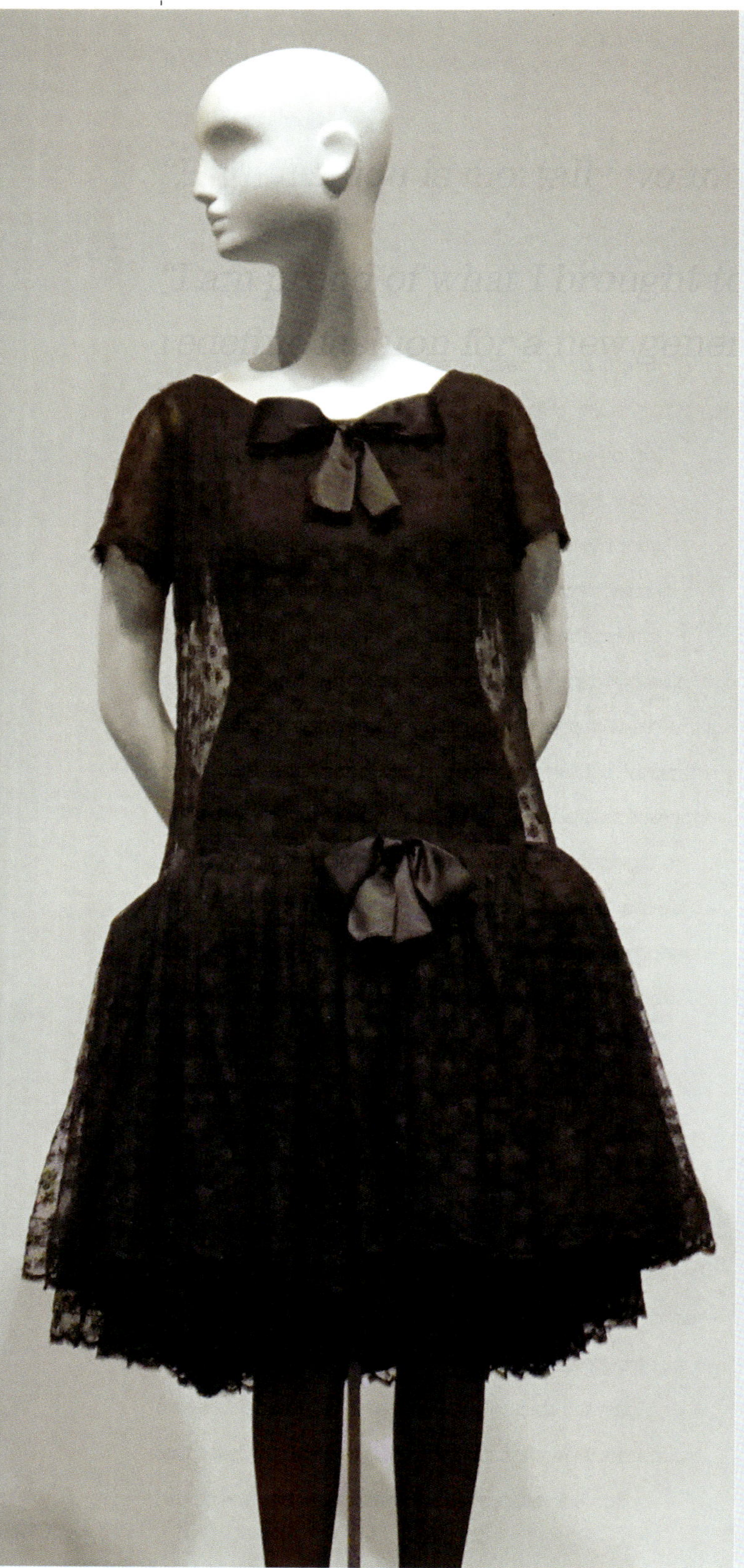

THE BABY DOLL DRESS, 1958

Youthful, high-waisted and skimming the knees, the Baby Doll dress was a precursor to the mini dress and mod styles of the 1960s. Though simple in appearance, its construction was complex, relying on invisible supports and expert pleating. Once again, Balenciaga was years ahead of the curve.

These garments were more about purity of line than decoration. Ornamentation was minimal or even absent altogether. A single bow, a stark colour or a dramatic sleeve was enough. The drama was in the cut.

Balenciaga was a contemporary of Christian Dior and Coco Chanel, and although they operated in the same world, their design philosophies could not have been more different. Dior, with his famous 'New Look', emphasized exaggerated femininity in the form of tiny waists, full skirts and romantic flourishes. His work celebrated opulence and a return to pre-war glamour. Chanel, on the other hand, was all about utility and ease. Her garments offered comfort and simplicity, challenging the rigid formality of earlier decades. Balenciaga, by contrast, was austere - almost spiritual - in his approach. He cared neither for commercial trends nor media attention. He believed in balance, silence and control. Despite their very different approaches to Balenciaga's way of working, both Dior and Chanel were in awe of his skill.

ABOVE: The Baby Doll dress by Balenciaga, 1958 at The Philadelphia Museum of Art
OPP PAGE: Didi Stone bringing the look with a vintage Baby Doll dress with a modern twist, Balenciaga Fall/Winter 2022

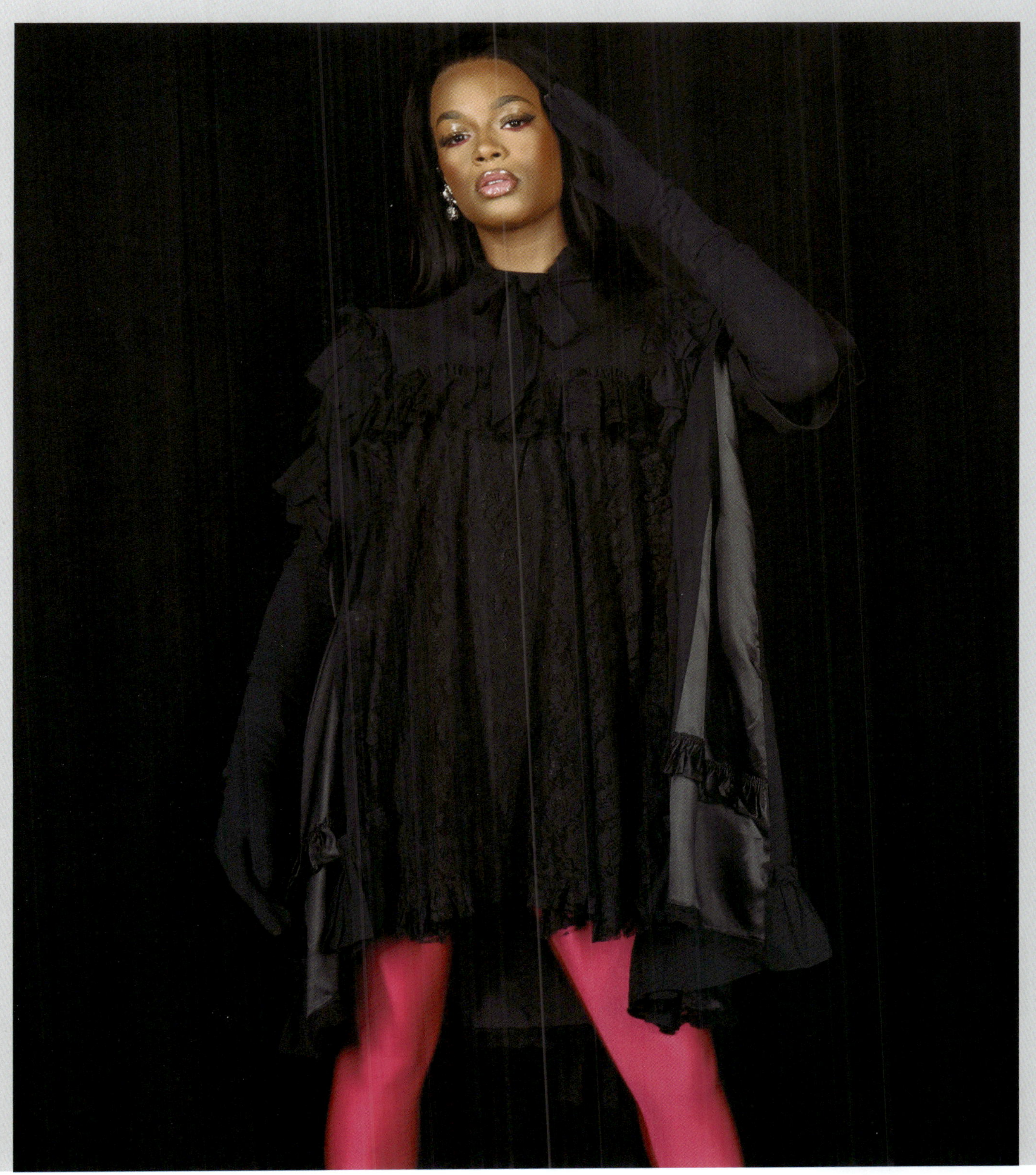

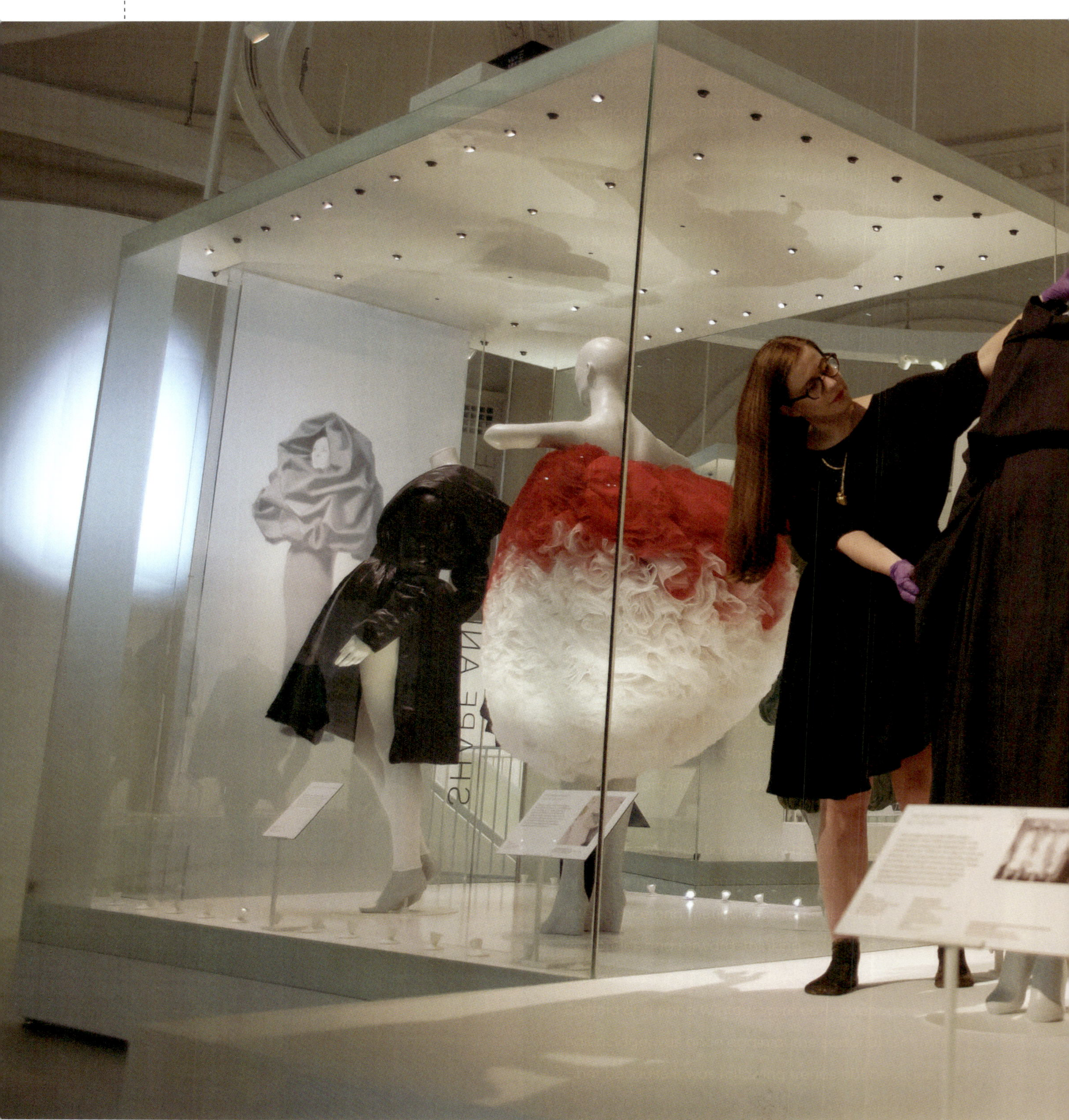

ABOVE: The first UK exhibition dedicated to Cristóbal Balenciaga, held at the Victoria and Albert Museum, London, on 24 May 2017, showcasing more than 100 garments and 20 hats

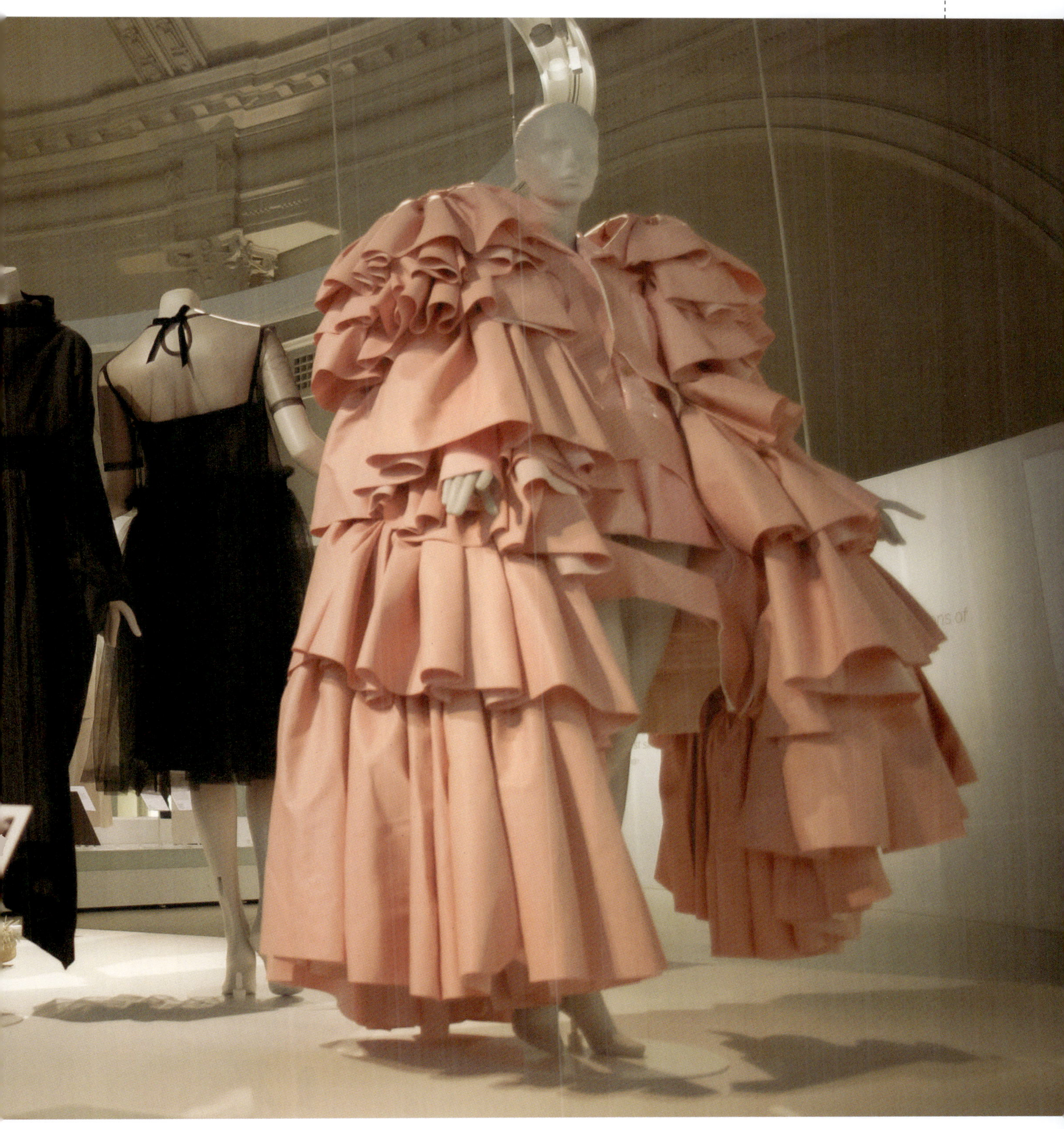

'*Haute couture is like an orchestra, and Balenciaga is its conductor. The rest of us are just the musicians,*' Dior once said.

While Chanel quipped, '*Only Balenciaga is a true couturier. The rest of us are just fashion designers.*'

By the end of the 1950s, the House of Balenciaga had changed the course of fashion and, in doing so, taught a generation of designers not just how to design but how to see. His garments were timeless. He had proven that fashion could be art, that restraint could be more powerful than extravagance and that true luxury lay in perfect precision. When he introduced a new silhouette, the world followed. Balenciaga didn't need to explain his work. He simply let it exist – perfectly cut, impeccably finished and immaculately silent.

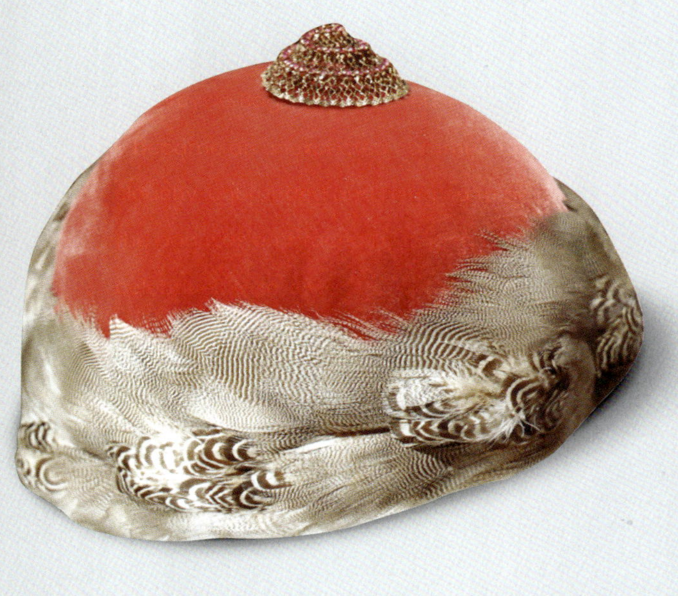

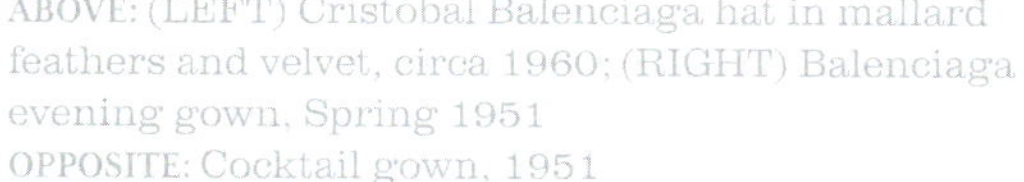

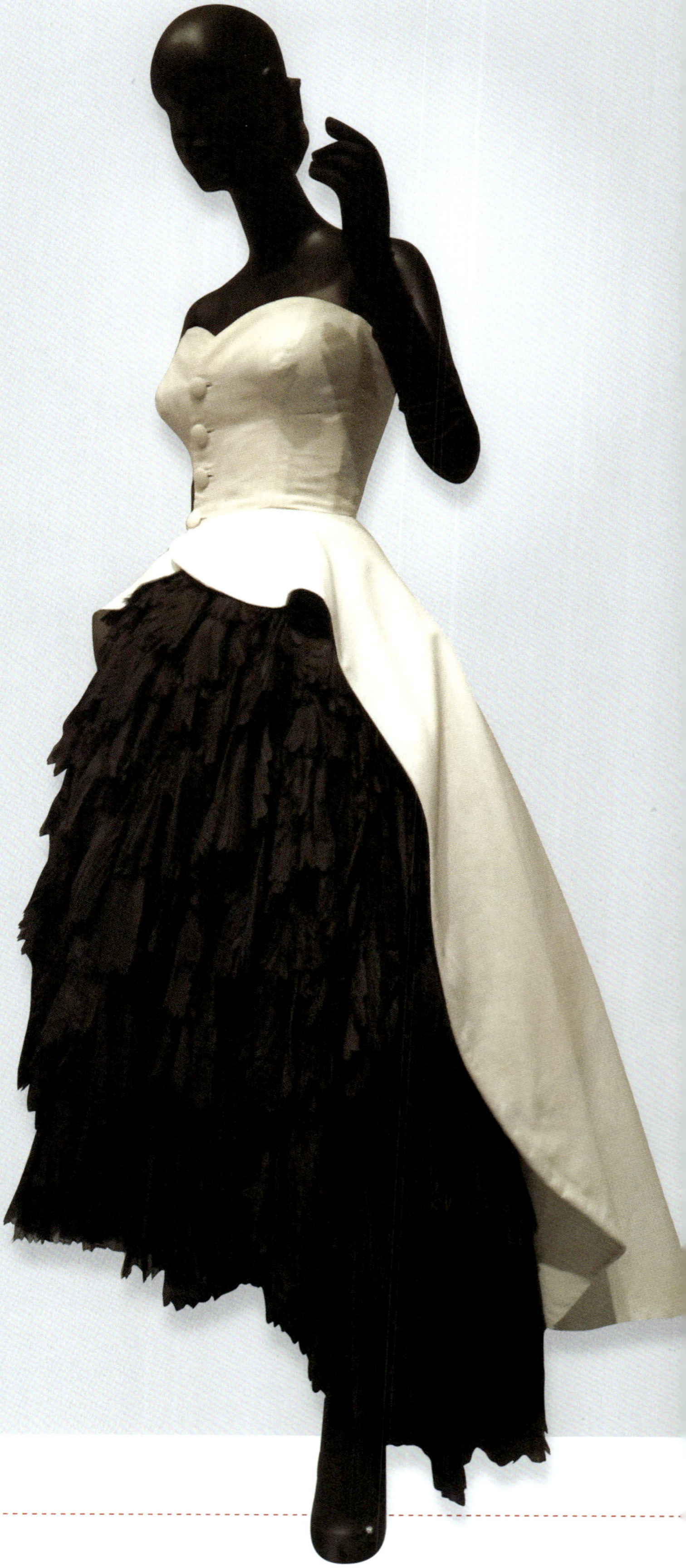

ABOVE: (LEFT) Cristobal Balenciaga hat in mallard feathers and velvet, circa 1960; (RIGHT) Balenciaga evening gown, Spring 1951
OPPOSITE: Cocktail gown, 1951

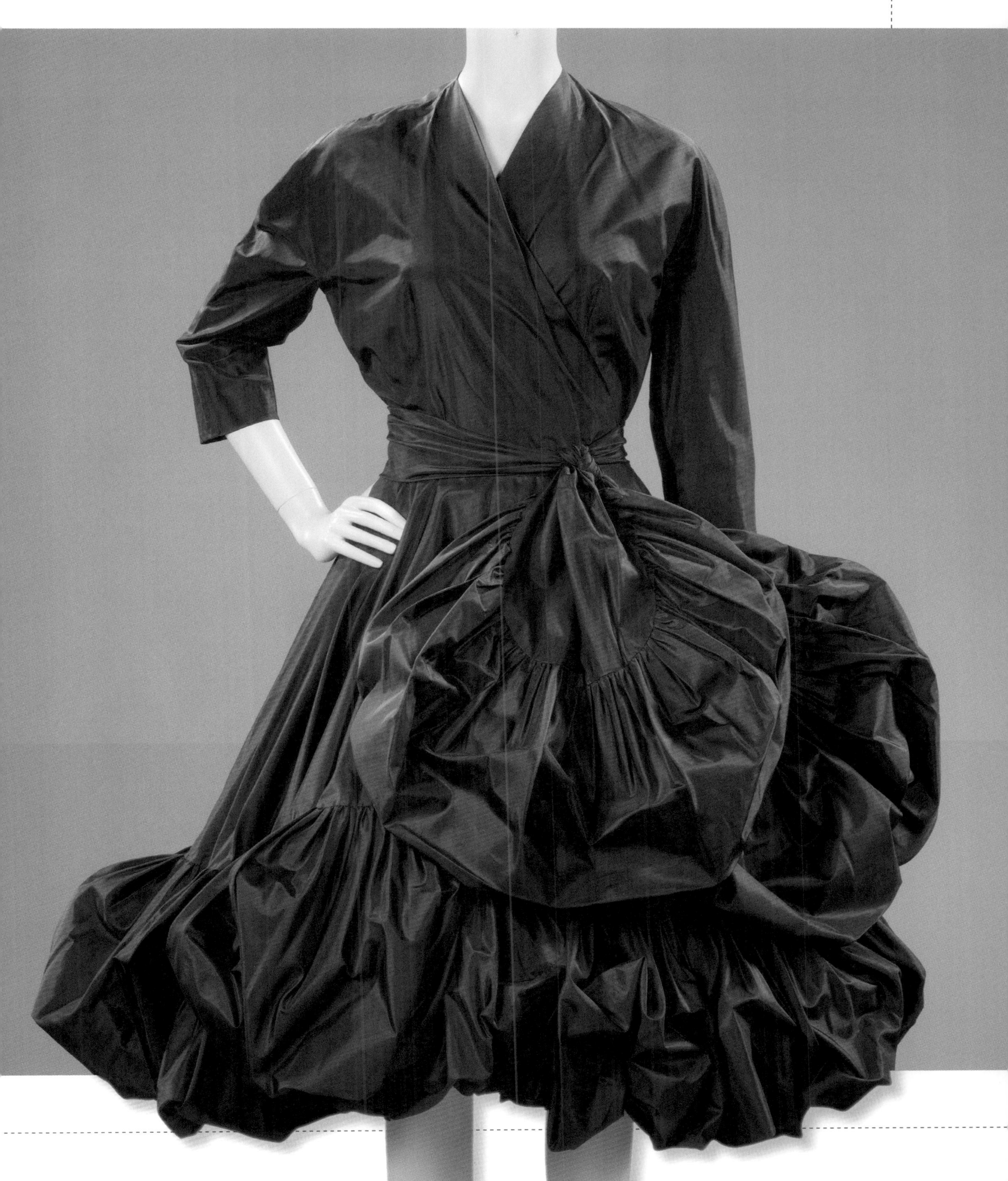

'GOLDEN AGE' ICONS

"Elegance is elimination"

Cristóbal Balenciaga

In the rarefied world of haute couture, it is not only the designer who defines the house but also the women who choose to wear those designs. To Cristóbal Balenciaga's Parisian salon flocked some of the 20th century's most powerful and enigmatic women - figures who were not merely famous but symbolic, too. A clientele not born of fleeting celebrity or public spectacle but of lineage, influence and aesthetic discernment. Together, Balenciaga and these women forged a new language of elegance in the decades following World War II.

GRACE KELLY (1929-82)

At the centre of this elite circle stood a Hollywood star whose quiet magnetism and natural elegance set her apart from her contemporaries. Her relationship with fashion evolved dramatically after her marriage to Prince Rainier III of Monaco in 1956, a union that elevated her from movie star to royalty. In this transformation, she sought out designers who could help bridge the worlds of American modernity and European tradition. Balenciaga, with his aristocratic sensibility and sculptural design philosophy, was an ideal match. Balenciaga's pieces for the

Princess were marked by restraint and refinement - unembellished yet architecturally complex garments that spoke to her new role as a European princess and public figure. Her Serene Highness did not require theatrics - she sought sophistication and symbolic weight. Whether attending diplomatic events in Monte Carlo or making appearances as a patron of the arts, Princess Grace wore Balenciaga to convey a calm and composed authority.

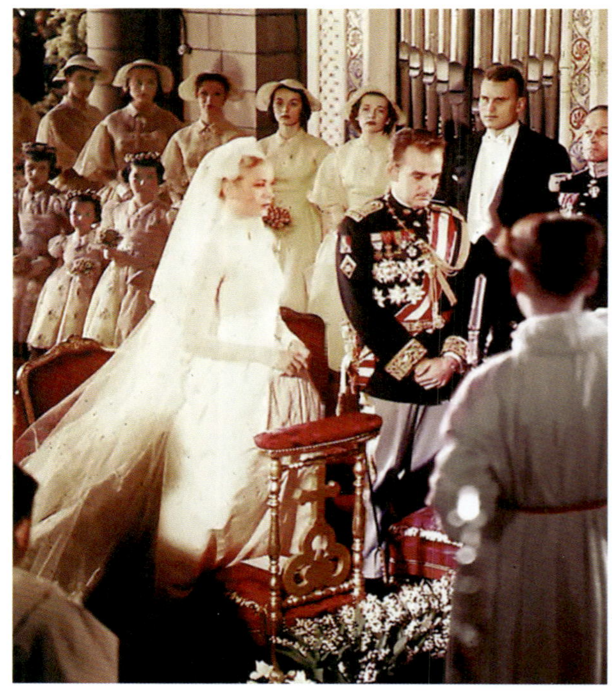

RIGHT: Wedding of Rainier III, Prince of Monaco, and Grace Kelly
OPP PAGE: Grace Kelly's wedding dress on display at 'Grace Kelly: From Movie Star to Princess' exhibition in 2011, Toronto, Canada

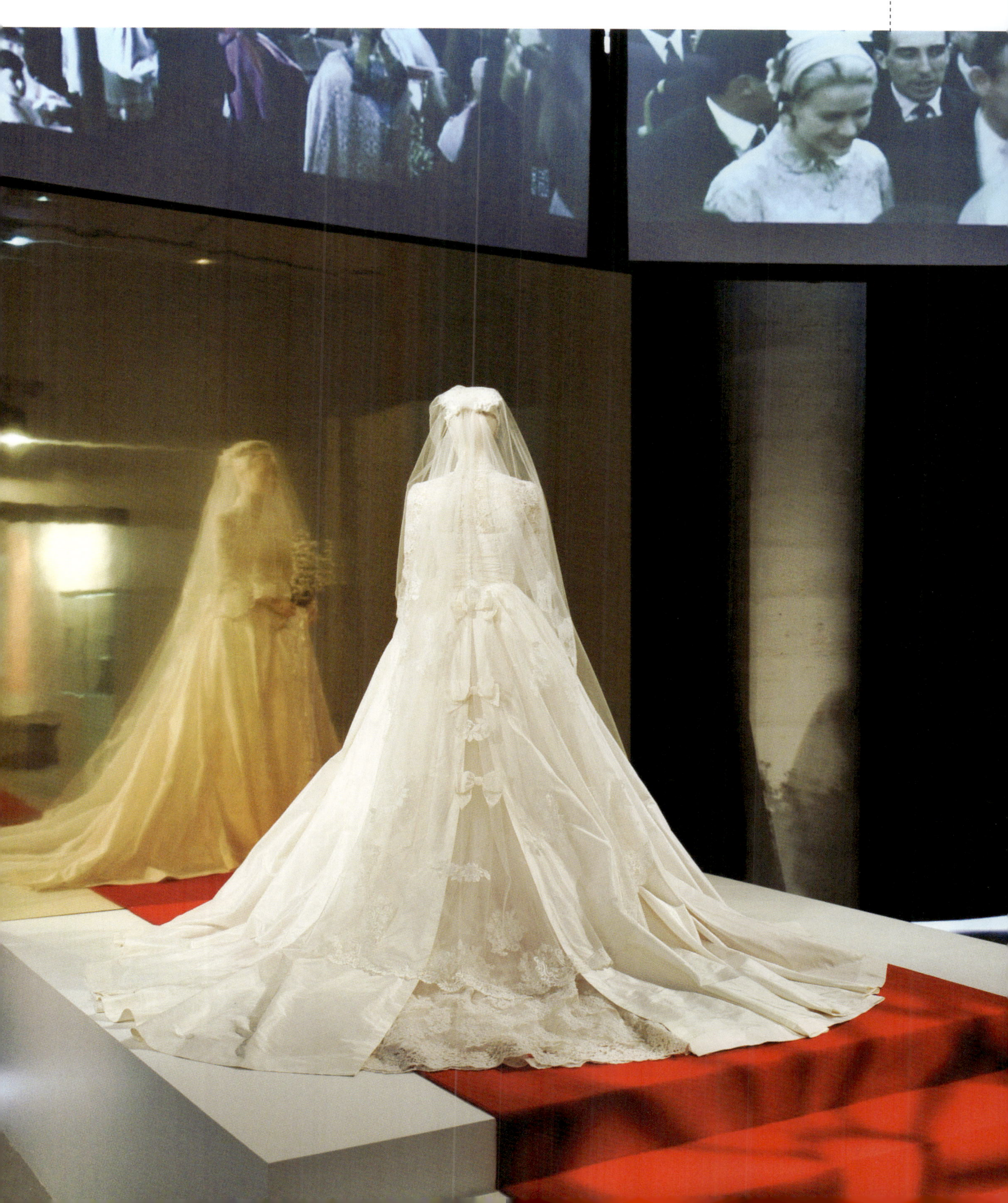

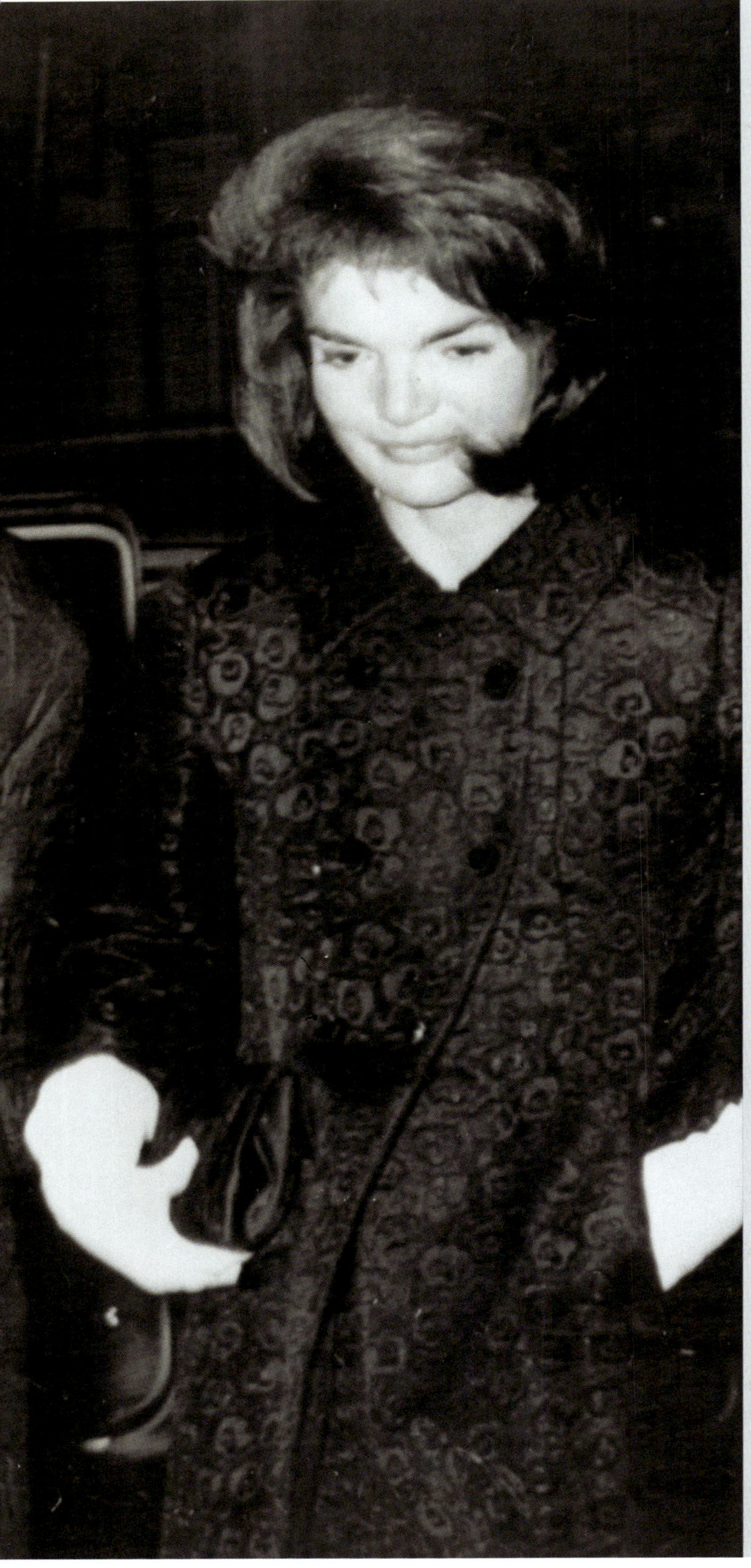

JACQUELINE KENNEDY
(1929-94)

Equally pivotal in cementing Balenciaga's place in the pantheon of elite fashion was the First Lady of the United States from 1961 to 1963. Though much of her public wardrobe was curated by American designers in deference to nationalist sentiment, Jackie privately admired and collected European haute couture. Her patronage of Balenciaga, though discreet, was significant. It reflected her cosmopolitan, European-influenced upbringing and her personal commitment to style. Kennedy's fashion choices were often strategic, subtle weapons in the cultural diplomacy of the Cold War. Balenciaga's austere elegance aligned perfectly with her vision of refined, forward-looking American womanhood. The clean lines, three-quarter sleeves, high boat necks and impeccable tailoring she favoured aligned perfectly with Balenciaga's vision.

THE DUCHESS OF WINDSOR
(1896-1986)

Wallis Simpson, the Duchess of Windsor, was renowned for her impeccable style, and one of the elite couturiers she favoured was Balenciaga. The Duchess's wardrobe featured Balenciaga pieces that exemplified her minimalist yet sophisticated style. This is exemplified in a 1950 photograph by Philippe Pottier, capturing the Duchess in a

ABOVE: Jackie Kennedy wears a Balenciaga black double-breasted coat in 1964

OPP PAGE: The Duchess of Windsor (centre) wearing a pinkish-red Balenciaga outfit with a mandarin collar, 10 October 1965, New York

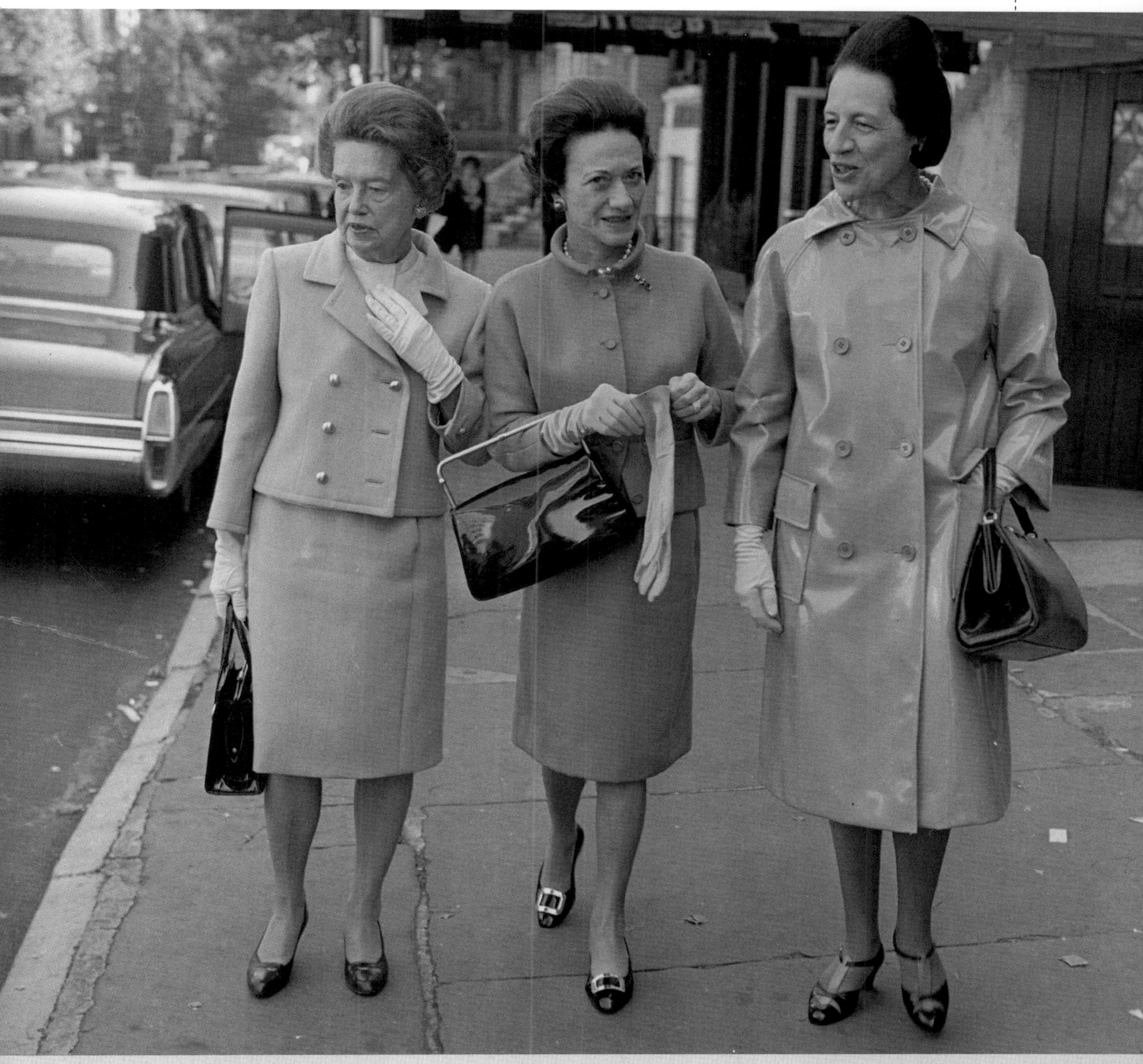

Balenciaga ensemble and highlighting her status as a fashion icon. Her collaboration with Cristóbal contributed to her reputation for elegance and influenced contemporary fashion.

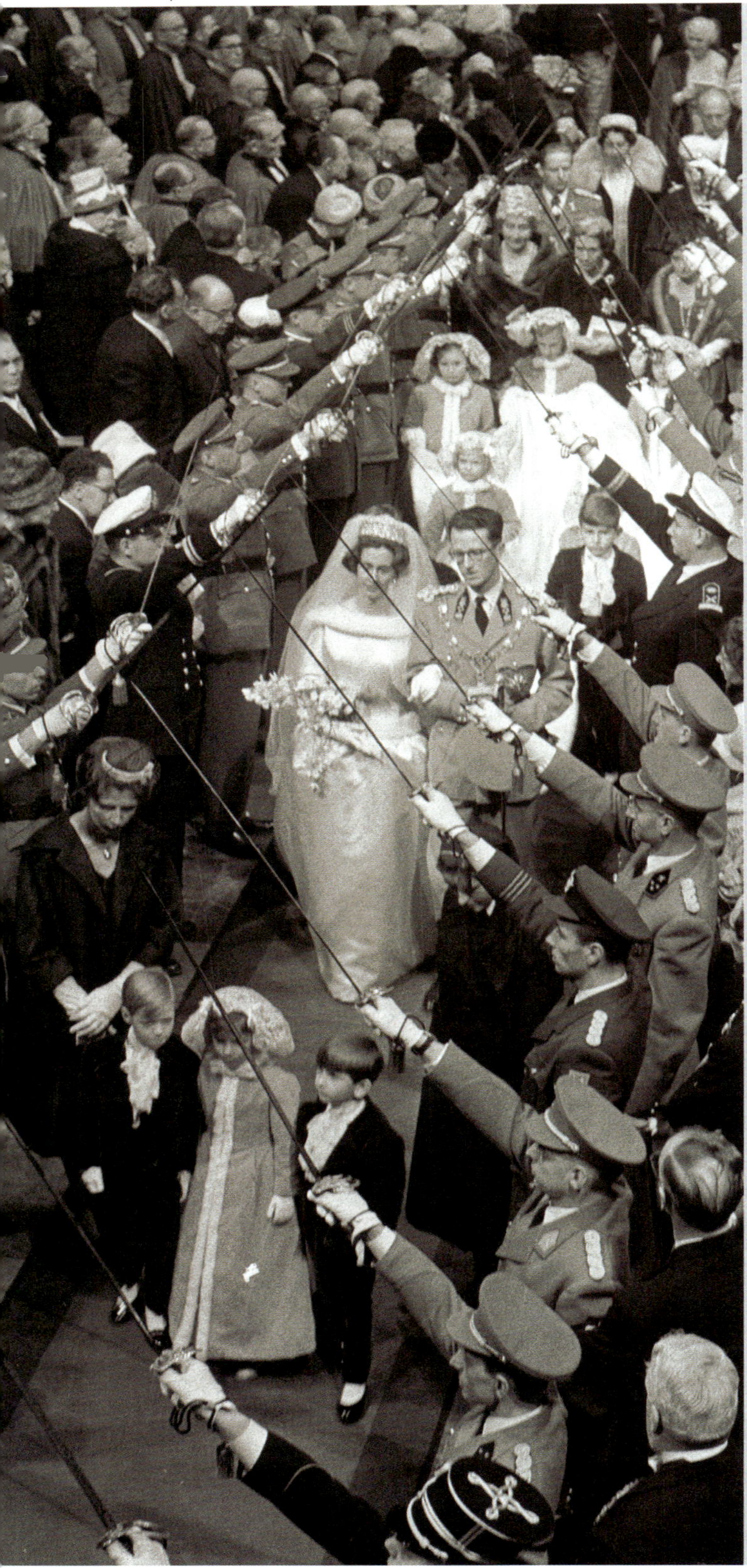

ABOVE & OPP PAGE: Fabiola in her wedding dress by Cristóbal Balenciaga, 15 December 1960

QUEEN FABIOLA OF BELGIUM (1928-2014)

The Belgium Queen Consort's collaboration with Cristóbal Balenciaga for her wedding to King Baudouin I in December 1960 has gone down as something of a pinnacle in royal fashion history. Their partnership culminated in a bridal gown that not only epitomised elegance but also showcased the connection between the Spanish designer and the Spanish-by-birth queen consort. Fabiola de Mora y Aragón, born into Spanish nobility, had familial ties to Balenciaga's early patronage. Her great-grandmother, the Marquess of Casa Torres, had been among Balenciaga's first supporters, greatly influencing his formative years in fashion. This shared heritage and mutual respect laid the foundation for their collaboration with regards to Fabiola's wedding dress. The gown - featuring a boat neckline, kimono sleeves and a dropped waist culminating in a voluminous skirt - was made from ivory satin with white mink at the collar and hips. A six-metre-long train flowing from the shoulders added regal grandeur. The gown is preserved and displayed at the Cristóbal Balenciaga Museum in Getaria, Spain, allowing future generations to appreciate this iconic piece of fashion history.

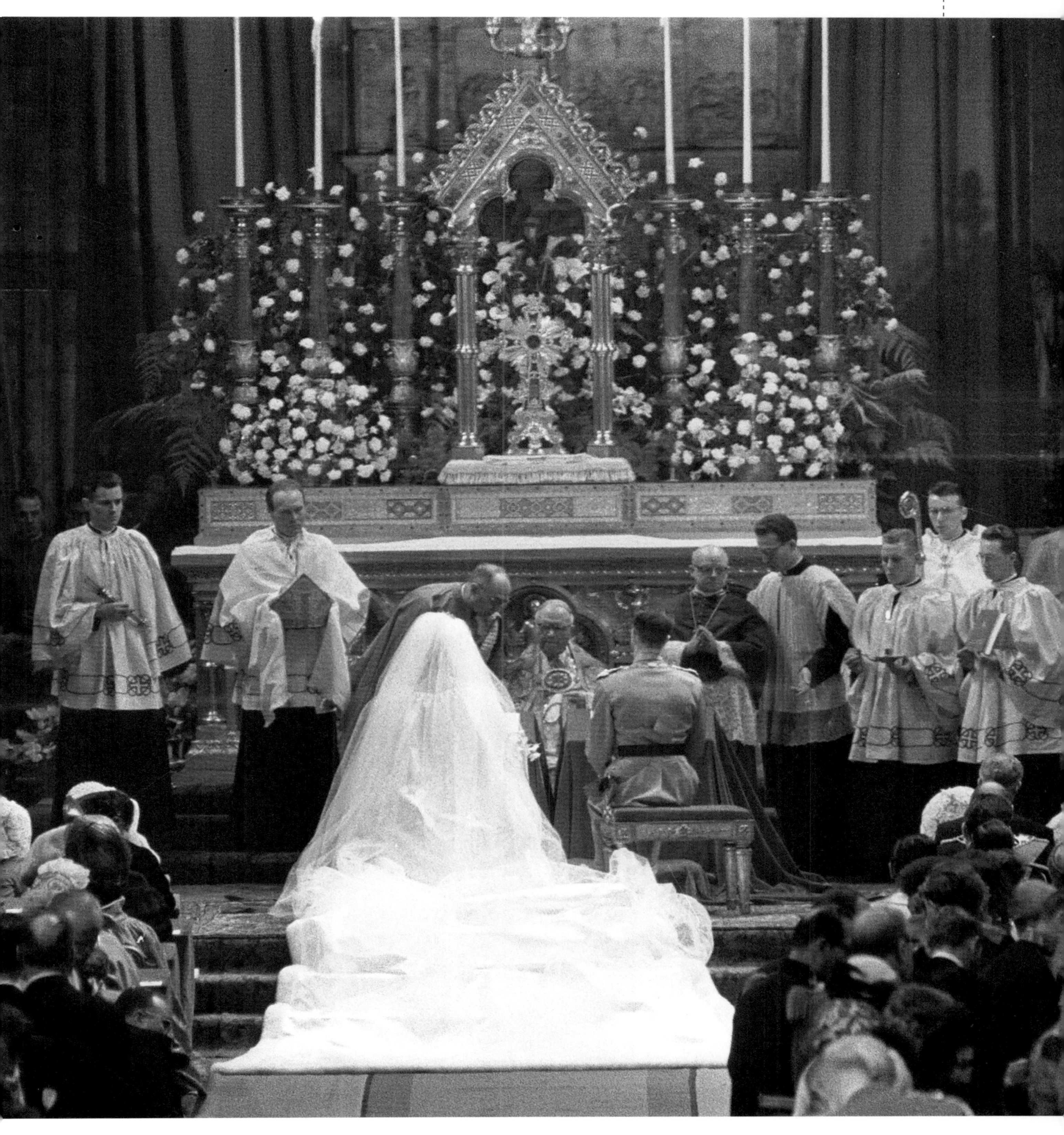

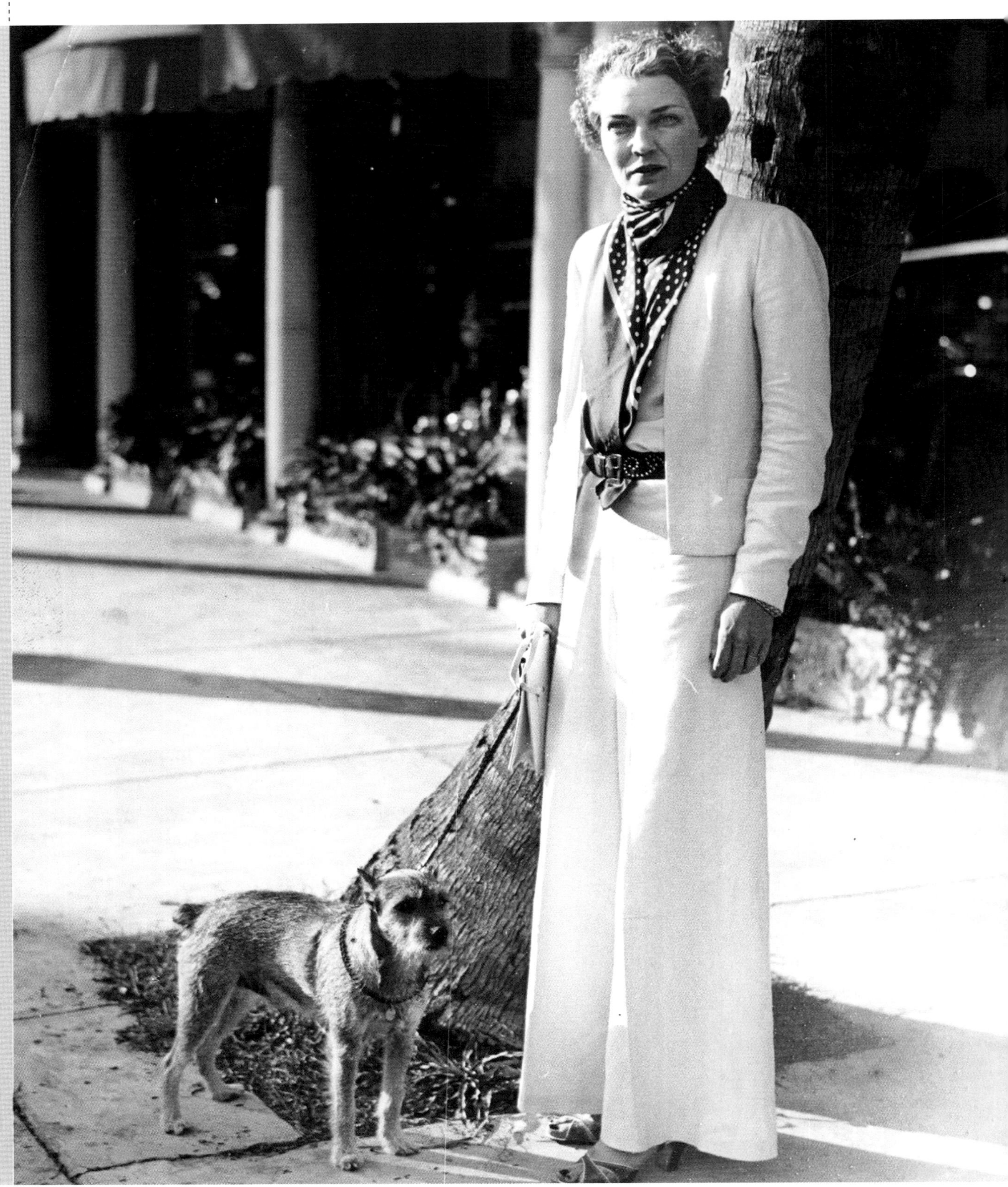

ABOVE: Mrs Harrison Williams (Mona von Bismarck),
socialite and fashion icon, 20 January 1933
OPP PAGE: 'The Kentucky Countess' (detail), painting of
Mona von Bismarck from 1943 by Salvador Dalí

MONA VON BISMARCK
(1897-1983)

Perhaps no client better illustrates the depth of Balenciaga's appeal among the aristocracy of style than Mona von Bismarck. An American heiress and socialite, von Bismarck was one of the wealthiest women of her era and a dominant figure on the international social scene. She commissioned entire wardrobes from Balenciaga, sometimes ordering dozens of gowns at a time. Her loyalty to him was not just passionate - it was absolute – and her devotion reached mythic proportions. When Balenciaga closed his couture house in 1968, she was devastated, reportedly locked herself in her suite at the Hôtel Lambert in Paris for three days. Diana Vreeland, the former editor of *American Vogue,* commented on this, saying, '*I mean, it was the end of a certain part of her life!*' Furthermore, Mona's admiration for Balenciaga was evident in her patronage - after a train accident destroyed much of her wardrobe, she ordered 150 garments from him in a single season. Balenciaga even designed her gardening attire!

Despite their fame and status, these women were drawn to the same qualities - Balenciaga's rare ability to blend innovation with dignity, structure with softness and silence with strength. He was a designer of few words yet his clothes spoke volumes.

Balenciaga's design process was intensely personal. Each garment was crafted to suit the specific needs, posture and poise of the woman who would wear it. He had a couturier's intuition – the capacity to understand, almost telepathically, how a woman wished to be seen as she moved through the world. For these women - whether navigating royal obligations, international diplomacy or the rigorous demands of social prominence - Balenciaga offered not just clothing but a definite identity. Each garment expressed character, aspiration and control. Balenciaga's post-war creations in particular offered a new visual language for women emerging from an era of deprivation. He replaced the frippery of pre-war couture with something more essential and sculptural - a future defined by clarity, strength and enduring grace.

In an age where fame could be fleeting, Balenciaga's clientele represented permanence. Through them, his vision of beauty was immortalized in state photographs, film stills, society pages and portraits. These women were not just the Muses of his 'Golden Age', they were the living embodiment of his artistic philosophy.

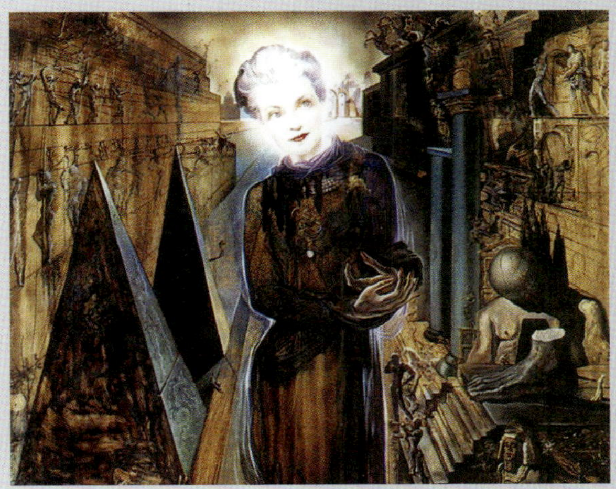

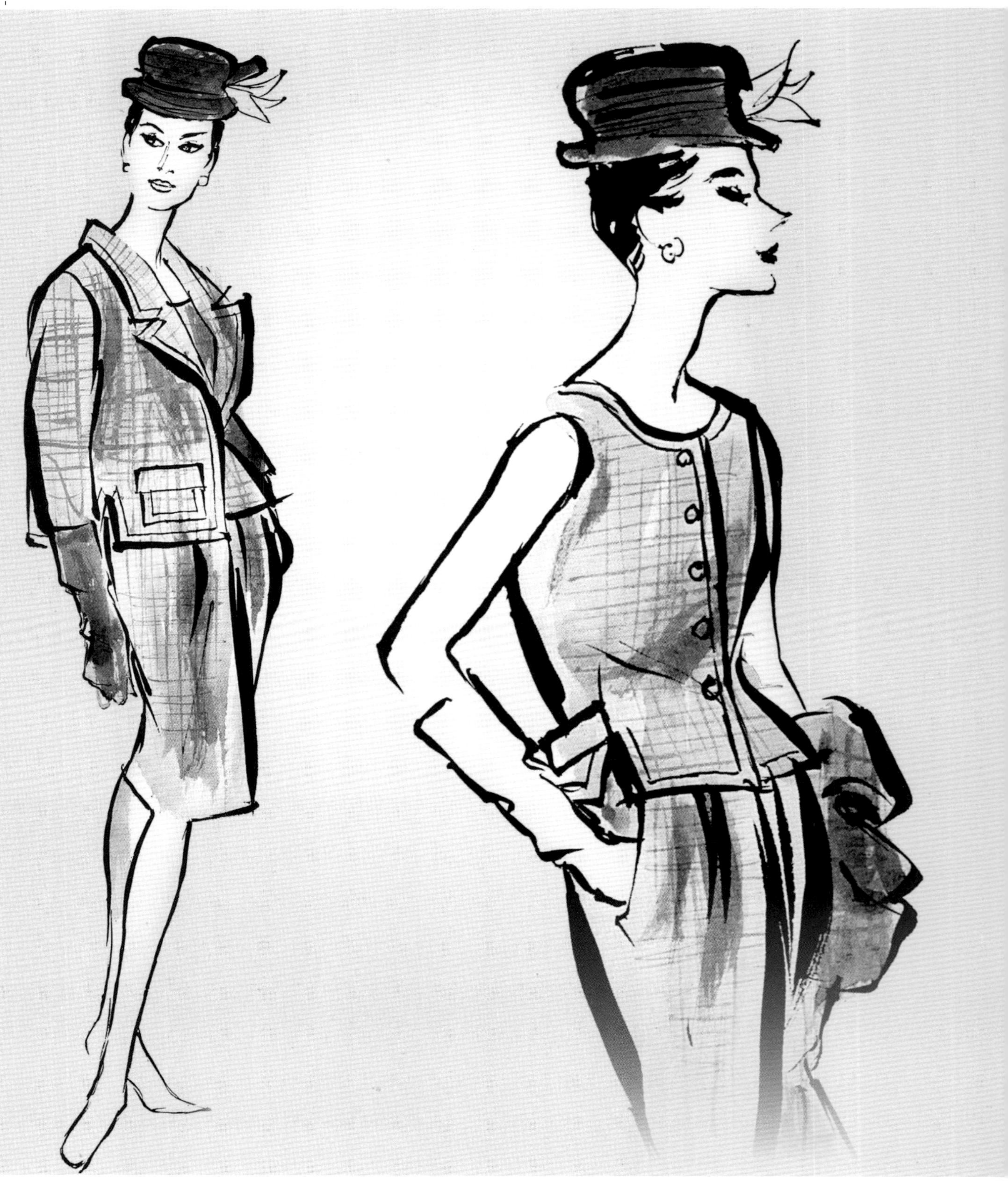

ABOVE: Balenciaga outfit sketches, 1960

ONE WOMAN'S WARDROBE
This week — Mrs Laurie Newton Sharp

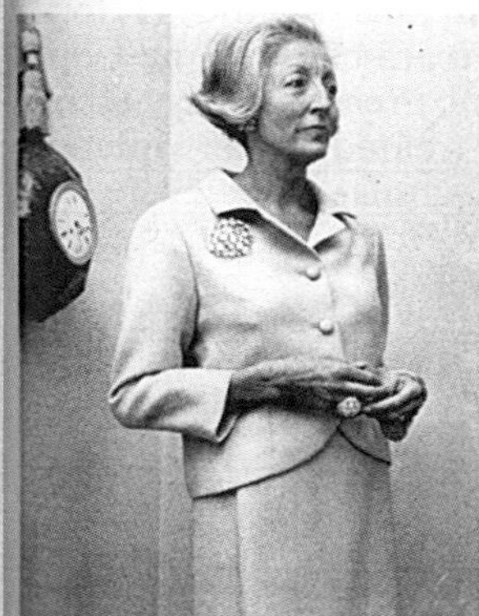

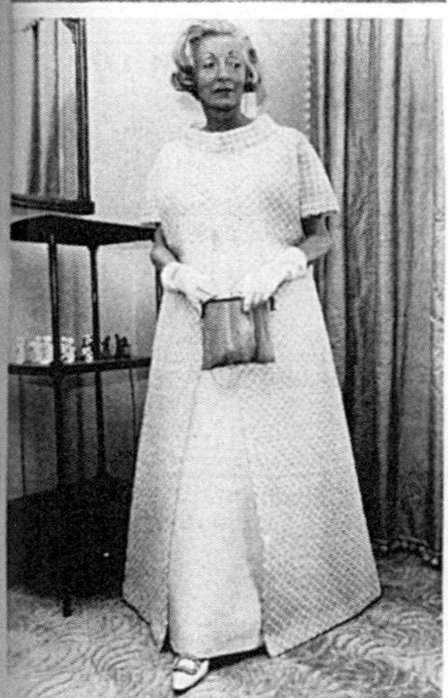

Mrs Newton Sharp is News Editor at Harrods, which involves directing publicity, handling entertainment and arranging receptions. Apart from the Press coverage, Mrs Newton Sharp is not associated with fashion, but she does not deny that a good dress sense has helped her in her career. She believes that women are ageless, and proves it by wearing the same type of clothes today that she did at the age of 20 – for example, her Molyneux dress. Now, some of her tips for elegance – good grooming, simplicity, cut and fabric all balancing, and important, choosing clothes that suit you, rather than following extreme fashion. Accessories are also very important and Mrs Newton Sharp will buy expensive gloves and shoes and the best stockings obtainable. She adores hats and never feels an outfit is complete without one. Although she does not think that Paris influences fashion as it used to, she still prefers to buy original models. Her favourites are Balenciaga and Yves Saint Laurent, but she also likes Italian clothes. She has no fur coat, but loves fur-lined coats and matching coats for evening. Her most coveted fur is sable. Much of her life is spent entertaining, and for this she wears long, flowing hostess gowns. But at weekends she likes trousers and tailored shirts.

In private life Mrs Newton Sharp is the wife of Dr P E Thompson Hancock, Director of Clinical Research at both the Royal Marsden Hospital and the Institute of Cancer Research, and apart from her full life at Harrods she is vice-chairman of the Ladies' Association of the Royal Marsden Hospital, a vice-chairman of the British Empire Cancer Campaign for Research and on the advisory committees of three art colleges.

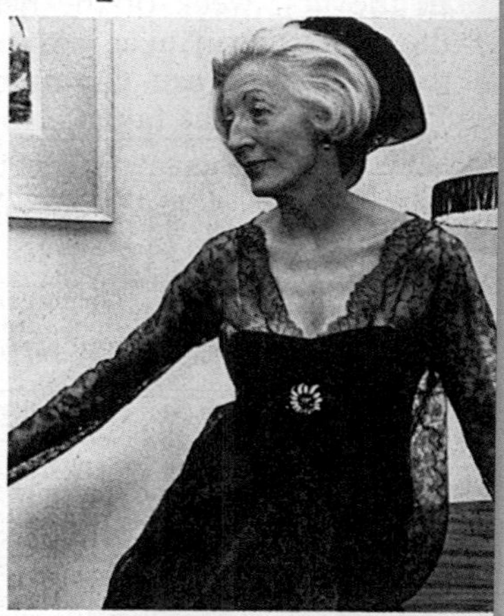

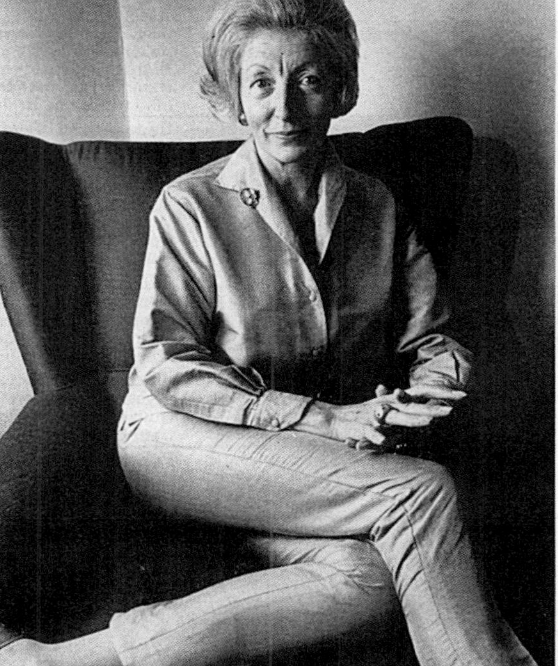

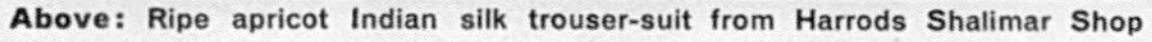

Above: Ripe apricot Indian silk trouser-suit from Harrods Shalimar Shop

Report NORMA MORICEAU Pictures PETER AKEHURST

Top: Palest blue wool hopsack suit by Balenciaga, from Harrods. **Above:** Ice-pink and white woven nylon evening coat worn over silk zibbeline dress. Original French models from Harrods. **Below:** Gabardine navy coat by Balenciaga with enormous bat-wing sleeves and trimmed with gold buttons. Worn with navy Balenciaga hat. From Harrods.

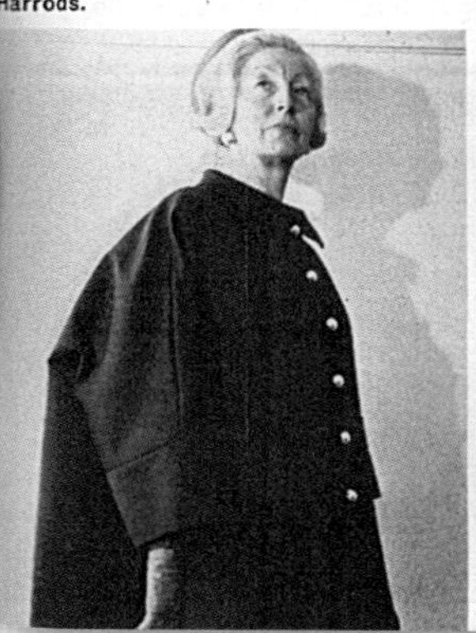

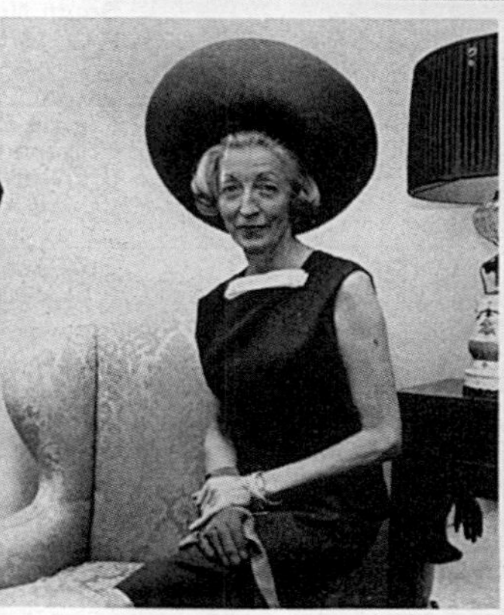

Top: Brown lace over black crepe strapless cocktail dress by Castillo. Large black organza rose hat by Dolores. From Harrods. **Above:** Brown linen and rayon dress with flat pique bow at neckline, by Molyneux. Huge coffee-coloured straw hat by Balenciaga. From Harrods. **Below:** Navy wool suit with white overcheck by Balenciaga. The navy felt hat is also Balenciaga. From Harrods.

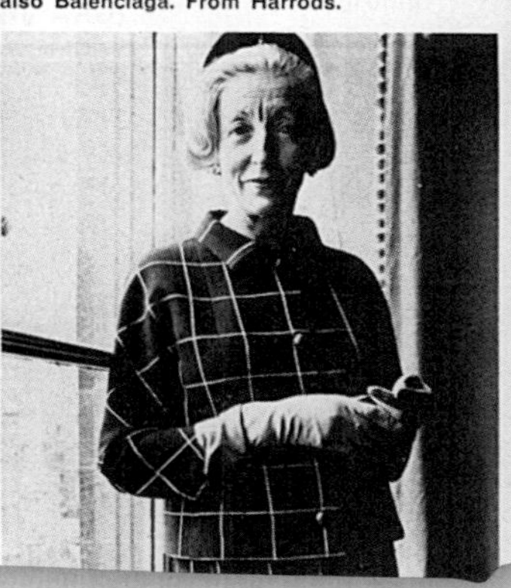

A SILENT EXIT

"High fashion is mortally wounded"
Cristóbal Balenciaga

As in every other area of life, the 1960s were a time of radical transformation in the world of fashion. The youth movement, led by designers such as the UK-based Mary Quant and Barbara Hulanicki of BIBA, were redefining what it meant to be stylish. Street fashion began to eclipse the rarefied air of haute couture. Ready-to-wear collections exploded in popularity, offering accessibility and adaptability in ways that couture never could. Cristóbal Balenciaga - ever the purist, ever the perfectionist - found himself increasingly at odds with the direction the industry was taking.

For decades, Balenciaga had operated with complete creative control, designing not for mass appeal but for aesthetic perfection. He viewed fashion as an art form, one that required solitude, craftsmanship and unwavering discipline. His atelier in Paris was a sanctuary of silence and precision – light years away from the burgeoning commercialism of the 1960s fashion scene. Balenciaga refused to compromise his vision. He would not dilute his artistry in order to fit into this new, fast-paced world. The ready-to-wear, faster-fashion revolution held no appeal for him. And so, in May 1968 - amid student protests in Paris and a broader social revolution that signalled the collapse of old hierarchies – Balenciaga, quietly and without fuss, closed his salons in Paris, Barcelona and Madrid. His decision was abrupt but not impulsive. Those close to him say he had long contemplated this retreat. He simply chose the moment when the world no longer aligned with his values.

After the closure of his fashion house, Balenciaga vanished from the public eye. He retreated to his beloved Spain, dividing his time between homes in Jávea and the Basque Country. Little is known about his final years, which he spent in almost monastic seclusion. He rarely granted interviews and declined public appearances. His once-bustling ateliers fell silent. The man who had once captivated the world's most discerning women - clients like Jacqueline Kennedy, Princess Grace of Monaco and the Duchess of Windsor - had exited the fashion stage for good. However, his designs continued to speak for him. Even in retirement, his influence was felt everywhere. Young designers continued to study his patterns, his construction, his revolutionary approach to volume and silhouette. They revered him as a master even if they had never met him. His retreat from public life was not an abdication but a quiet assertion of control - a final design decision from a man who had spent his

OPP PAGE: The new uniform created by Cristóbal Balenciaga for Air France flight attendants, worn from June 1969

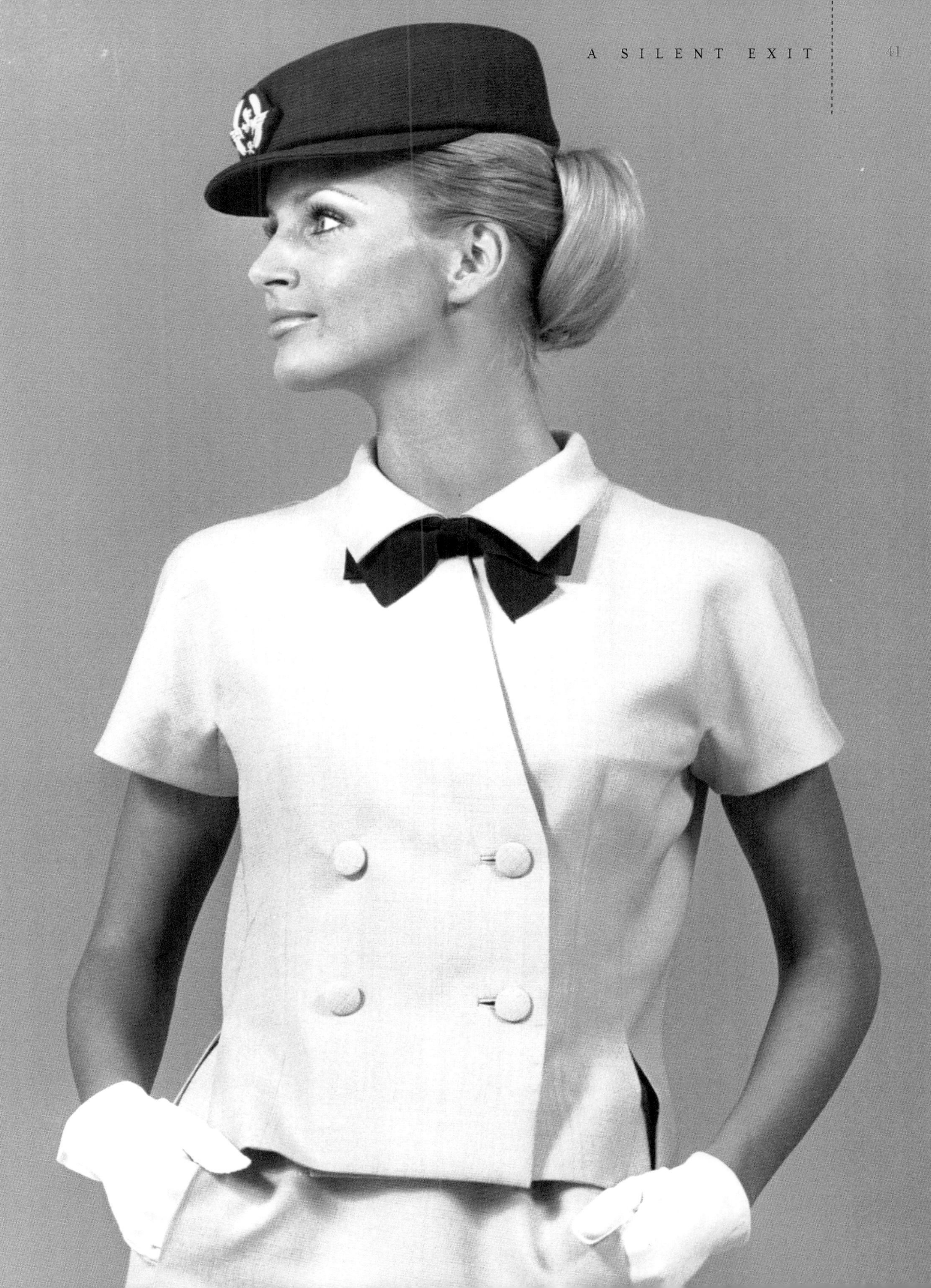

life perfecting silhouettes and sculpting elegance out of fabric. It was, in essence, his last masterpiece. The closing of the Balenciaga fashion house in 1968 was not just a business decision - it was a philosophical stance. Cristóbal Balenciaga chose to exit a world that no longer reflected his values, doing so with the same integrity that had defined his life's work.

Cristóbal passed away in 1972 aged 77, four years after his retirement. His death was deeply mourned in the industry, not just for the loss of a genius but for the closing chapter of haute couture's golden age. However, he left behind a body of work that would become foundational to modern fashion.

Balenciaga's impact continued to be felt in the fashion world long after his departure. Perhaps his most profound legacy lay in the designers he mentored or inspired - figures like Hubert de Givenchy, André Courrèges and Oscar de la Renta, each of whom carried forward elements of his vision in their own work.

HUBERT DE GIVENCHY

One of Balenciaga's most devoted protégés, Givenchy often spoke of the Spaniard with reverence. He had long admired Balenciaga's command of structure and form, his ability to strip away excess and arrive at something eternal. Though the two never officially collaborated, Balenciaga's advice and influence were pivotal in shaping Givenchy's approach. Givenchy

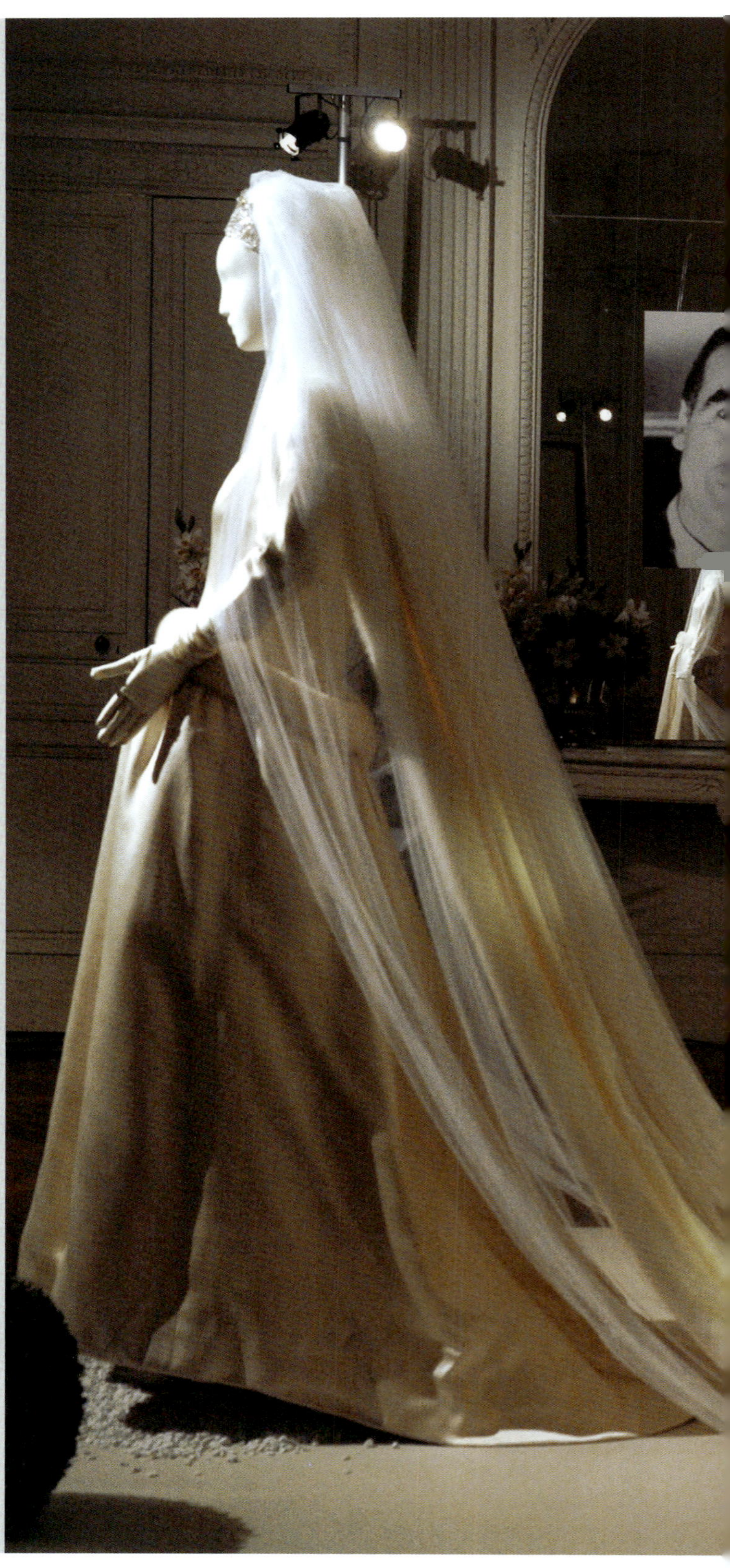

ABOVE: Two Hubert de Givenchy dresses (right) on display alongside the Balenciaga-designed Queen Fabiola wedding dress

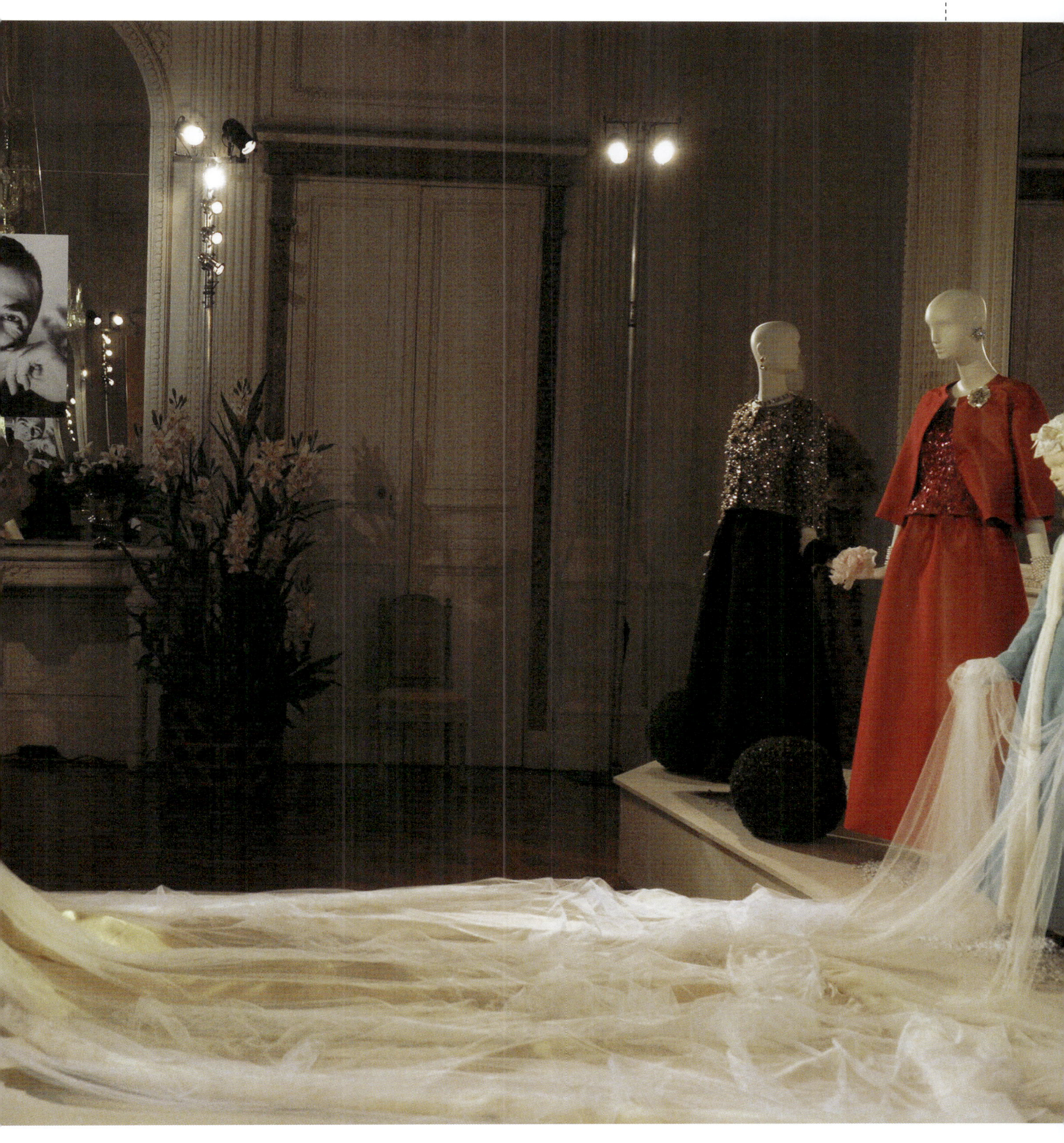

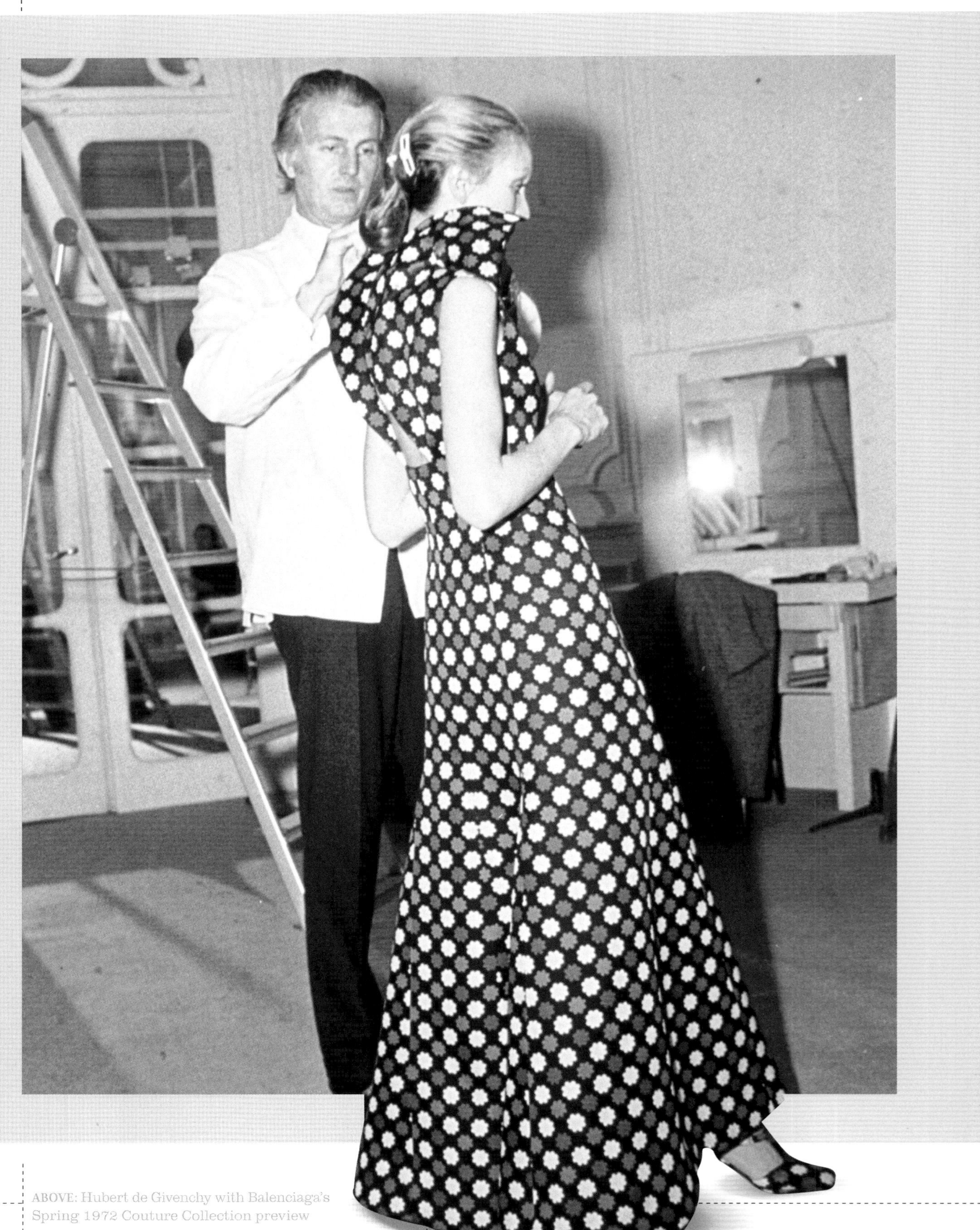

ABOVE: Hubert de Givenchy with Balenciaga's
Spring 1972 Couture Collection preview

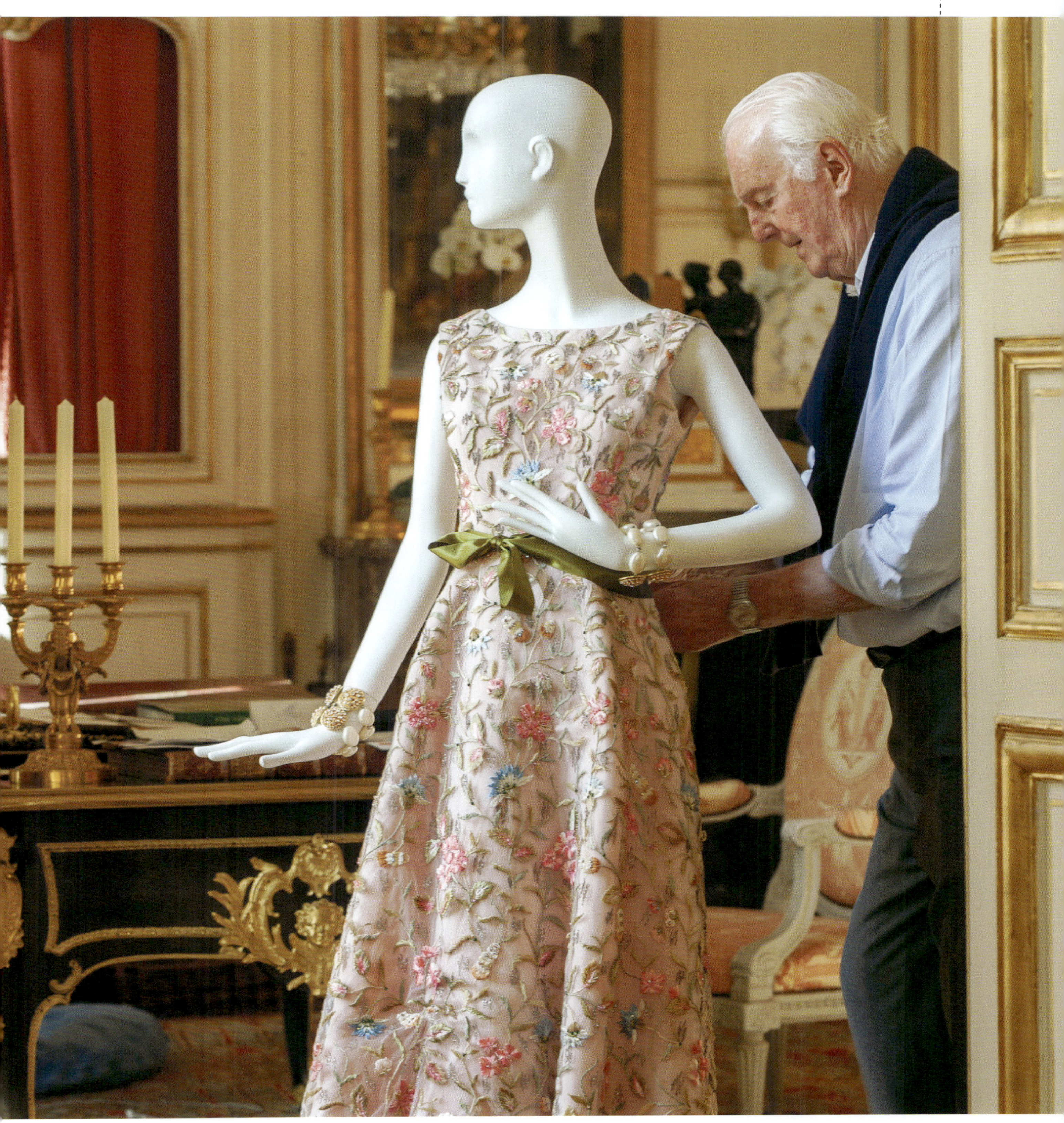

ABOVE: Hubert de Givenchy alters a Cristóbal Balenciaga dress during the shooting of an exhibition catalogue

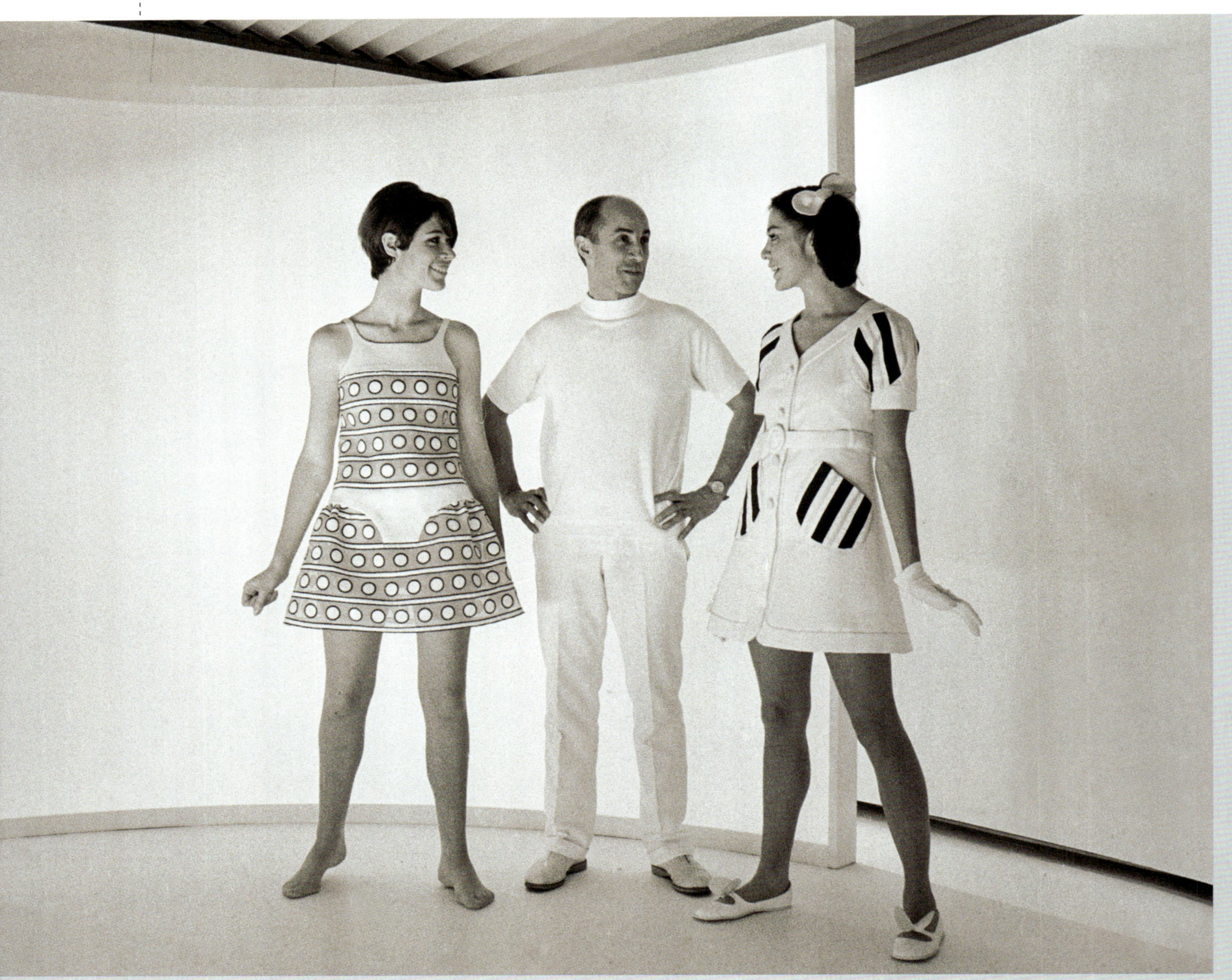

once said, *'Balenciaga was my religion'*. His minimalist aesthetic, refined lines and insistence on quality can be traced directly to the master's teachings. Most notably, Givenchy applied Balenciaga's principles to the modern woman's wardrobe, blending elegance with practicality in ways that captivated clients like Audrey Hepburn.

ANDRÉ COURRÈGES

Former pupil Courrèges took the maestro's architectural foundations and propelled them into the future. After spending years under Balenciaga's tutelage, Courrèges struck out on his own in the early 1960s, becoming one of the leading figures of

ABOVE: André Courrèges with models, 26 January, 1968
OPP PAGE: Oscar de la Renta fashion show, 13 September 2004

space-age fashion. Though his designs - marked by geometric shapes, short skirts and futuristic materials - seemed a stark departure from Balenciaga's, the connection lay in technique. Courrèges adopted Balenciaga's obsession with form and construction and applied it to a new, modern context. He proved that the master's teachings could adapt, evolve and remain relevant in an entirely different fashion language.

OSCAR DE LA RENTA

Another heir to Balenciaga's aesthetic lineage, De la Renta brought the elegance and sophistication of

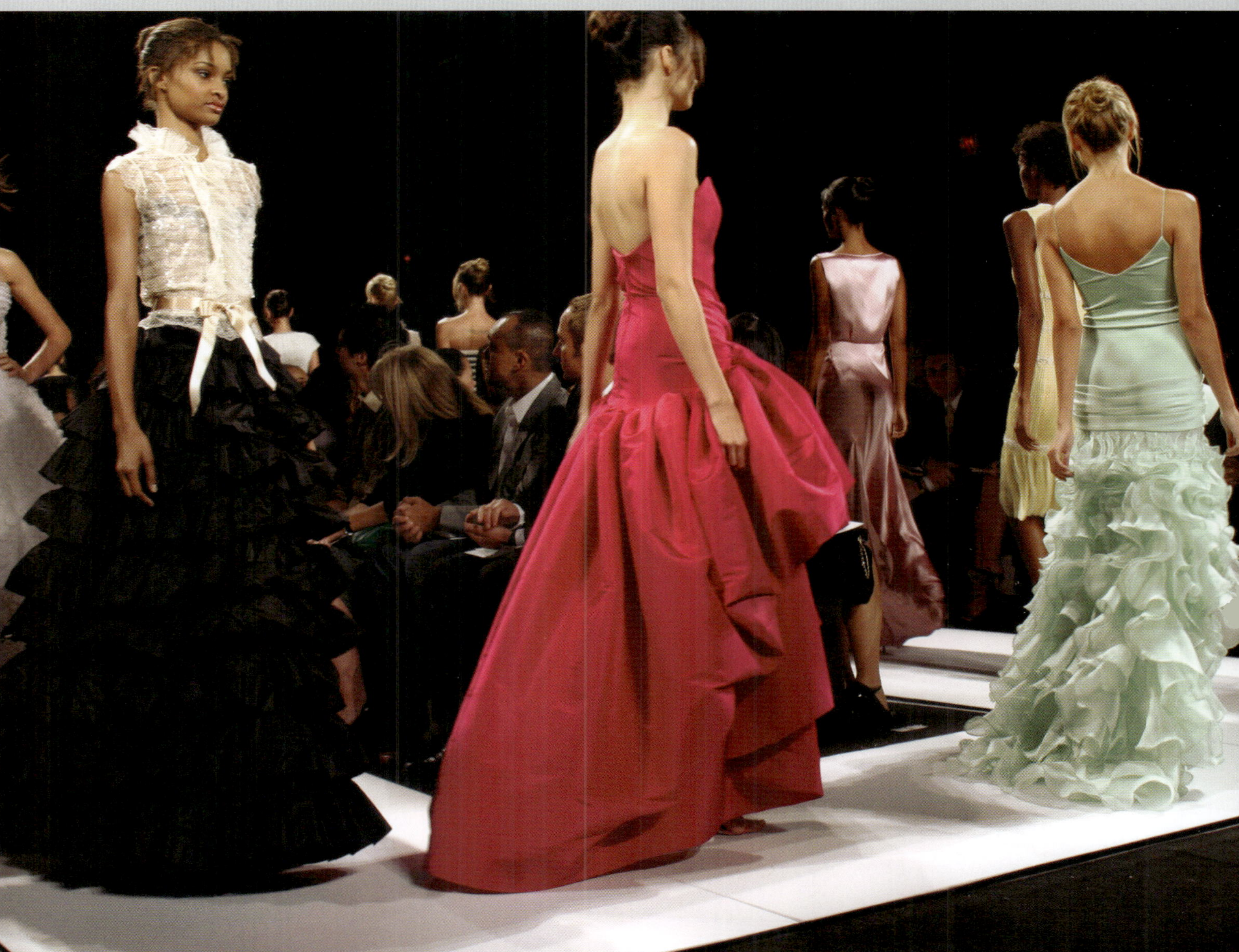

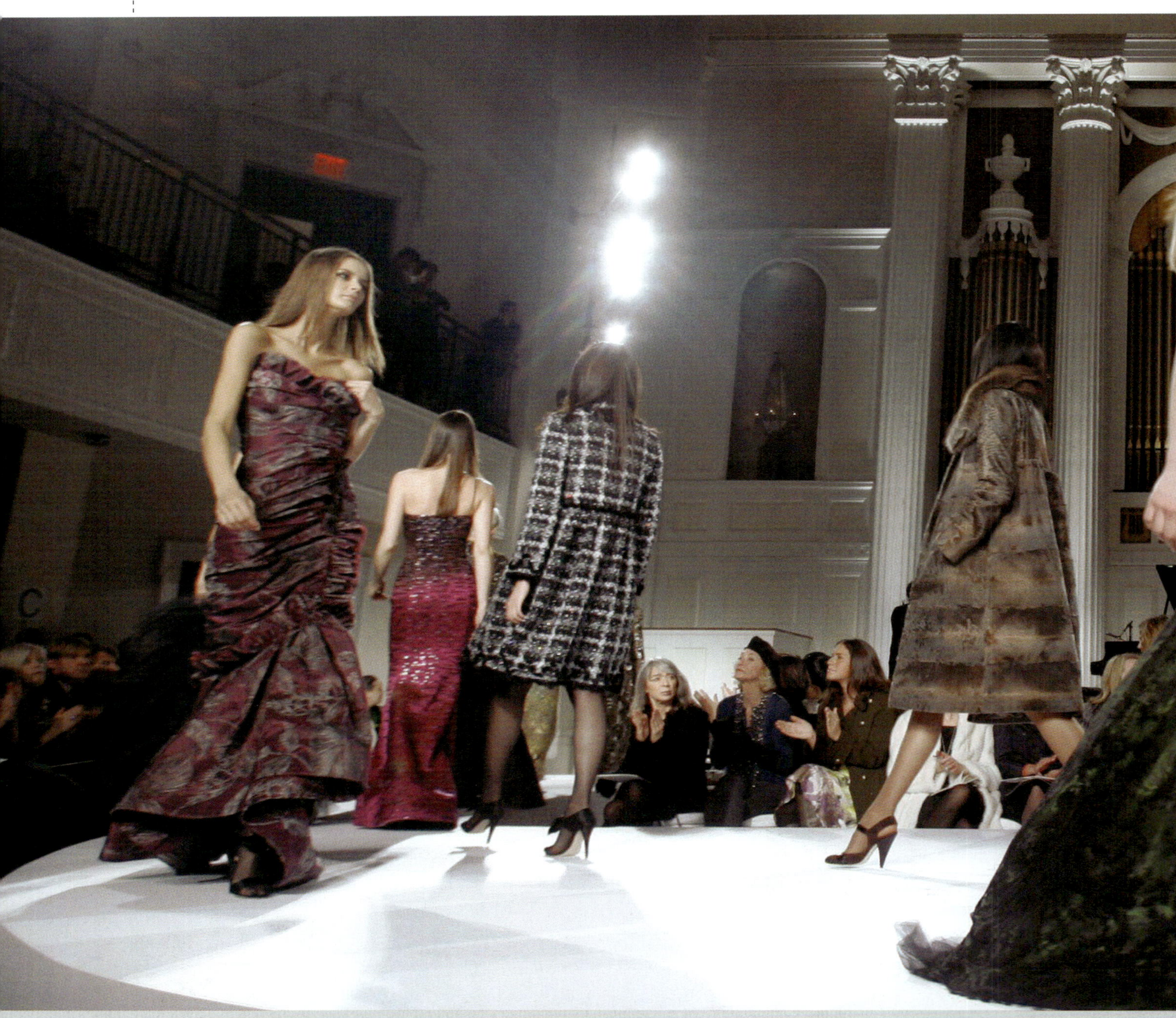

haute couture into the American fashion lexicon, and considered Balenciaga a spiritual mentor. His designs - graceful, feminine and immaculately tailored - often echoed Balenciaga's reverence for beauty and precision. De la Renta managed to bridge the old world and the new, bringing the craftsmanship of European couture to the ready-to-wear arena.

Beyond these three designers, countless others – including Yves Saint Laurent and Emanuel Ungaro

ABOVE: Models walk the finale of Oscar de la Renta's Fall 2008 collection at New York Fashion Week, 4 February 2008

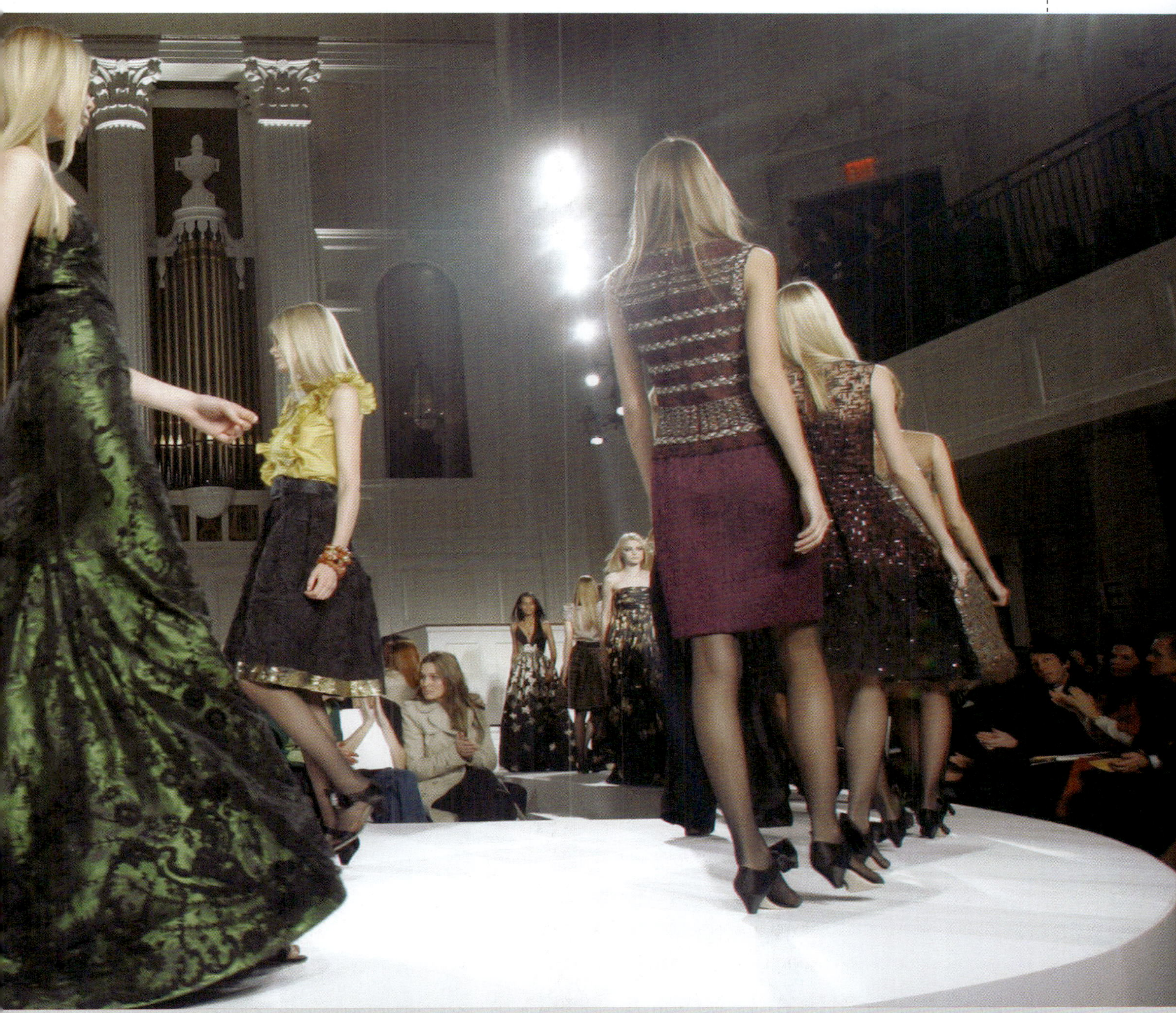

- cited Balenciaga as an inspiration. His methods, particularly the use of innovative fabrics and sculptural cuts, remain as something of a benchmark. Cristóbal's philosophy - that fashion should serve form, that beauty lies in restraint, that elegance is eternal - continues to resonate. But one of the great paradoxes of Cristóbal Balenciaga's legacy has to be that, while he rejected the commercialisation of fashion, his name became a global brand long after his death.

CRISTÓBAL BALENCIAGA MUSEOA

Nestling in the coastal town of Getaria, Spain - the birthplace of the legendary couturier - the Cristóbal Balenciaga Museoa or Cristóbal Balenciaga Museum stands as a testament to the enduring legacy of one of fashion's most influential figures. Inaugurated on 7 June 2011, the institution offers an immersive journey into Balenciaga's life, artistry and his profound impact on haute couture.

At the heart of the museum lies an extensive collection of over 1200 pieces, encompassing garments, accessories, sketches and personal artifacts. These items chronicle Balenciaga's evolution from his early days in Spain to his illustrious career in Paris. The collection includes rare pre-Paris designs from the 1910s to the 1930s, showcasing his foundational techniques and aesthetic development. Notable donations from prominent figures such as Rachel L. Mellon, Hubert de Givenchy, the Belgian Royal Family and the heirs of Princess Grace of Monaco enrich the museum's holdings, offering insights into Balenciaga's relationships with his elite clientele.

The museum curates a dynamic program of exhibitions and events aimed at highlighting Balenciaga's role in

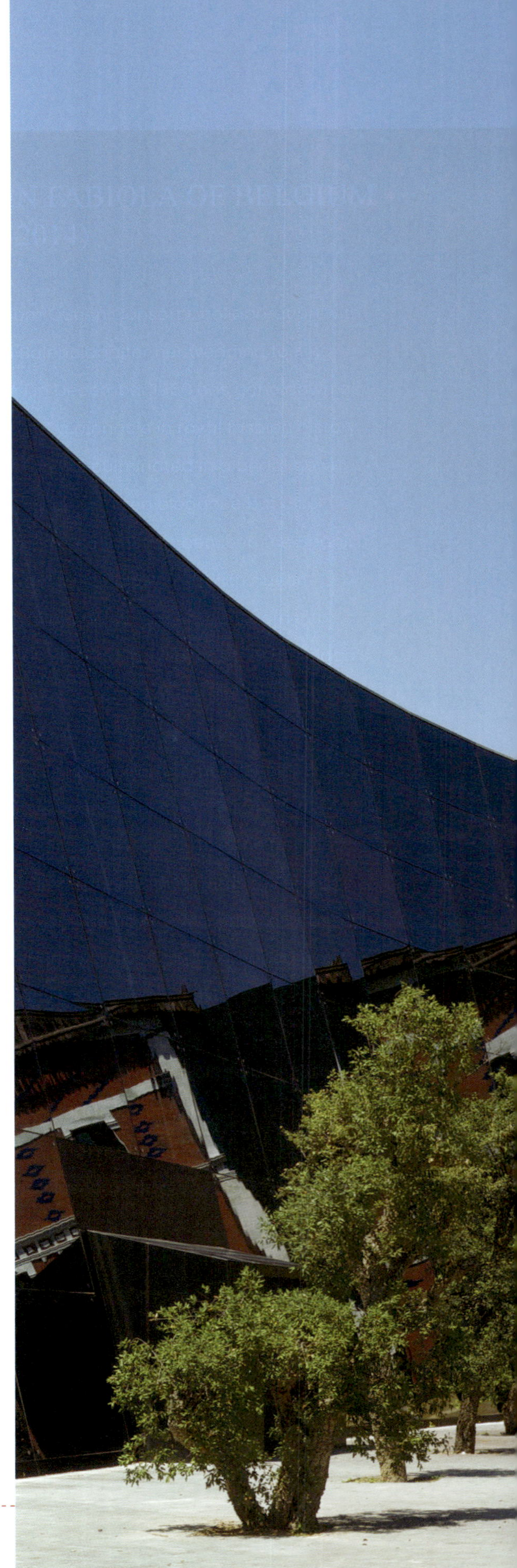

RIGHT: Cristóbal Balenciaga Museum, Getaria, Spain

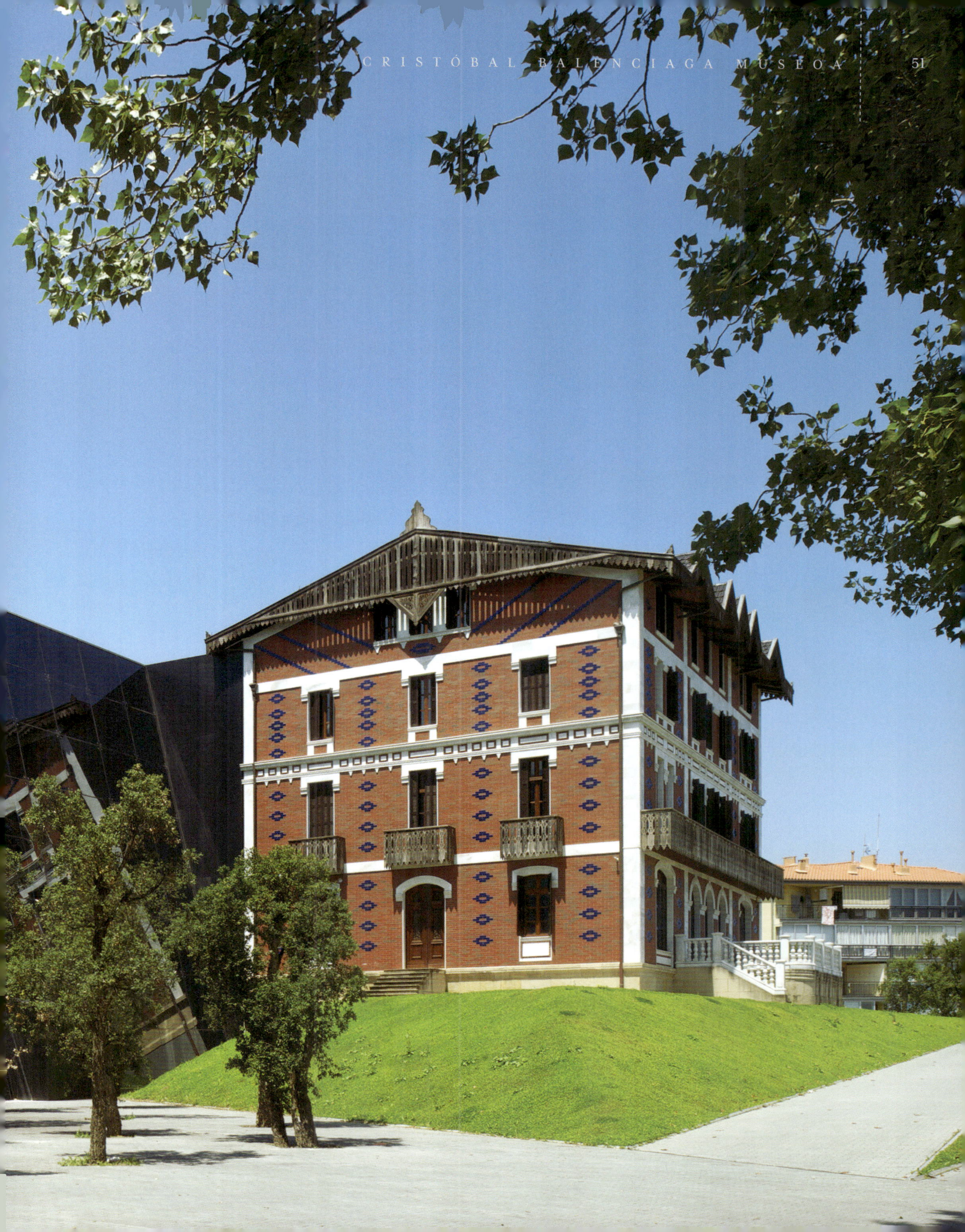

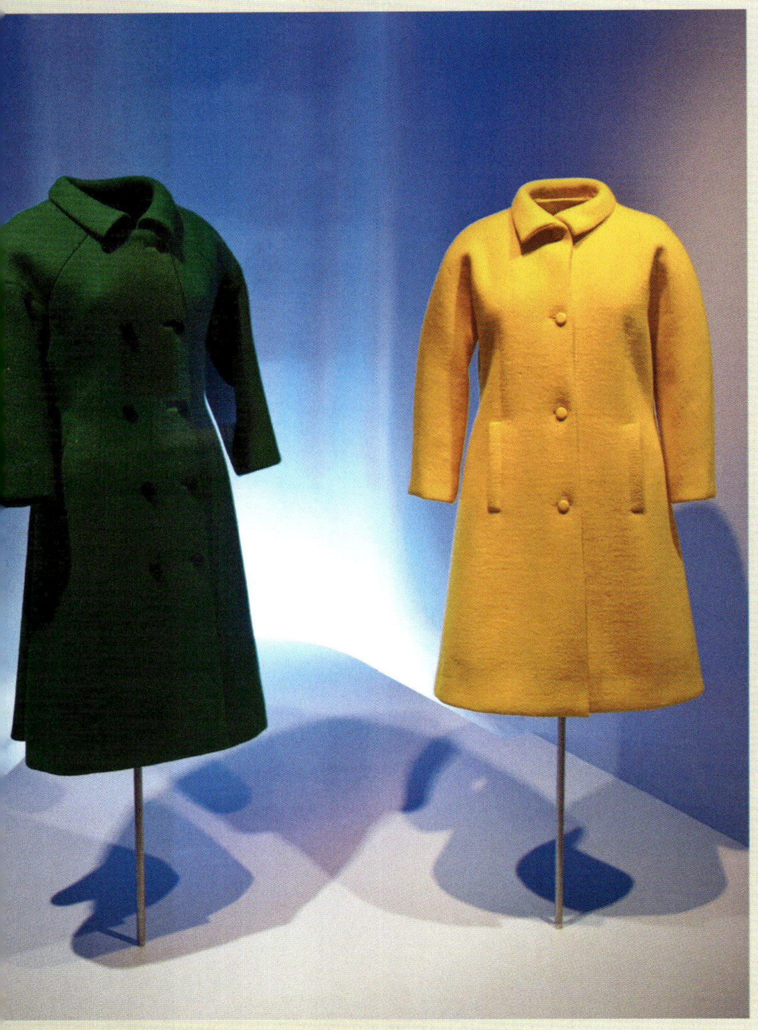

The museum's location is steeped in personal significance. It adjoins the historic Palacio Aldamar, a 19th-century villa once frequented by Balenciaga's seamstress mother as it had been the home of the Marquesa de Casa Torres. The museum's modern annexe, designed by Cuban architect Julián Argilagos and the AV62 Arquitectos team, features a sleek, curved façade of dark glass and steel. This contemporary structure harmoniously contrasts with the traditional villa, symbolizing the fusion of Balenciaga's classical roots and innovative spirit. The museum's architectural design reflects Balenciaga's principles of structure and form. The interior features three suspended gallery spaces within the modern annex, creating an atmosphere of calm and contemplation. This spatial arrangement allows visitors to engage intimately with the exhibits, mirroring the designer's meticulous attention to detail and preference for understated elegance.

Beyond preserving historical artifacts, the Cristóbal Balenciaga Museum serves as a vibrant centre for cultural exchange and scholarly research. Through its exhibitions, educational programmes and architectural embodiment of Balenciaga's ethos, the museum not only honours the past but also inspires future explorations in fashion and design. It stands as a beacon of Balenciaga's enduring legacy, inviting visitors to experience the artistry and innovation that defined his remarkable career.

fashion history and his enduring influence. Exhibitions, such as 'Cristóbal Balenciaga: Technique, Material and Form' have delved into the couturier's innovative methods and design philosophy. Additionally, the museum offers educational programmes, including advanced courses in haute couture tailoring techniques - fostering the transmission of Balenciaga's craftsmanship to new generations of fashion professionals.

ABOVE: Two Balenciaga coats at the Cristóbal Balenciaga Museum
OPP PAGE: Balenciaga Haute Couture exhibition

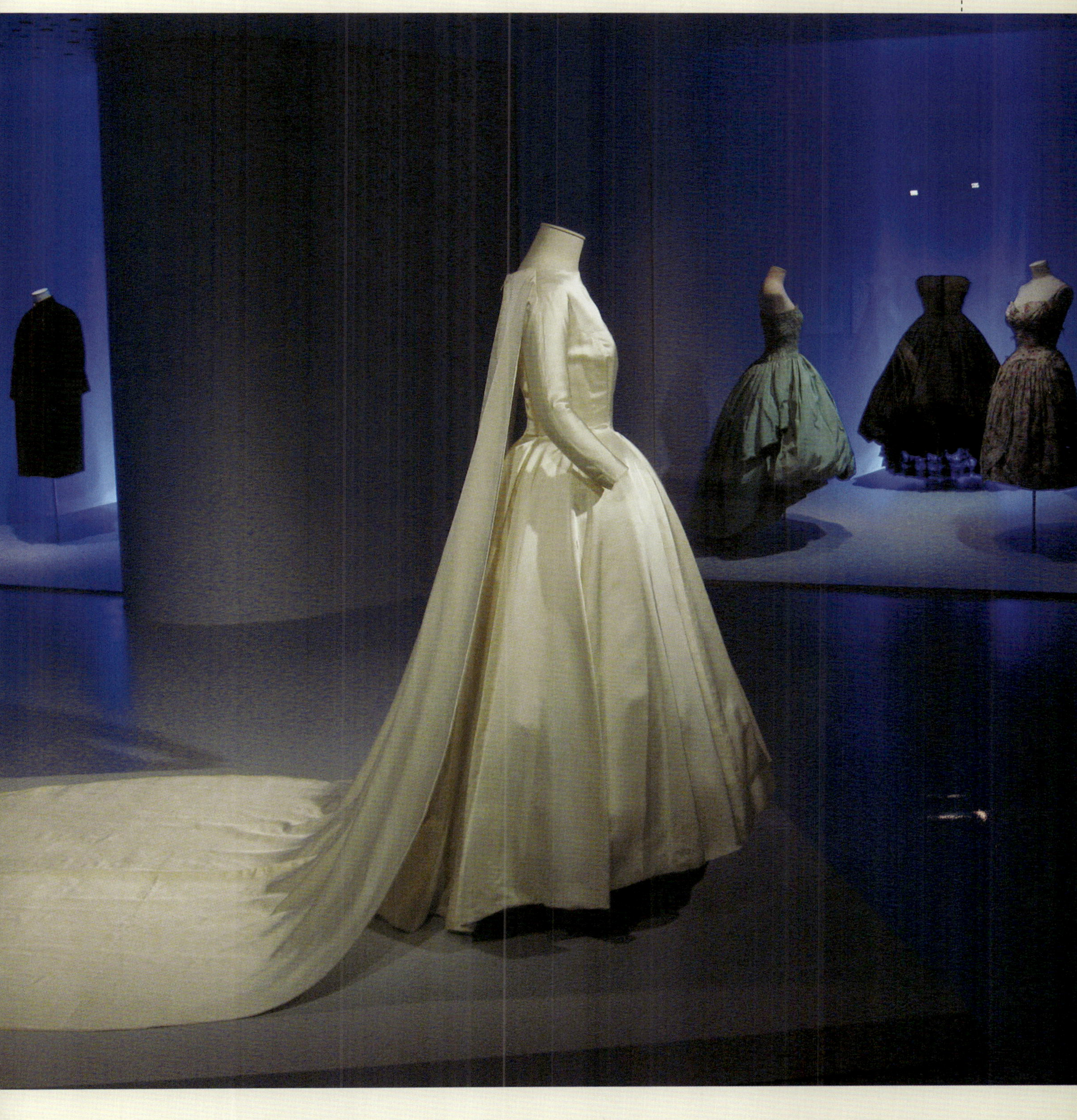

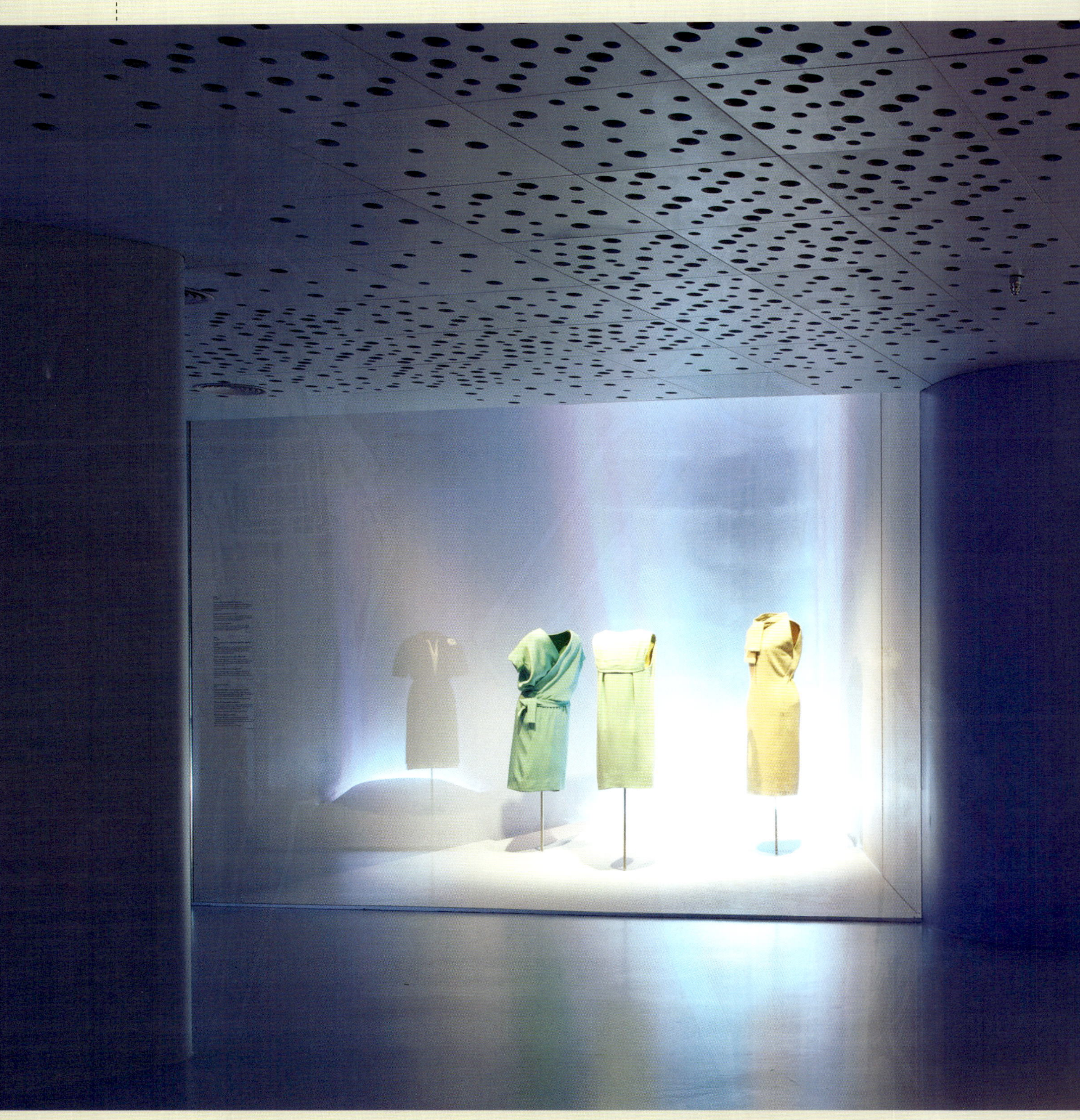

ABOVE: A stunning display at the Cristóbal Balenciaga Museum

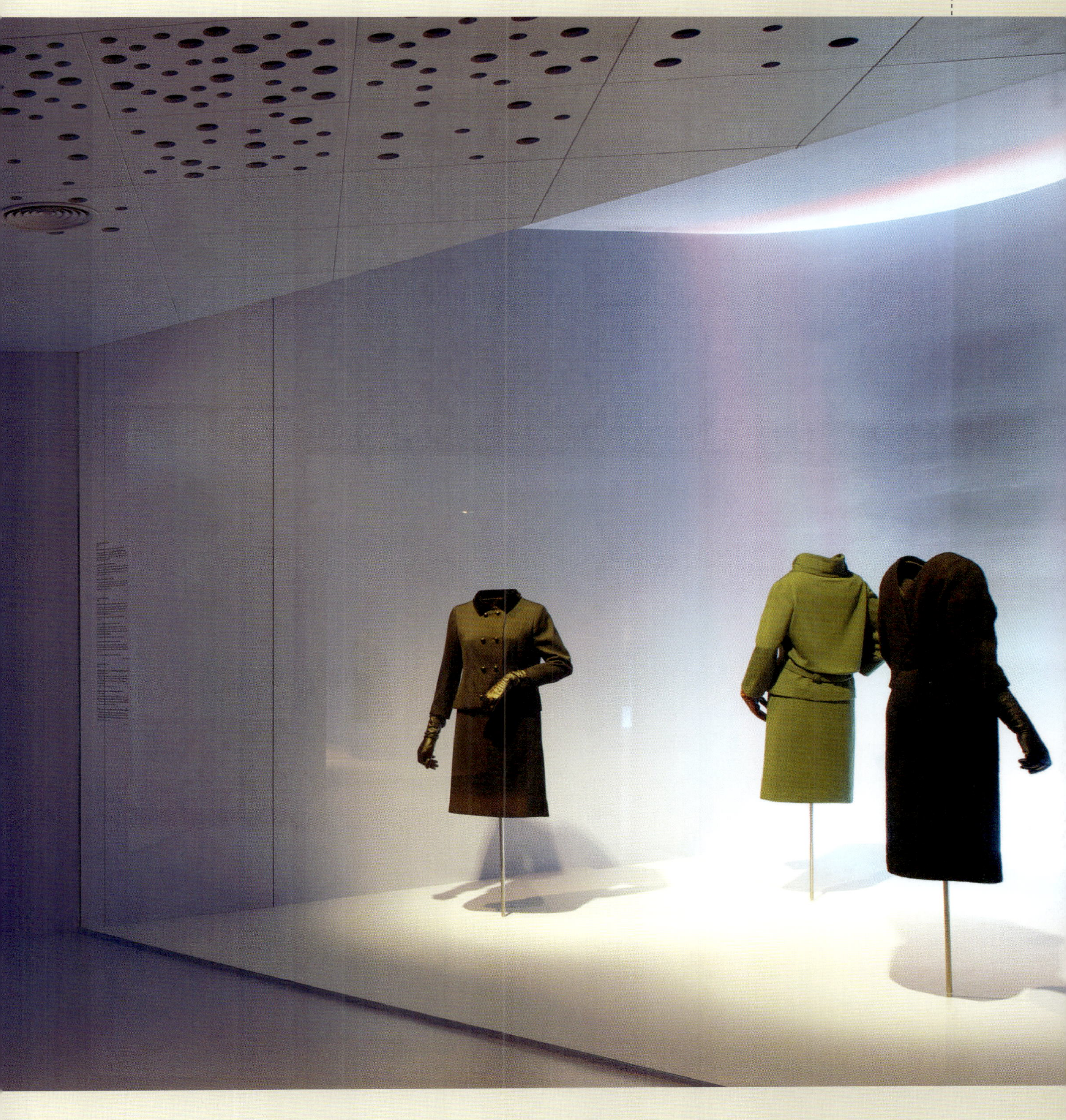

REVIVAL AND REBIRTH

"I am proud of what I brought to Balenciaga. I believe we helped redefine fashion for a new generation"

Nicolas Ghesquière, Creative Director of Balenciaga 1997-2012

The House of Balenciaga lay virtually dormant for almost 20 years. Then in 1986, the French company Jacques Bogart S.A. acquired the rights to the brand, marking the beginning of its revival. The following year Michel Goma, former artistic director at Jean Patou, was appointed creative director at the newly revived brand. Under his leadership, the House introduced a new ready-to-wear line called 'Le Dix', named after the house's first perfume launched in 1947. Goma's designs were characterised by a sleek, minimalist aesthetic that modernised the brand while respecting its heritage. His tenure helped Balenciaga regain some status within the industry. However, it wasn't until relatively unknown designer Nicolas Ghesquière, who had been working within Balenciaga's licensing wing, took over in 1997 that the brand once again became a fashion force to be reckoned with. Ghesquiere was appointed creative director of women's ready-to-wear, and what followed was one of the most acclaimed creative renaissances in modern fashion history.

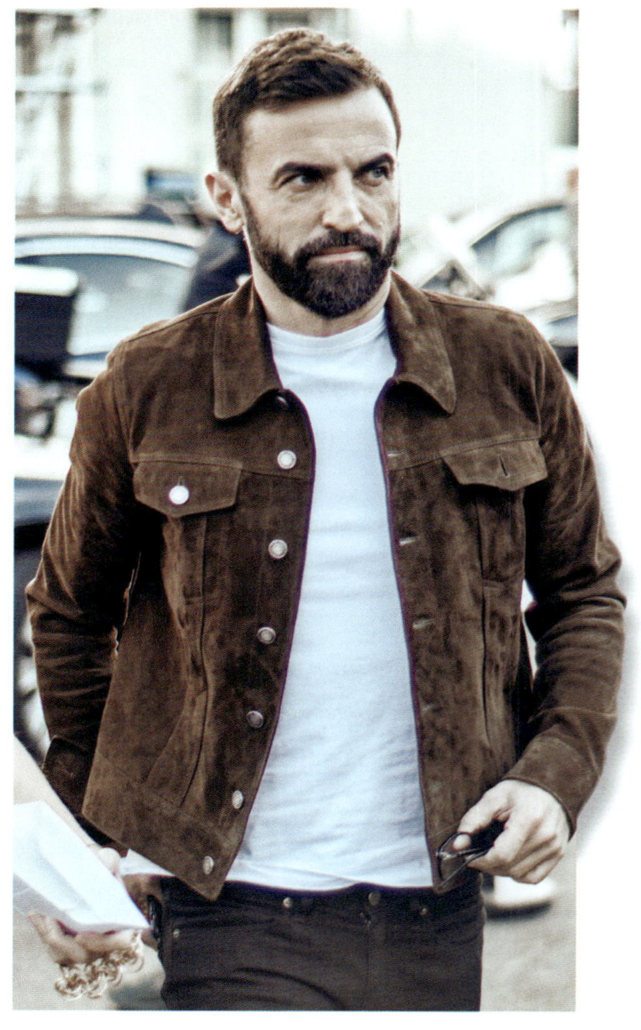

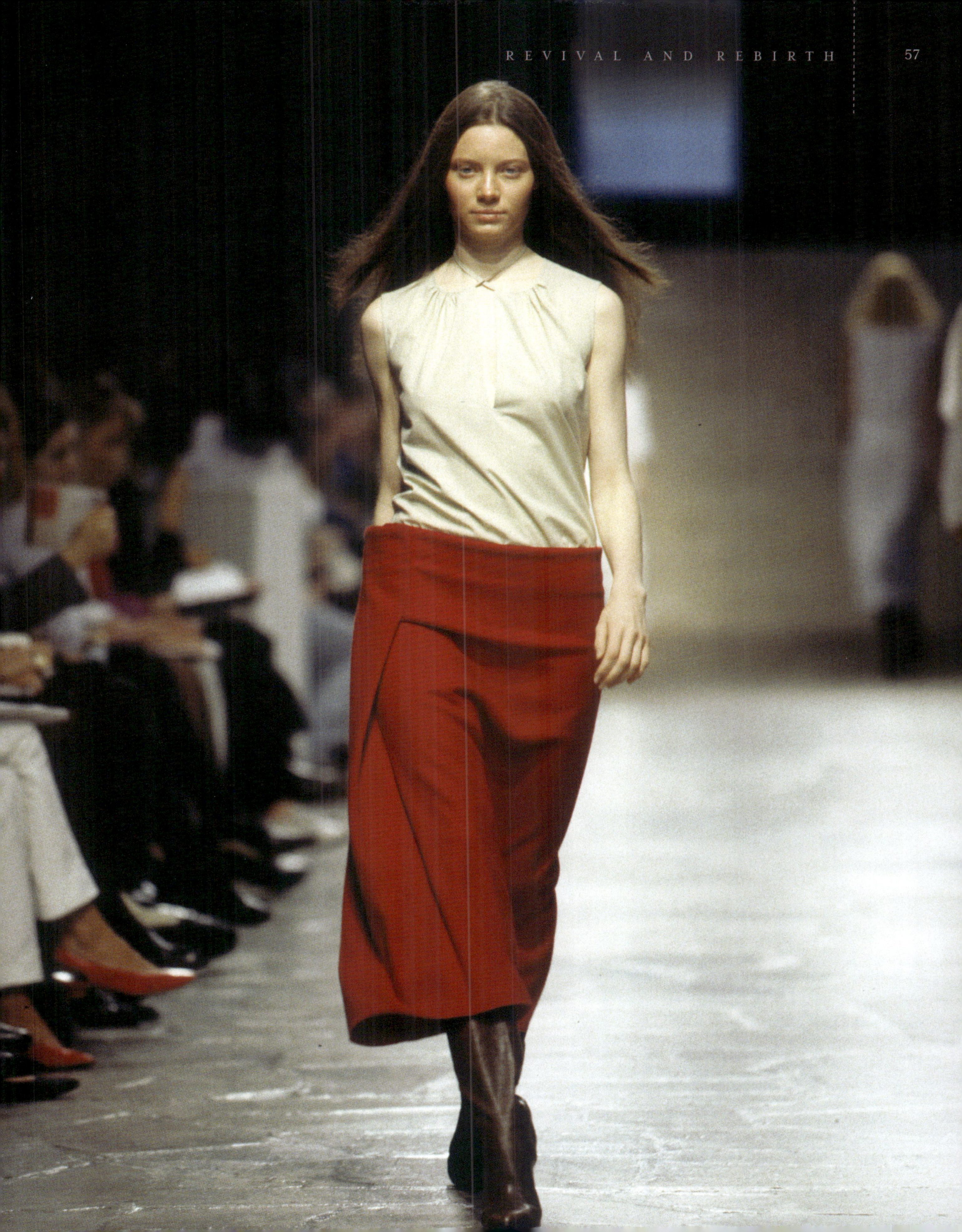

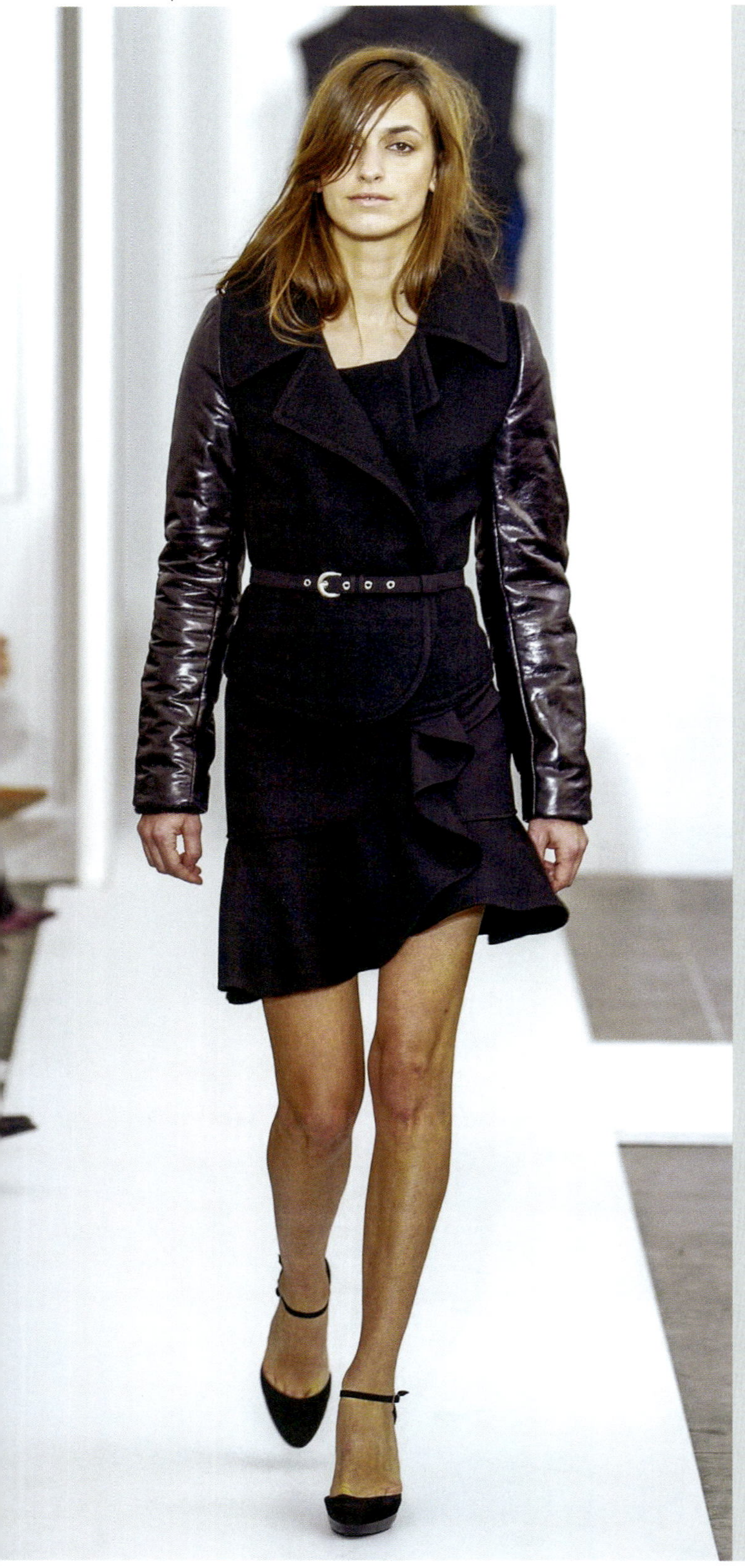

From his very first collections, Ghesquière reinvigorated Balenciaga with an aesthetic that was rooted in structure and experimentation. He paid homage to Cristóbal's architectural silhouettes - such as cocoon coats, barrel lines and dropped shoulders - but infused them with futuristic materials, synthetic fabrics and tech-inspired cuts. The interplay of past and future became his signature. Ghesquière did not simply modernise Balenciaga - he deconstructed it and reassembled it through a contemporary lens.

One of his most defining collections arrived in Fall/Winter 2002 – the year after he'd been named Designer of the Year by the Council of Fashion Designers of America or CFDA.

Ghesquière presented a collection of sculptural, space-age garments that blended neoprene, vinyl and metallic finishes. The silhouettes were severe and precise yet graceful. Fashion journalists, critics, and buyers hailed him as a saviour with Janet Ozzard of *Vogue* noting that Ghesquière's designs were *'inventive, original—and commercially viable'*.

Under Ghesquière, Balenciaga became a cult phenomenon. Fashion insiders revered his intelligence and meticulous craftsmanship, while celebrities and forward-thinking stylists championed his bold designs. Top fashion editors like Carine Roitfeld and Anna Wintour were early supporters. Balenciaga was once again at the sartorial forefront - not because it was following trends but because it

ABOVE & OPP PAGE: Models walk the runway during Balenciaga's Fall/Winter 2002 ready-to-wear show at New York Fashion Week, 12 February 2002

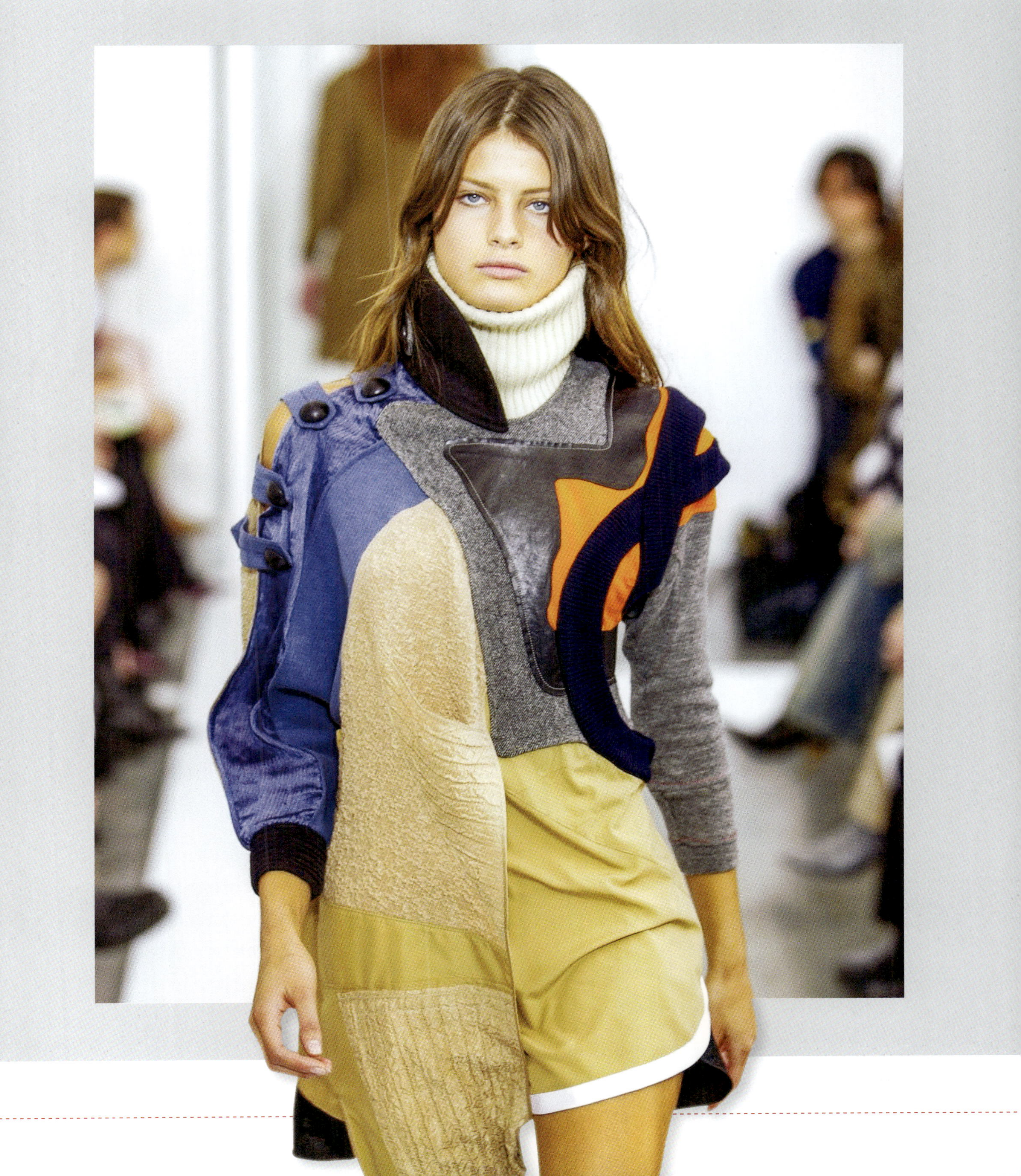

was creating them. Balenciaga's reinvention under Ghesquière was not just a matter of silhouette or fabric - it was philosophical. At a time when many luxury houses were leaning into sex appeal, heritage nostalgia or blatant commercialism, Balenciaga offered an alternative - fashion for the thinking elite. Ghesquière's collections were futuristic but grounded in historical awareness. He referenced science fiction, 1960s futurism, Japanese anime, cyberpunk culture and industrial design - melding these influences into collections that were truly ground-breaking. His clothing often challenged the body's proportions as he produced hyper-shouldered jackets, low-slung trousers, voluminous skirts with narrow waists and armour-like dresses. Balenciaga's pieces under Ghesquière weren't just meant to flatter. They were meant to provoke.

Ghesquière also redefined fashion accessories. His Motorcycle Bag - initially released with little fanfare - became an unexpected commercial success. Soft, slouchy, unbranded and begging to be customised, the bag was embraced by It-girls, models, and celebrities alike. It was the anti-logo bag in an era obsessed with monograms which made it subversively chic. He experimented with footwear, too, playing with form and function to create Lego heels – so called due to the multicoloured, glossy plastic components they featured - metallic space boots and hybrid trainers that blurred the line between utility and ornament. Even Balenciaga's campaigns and look-books adopted a mood of cool detachment – shot in stark environments with models styled in offbeat, almost alien ways. Ghesquière's creations spoke of identity in the digital age, of the tension between human and machine, between the past and

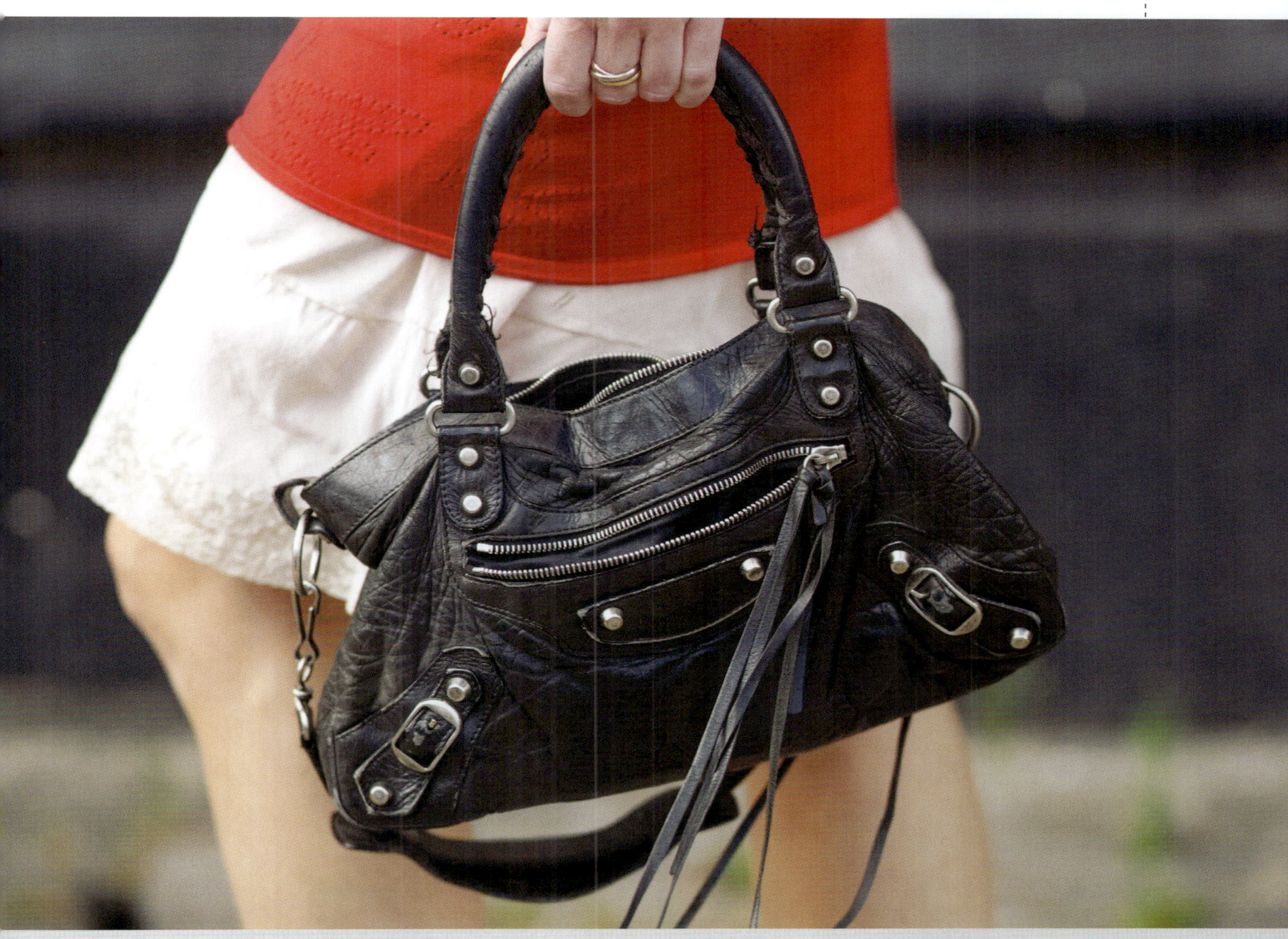

the future. His Balenciaga woman was intellectual, fashion-literate and fiercely independent. A trail blazer – just as Princess Grace and the Duchess of Windsor had been in their time.

By the mid-2000s, Balenciaga had fully re-entered the fashion conversation. Ghesquière received multiple awards and his shows were consistently listed among the most innovative of each season.

The house's financial health improved steadily and it regained its place among fashion's most respected names. Notably, Ghesquière was not content with mere aesthetic success. He insisted on using sustainable practices where possible, advocated for innovation in textiles and maintained a close relationship with the brand's atelier - ensuring that every design, no matter how radical, was impeccably constructed.

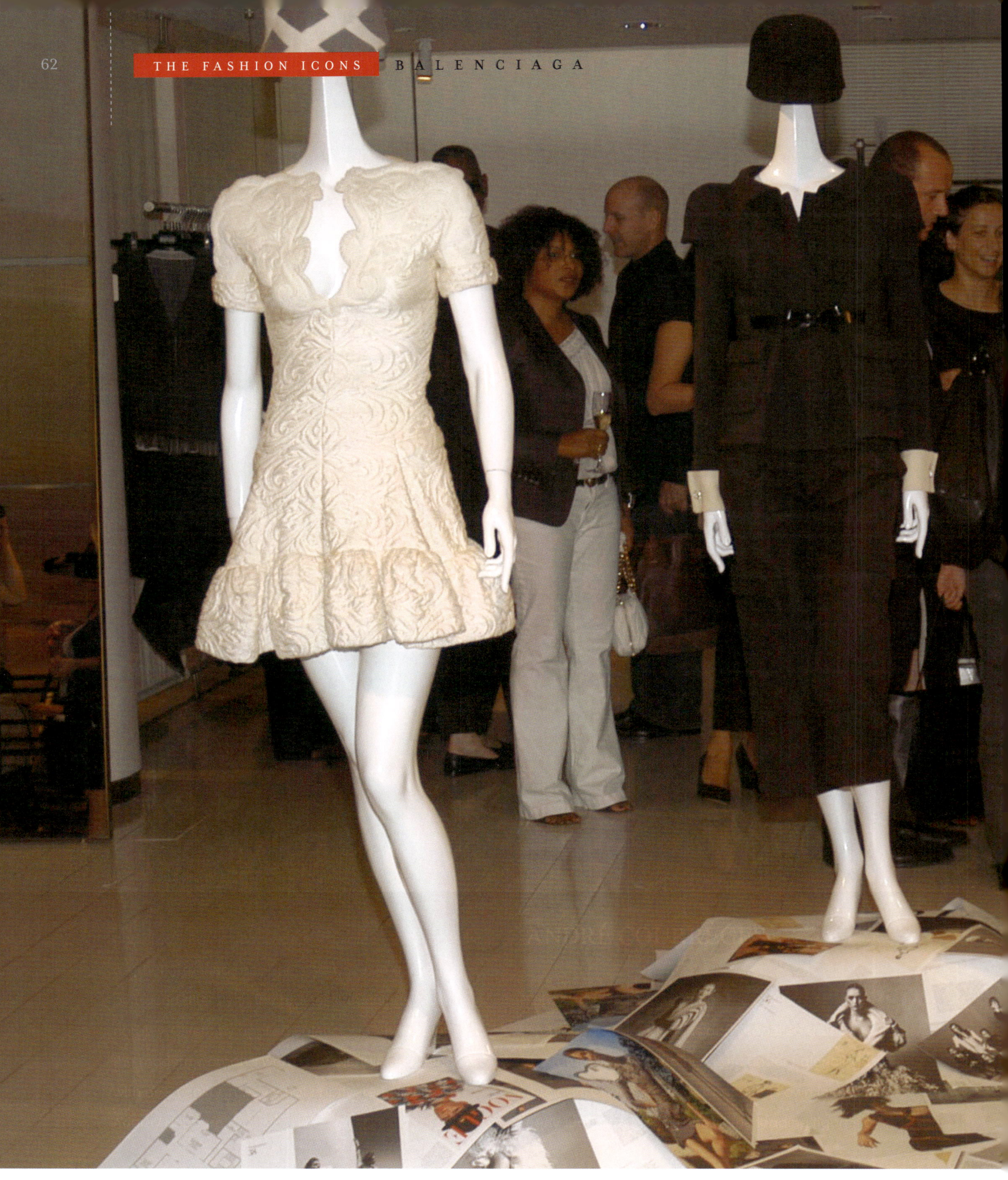

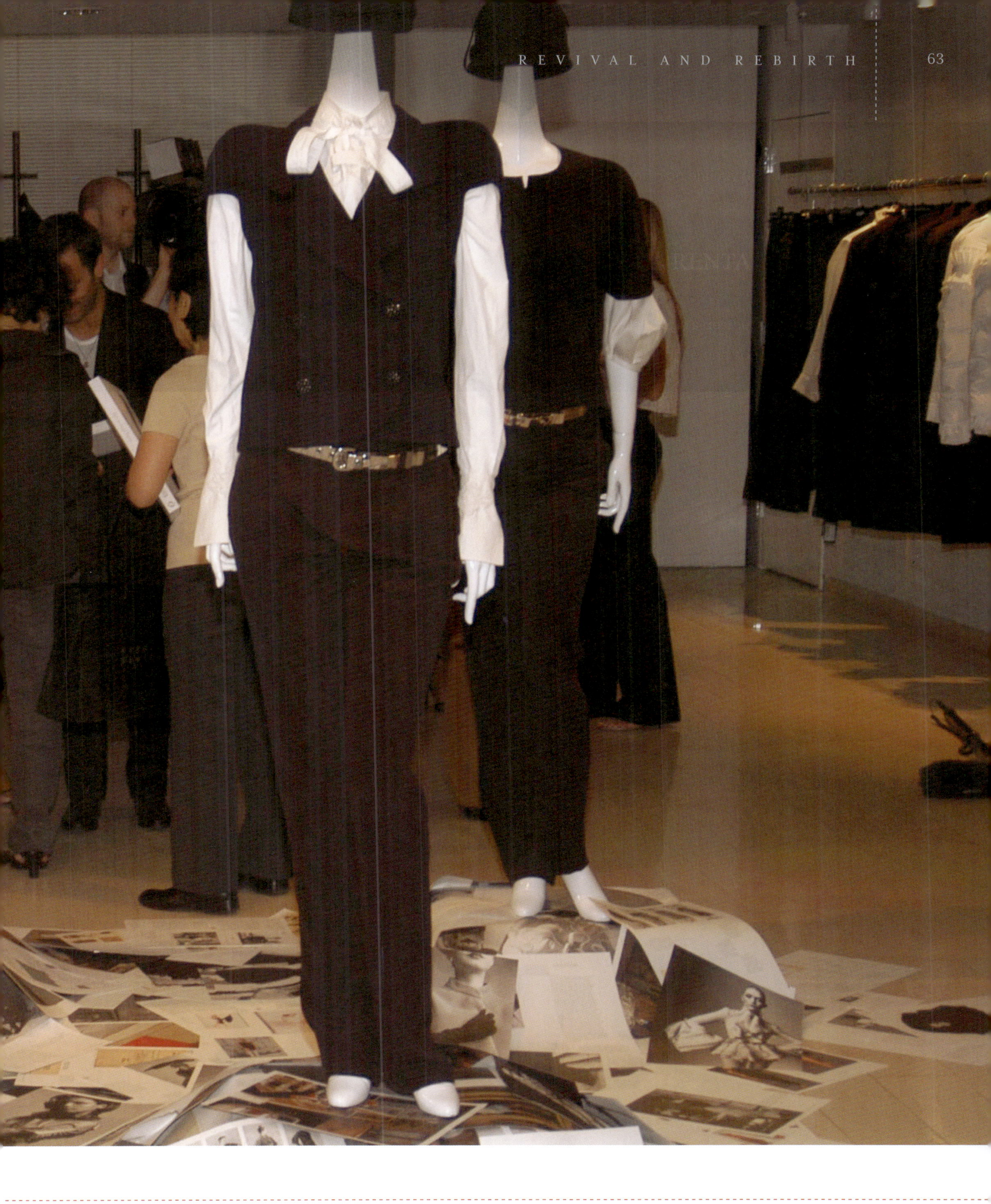

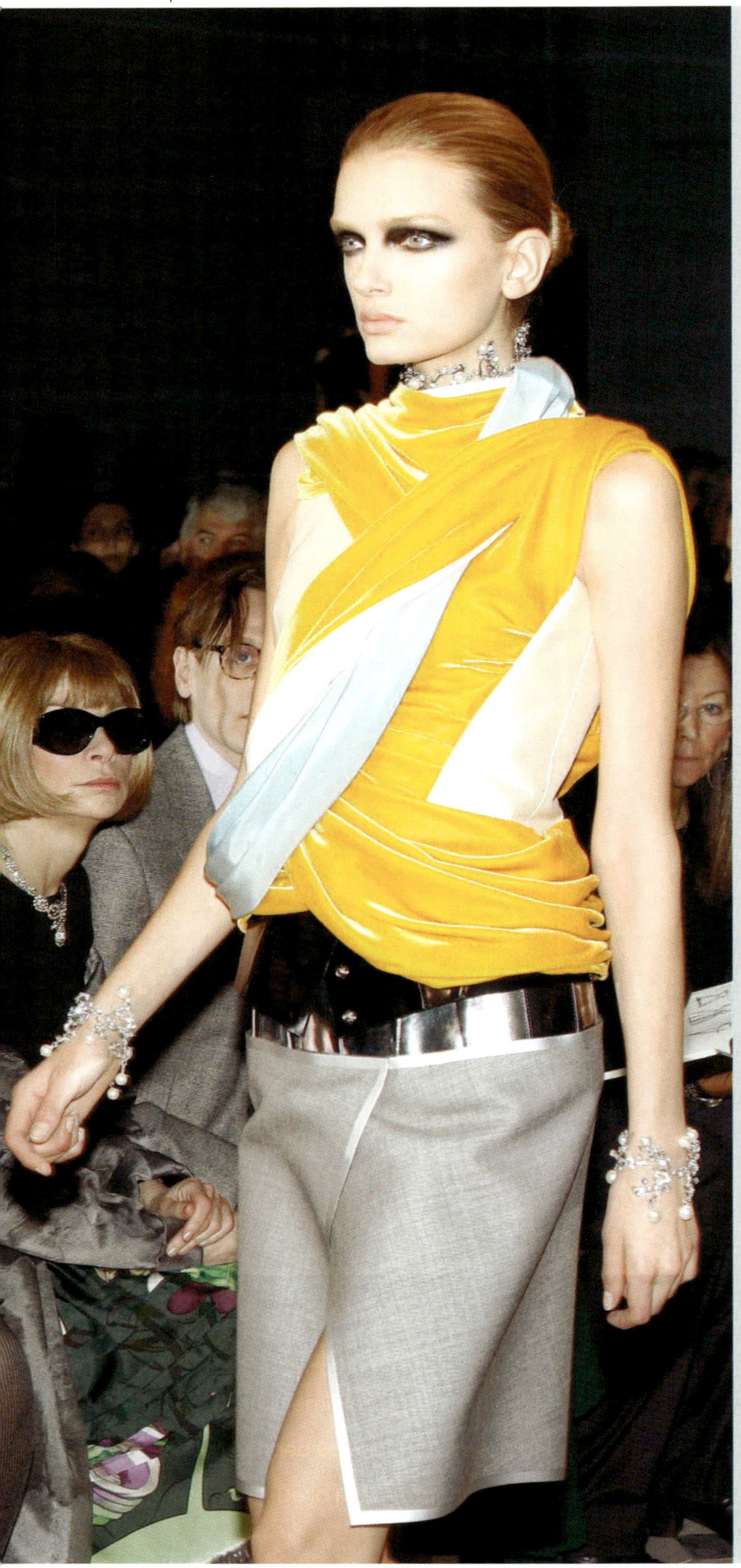

Beyond the runway, Balenciaga once again became culturally influential. Celebrities like Cate Blanchett, Charlotte Gainsbourg and Nicole Kidman became ambassadors for the brand; stylists turned to Balenciaga for red carpet looks that defied the mainstream; and musicians referenced Balenciaga in lyrics.

Ghesquière remained with the house until 2012. Though his departure was sudden, his legacy was unshakable. He had given Balenciaga a new voice - one that resonated far beyond the confines of Parisian fashion houses. The Balenciaga that would dominate headlines for years to come - with its dystopian runway shows, viral trainers and politically charged designs - owes much of its modern identity to Ghesquière. Without his ability to meld heritage and modernity, and to regard fashion as culture, this rebirth would never have been possible.

Ghesquière's departure – for Louis Vuitton as it would eventually turn out - left big shoes to fill. His successor, American designer Alexander Wang, aimed to bring a more urban, accessible feel to the brand but struggled to maintain the delicate balance between innovation and legacy. It wasn't until Georgian designer Demna Gvasalia took over in 2015 that Balenciaga entered its next mind-blowing and ground-breaking phase.

ABOVE: Balenciaga 2008–2009 Ready-to-Wear, Paris
OPP PAGE: Balenciaga Fall 2010 Show, Hôtel de Crillon, Paris

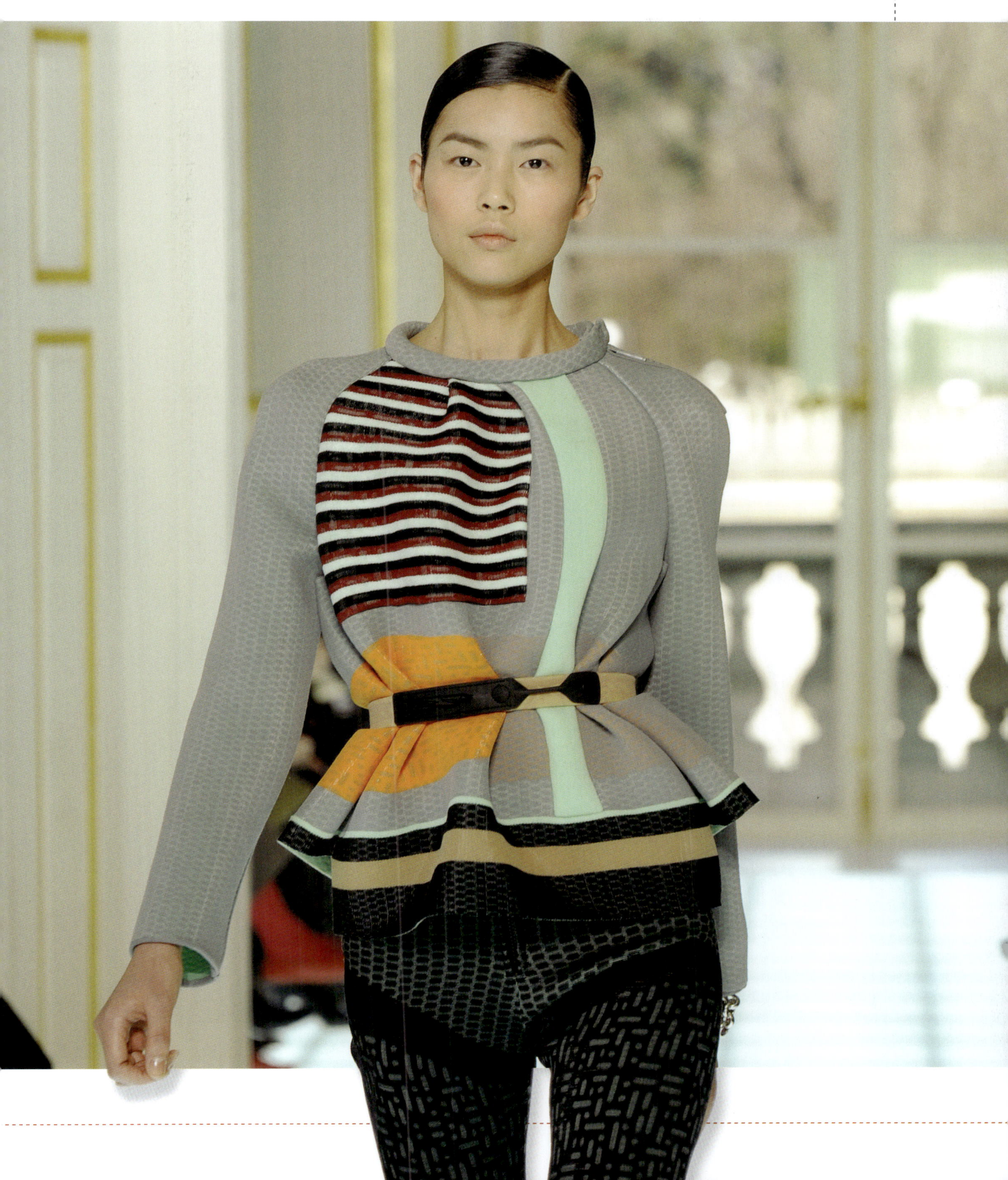

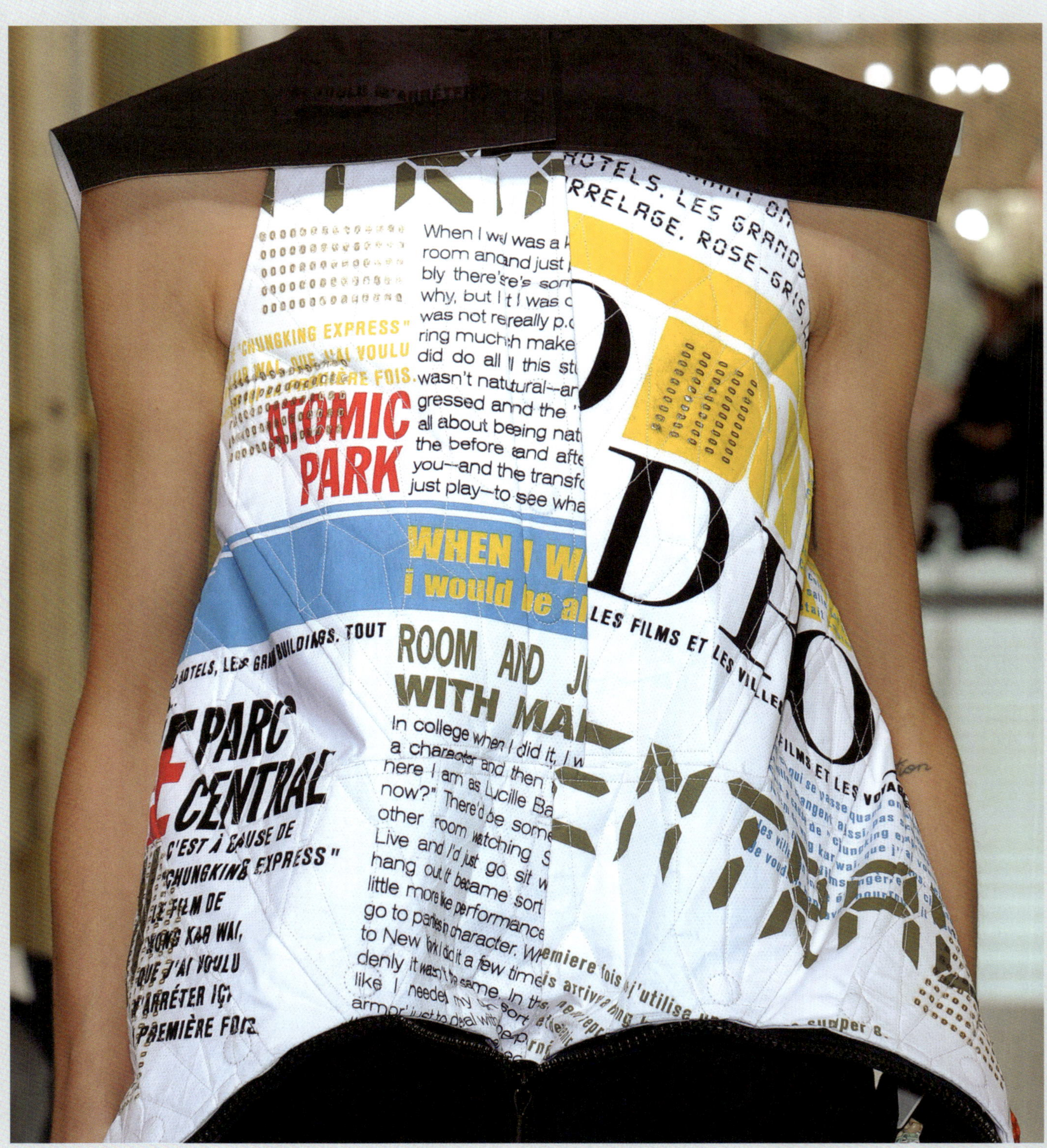

ABOVE: A piece from the Balenciaga Fall/Winter
2010/2011 Ready-to-Wear collection
OPP PAGE: A creation by Nicolas Ghesquière for Balenciaga
Spring/Summer 2013 Ready-to-Wear collection

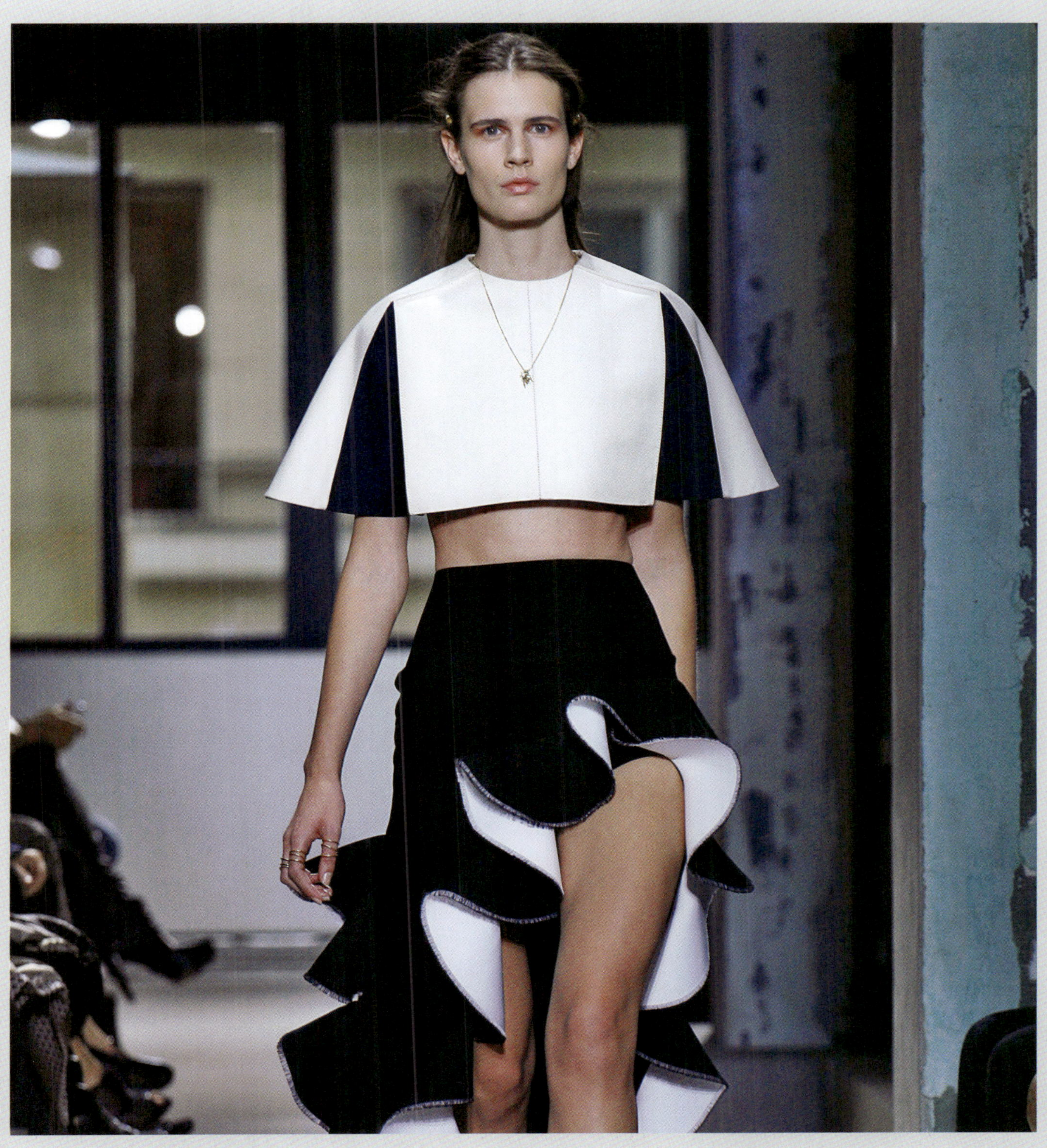

HOMAGE TO THE MASTER

Cristóbal Balenciaga would barely recognise the fashion house that today bears his name yet decades after his retirement and passing, his influence continues to shape not just the label but the world of fashion as a whole. The designers who have taken on the Balenciaga mantle since the 1990s - Nicolas Ghesquière, Alexander Wang, and Demna (it is, perhaps, too soon to speculate in detail on Pierpaulo Piccioli's tenure) - have each found their own, sometimes obscure, way to honour his legacy while pursuing their own vision.

NICOLAS GHESQUIÈRE

Creative director from 1997 to 2012, Ghesquière is credited for bringing the label back to life. While he didn't copy Cristóbal's designs, he studied them diligently – using similar concepts of shape, volume and structure but with a modern twist. In his Fall/Winter 2006 collection, for instance, Ghesquière displayed bubble skirts and high collars - details that clearly came from Cristóbal Balenciaga's 1950s

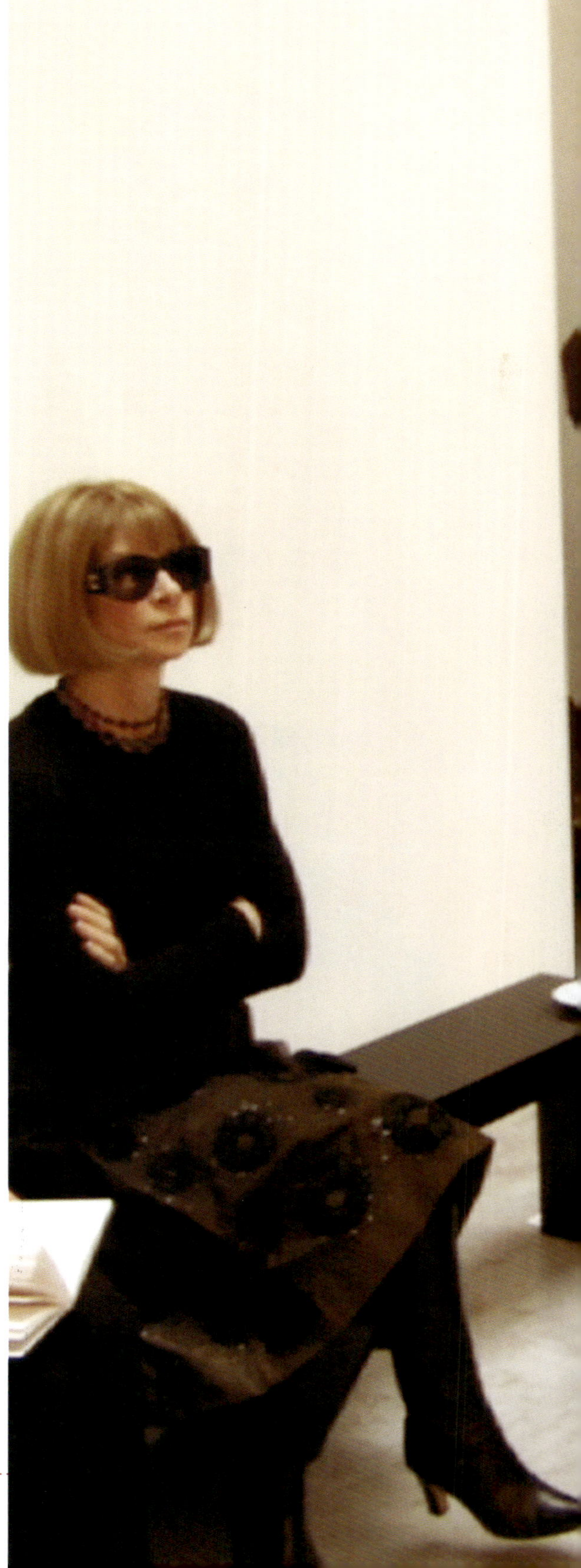

RIGHT: Nicolas Ghesquière in 2009

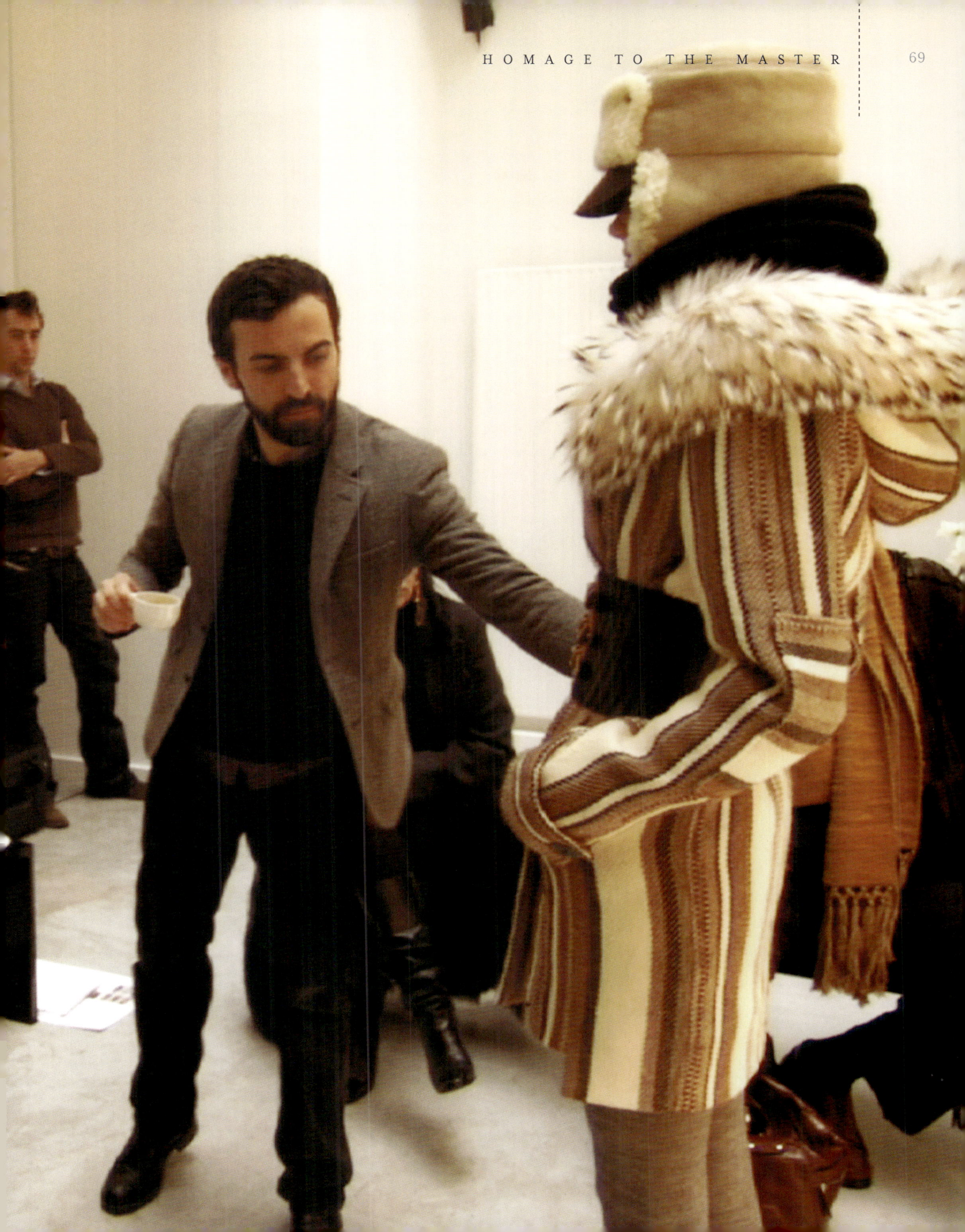

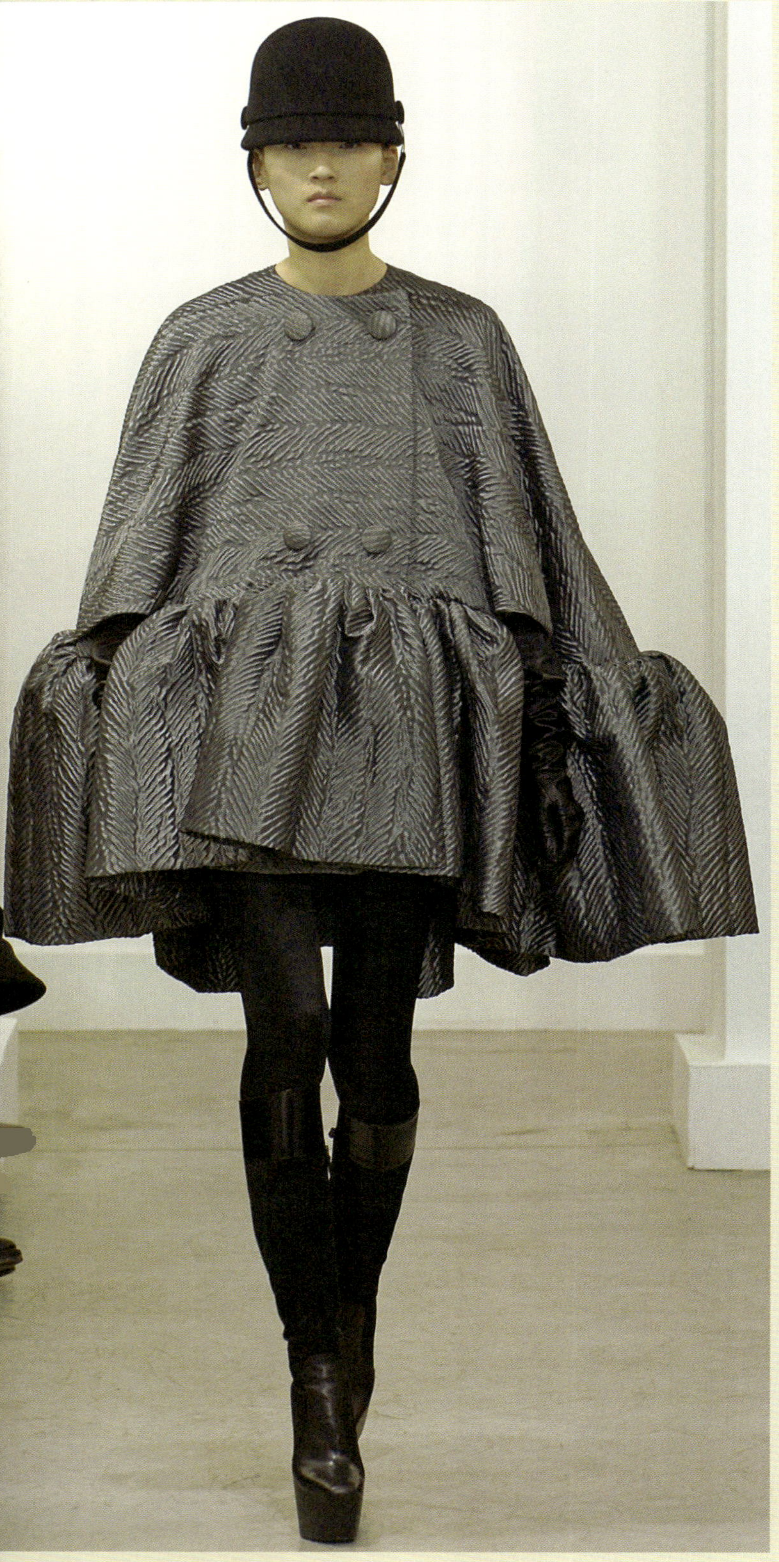

designs. But instead of using traditional fabrics, he worked with modern materials like neoprene. This gave the clothes a futuristic edge while still honouring the original styles. Ghesquière respected Cristóbal's legacy but wanted to move the brand forward. He once said he was trying to have a *'conversation'* with Cristóbal rather than just recreate his work. This approach helped Ghesquière make Balenciaga exciting and relevant for a new generation.

ALEXANDER WANG

Alexander Wang took over from Ghesquière in 2012. Known for his streetwear-inspired designs, many were unsure if he was the right choice for such a historic brand. While his tenure ultimately had mixed reception, during his two years as creative director, Wang was seen to be referencing Cristóbal by focusing on clean lines, sharp tailoring and simple but strong shapes. In his Spring 2014 collection, Wang used a lot of black and white, reminiscent of Balenciaga's 1960s monochrome designs. He also gave a nod to Cristóbal's famous 'envelope dress' by playing with structure in a more understated way. Wang's tribute to Balenciaga was not loud or dramatic. It showed itself in the way the American shaped his clothes, and focused on craftsmanship and precision.

ABOVE: Balenciaga Fall/Winter 2006 Ready-to-Wear, Paris Fashion Week
OPP PAGE: Alexander Wang Spring 2014 Collection, New York Fashion Week

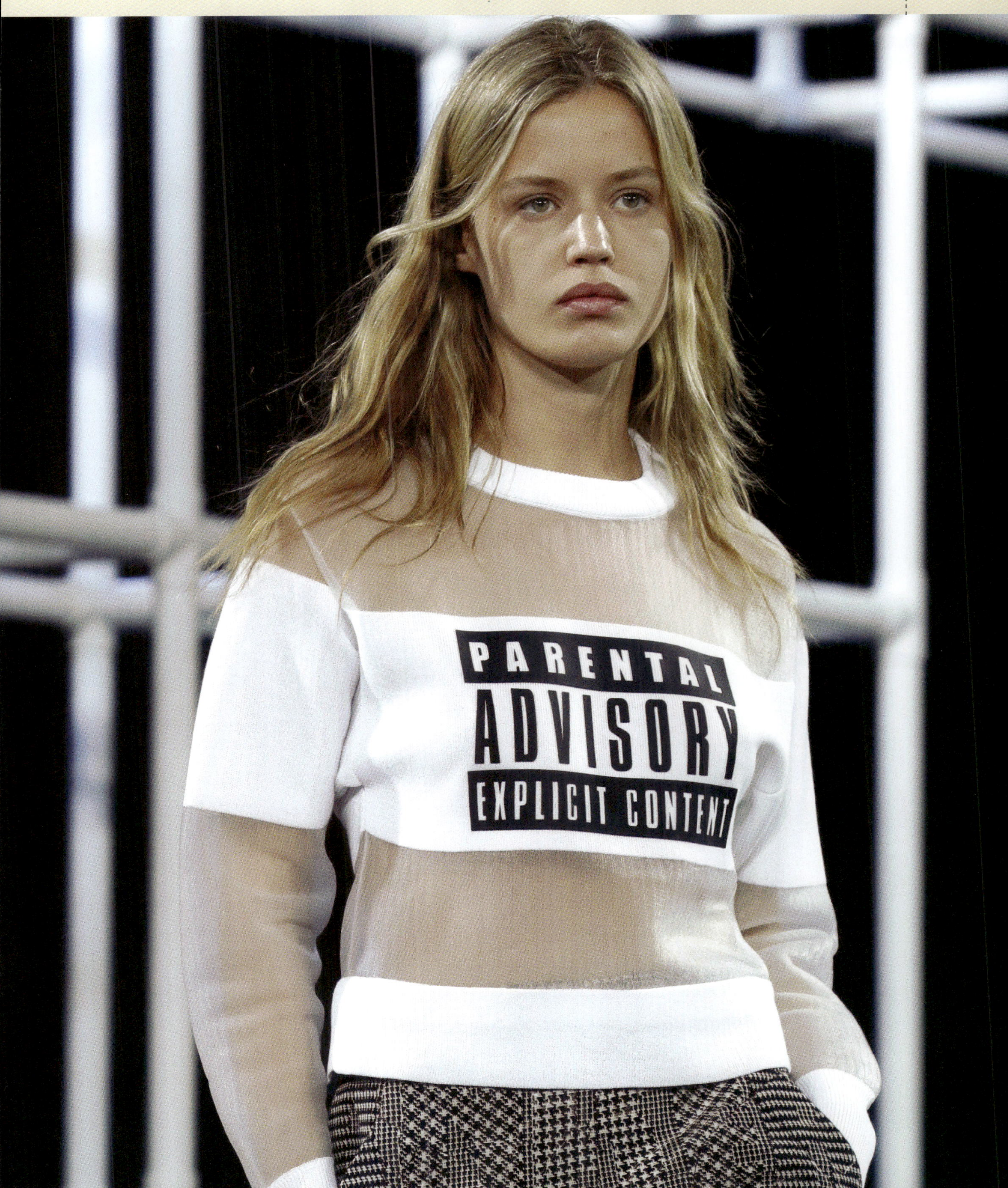
PARENTAL
ADVISORY
EXPLICIT CONTENT

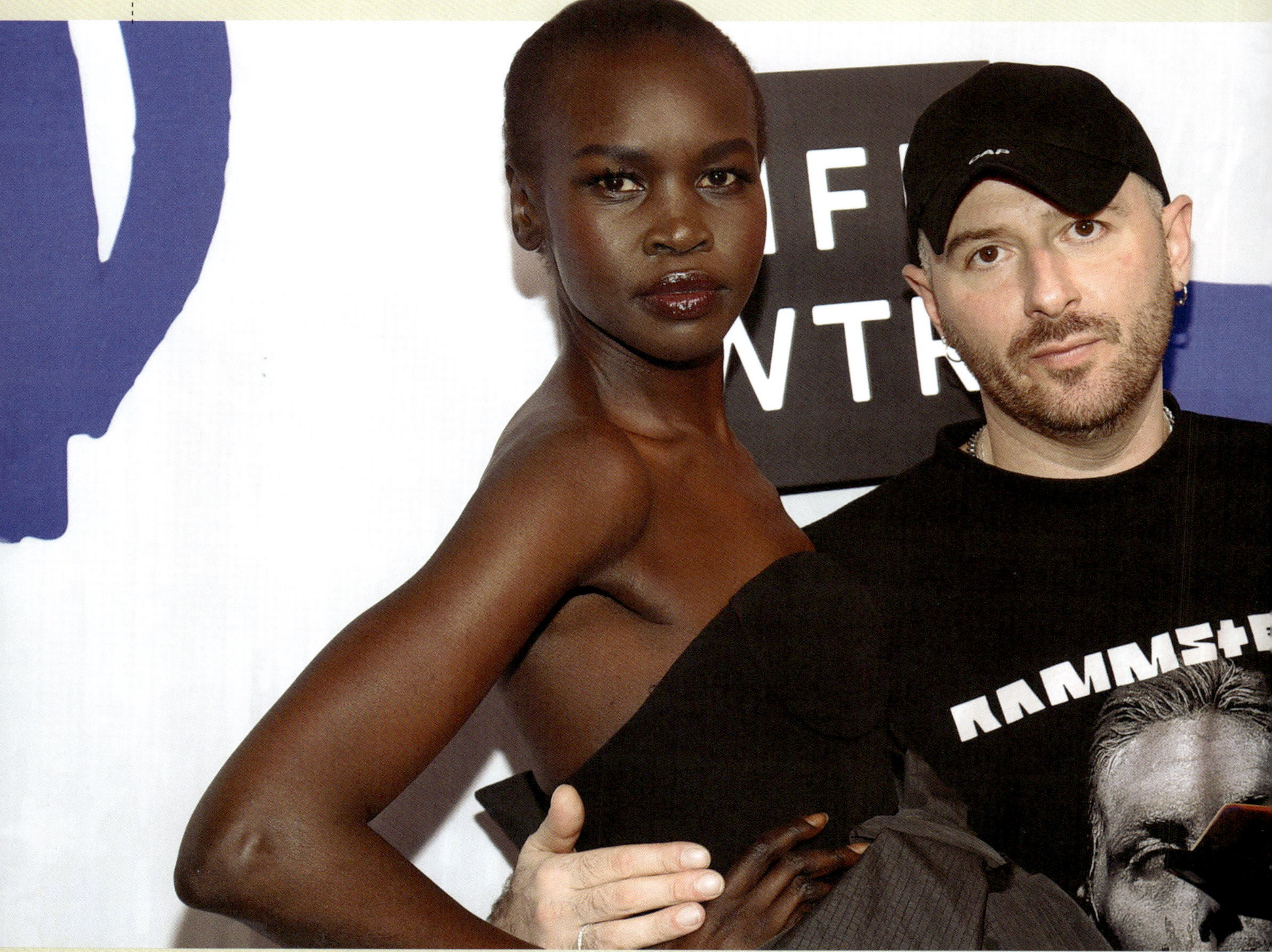

DEMNA

Demna (formerly Demna Gvasalia) became creative director in 2015 and brought a completely different energy to Balenciaga. Known for his edgy, experimental style Demna shocked many people with his oversized clothes, ironic graphics and streetwear influences. But beneath this boldness was a genuine admiration for Cristóbal Balenciaga. Demna commented many times that he deeply respected the founder's work. In fact, many of his designs were actually modern versions of Cristóbal's originals. Like Balenciaga, he used dramatic silhouettes. Huge shoulders, cocoon coats and sculptural shapes all made a comeback in Demna's collections but on a much bigger, more extreme scale. In 2021, Demna brought back Balenciaga's haute couture line for the first time in over 50 years. The collection was

ABOVE: Alek Wek (left) with Demna Gvasalia, winner of the international award, at the CFDA Fashion Awards at the Hammerstein Ballroom, 5 June, 2017, in New York

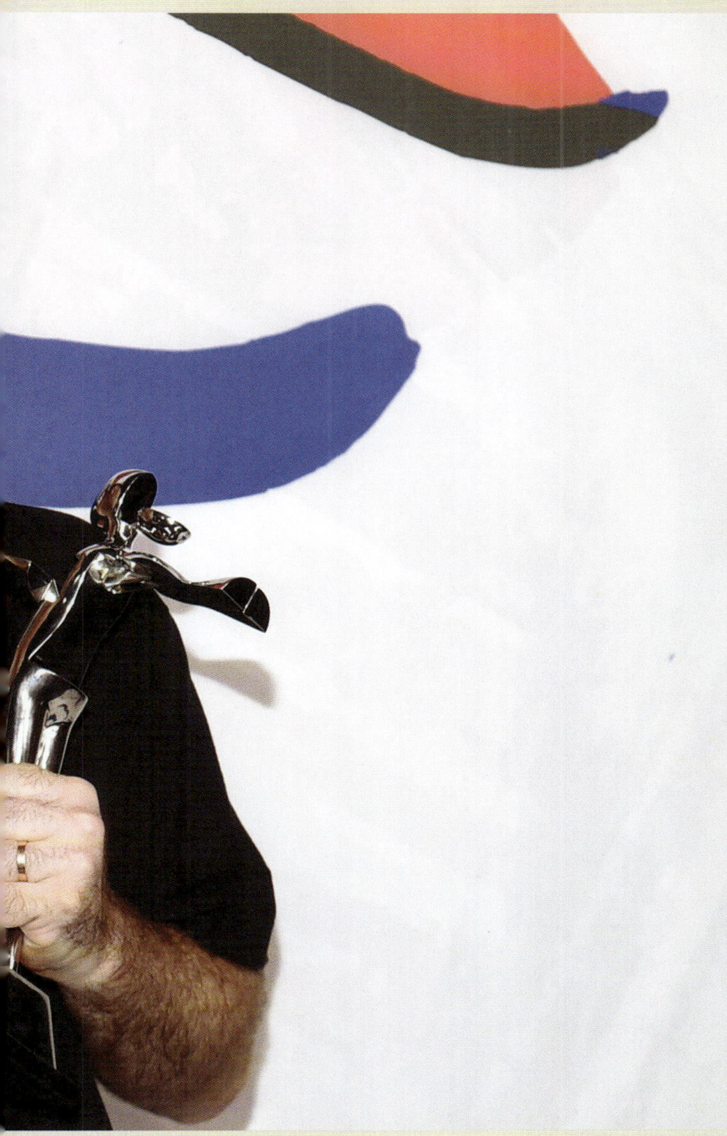

different styles, in a number of respects the three respected Cristóbal Balenciaga's legacy in a similar way. Firstly, they all cared about shape and structure. Balenciaga was known for his dramatic silhouettes and this trio of successors demonstrated this in their own, individual way - whether through clean tailoring, futuristic shapes or oversized designs. Secondly, they valued craftsmanship. Cristóbal was a perfectionist who paid attention to every detail and this ideal has been kept alive, especially in Balenciaga's couture and ready-to-wear pieces. Finally, each understood that honouring Balenciaga didn't mean copying him. Instead, they used his ideas as inspiration to pushed forward in new directions. This balance between tradition and innovation is what keeps the brand strong and interesting. Ghesquière modernised his ideas with a futuristic twist. Wang offered a quiet, minimalist tribute. And Demna has transformed the brand with bold new visions while still respecting the past. Together, they have kept the spirit of Balenciaga alive - not by looking backward but by continuing the founder's mission of innovation, craftsmanship, and creativity.

a major tribute to Cristóbal. It included new versions of classic Balenciaga shapes like the balloon skirt and the cape dress – all exquisitely made with the same high level of craftsmanship. Demna said he didn't want to copy the past but continue the story. This couture collection demonstrated that, even with his bold 'out there' ideas, Demna still honoured the founder's vision.

Athough Ghesquière, Wang, and Demna had very

Pierpaolo Piccioli's appointment at Balenciaga suggests a return to the spirit of Cristóbal Balenciaga, especially when compared to Demna's provocative, streetwear-heavy era. Piccioli is deeply rooted in couture traditions - at Valentino, for instance, he emphasised artisanal craftsmanship, romance and elegance. Piccioli believes in *'fashion as poetry'* using colour and shape to evoke emotion - an ethos much closer to Balenciaga's refined vision than Demna's irony.

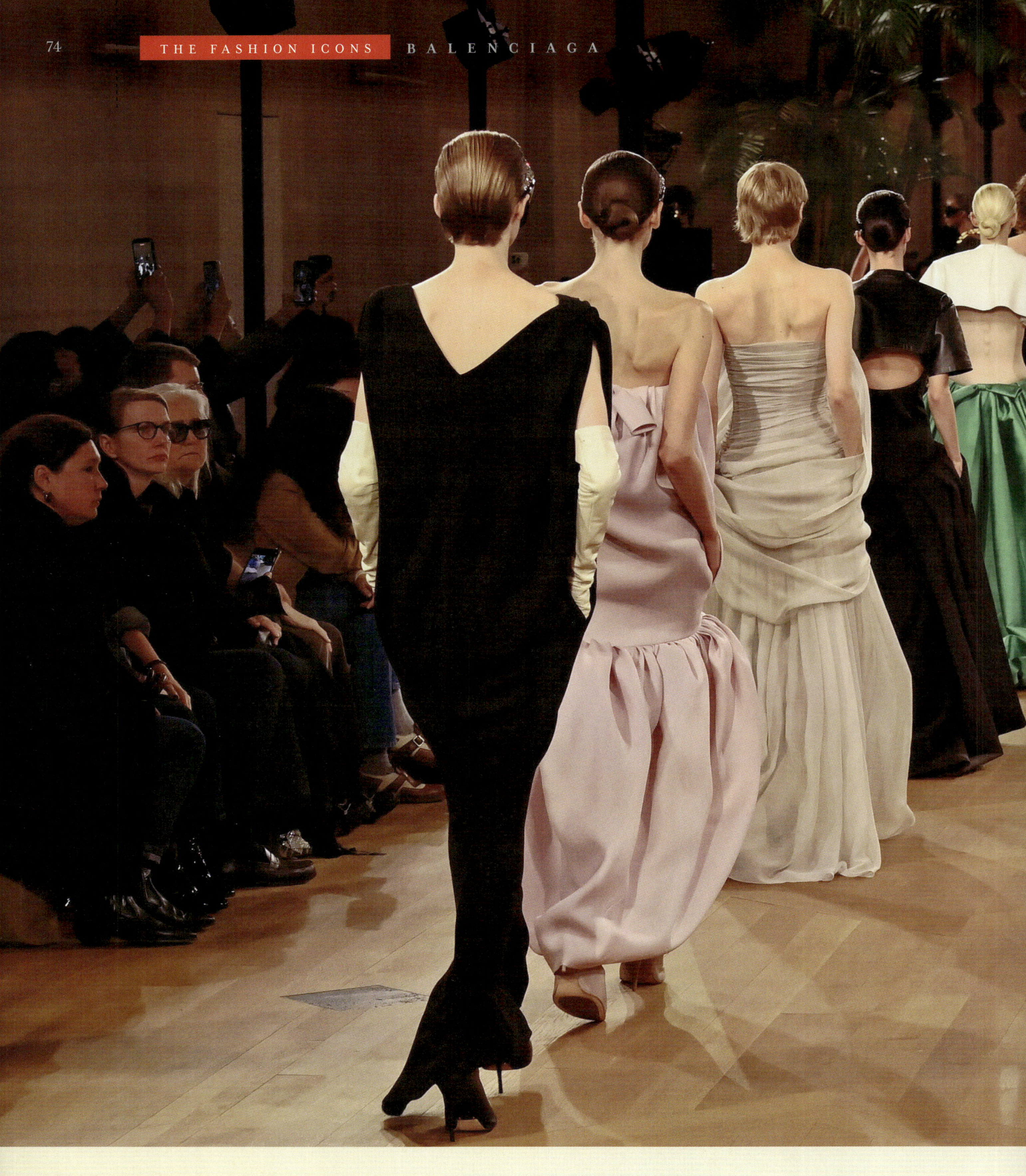

ABOVE: Balenciaga Spring/Summer 2026 Ready-to-Wear,
Paris Fashion Week, October 2025

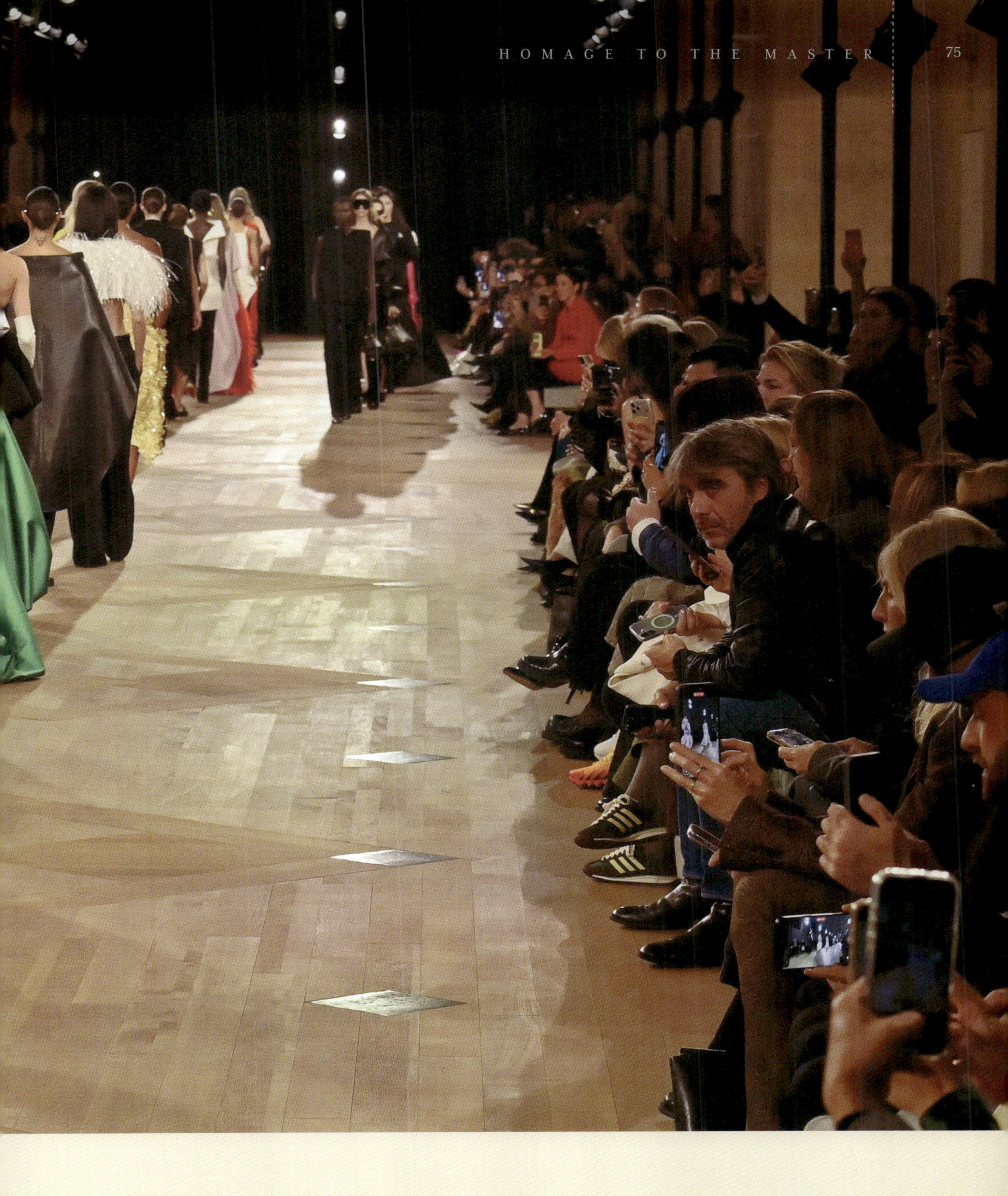

THE DISRUPTER

"Fashion should not please"

Demna Gvasalia

Demna Gvasalia's decade as creative director of Balenciaga was not just a time of bold reinvention for the historic fashion house - it was a radical shift in the way luxury itself was understood, communicated and consumed. Born in post-Soviet Georgia, shaped by political upheaval and sharpened in the subversive classrooms of Antwerp's Royal Academy of Fine Arts, Demna, as he preferred to be known, arrived at Balenciaga in 2015 with a perspective far from that of a traditional couturist. He was an outsider looking in and recognised both the absurdities and the allure of the fashion world. He used this vantage point to unpick and then reassemble one of fashion's most revered names.

When Demna took the reins from Alexander Wang, the fashion press was quick to speculate. Could the co-founder of 'Vetements', the label known for DHL-branded T-shirts and deconstructed hoodies, really translate his streetwise irreverence into the rarefied air of Balenciaga with its history of sculptural elegance and aura old-world discipline? From his

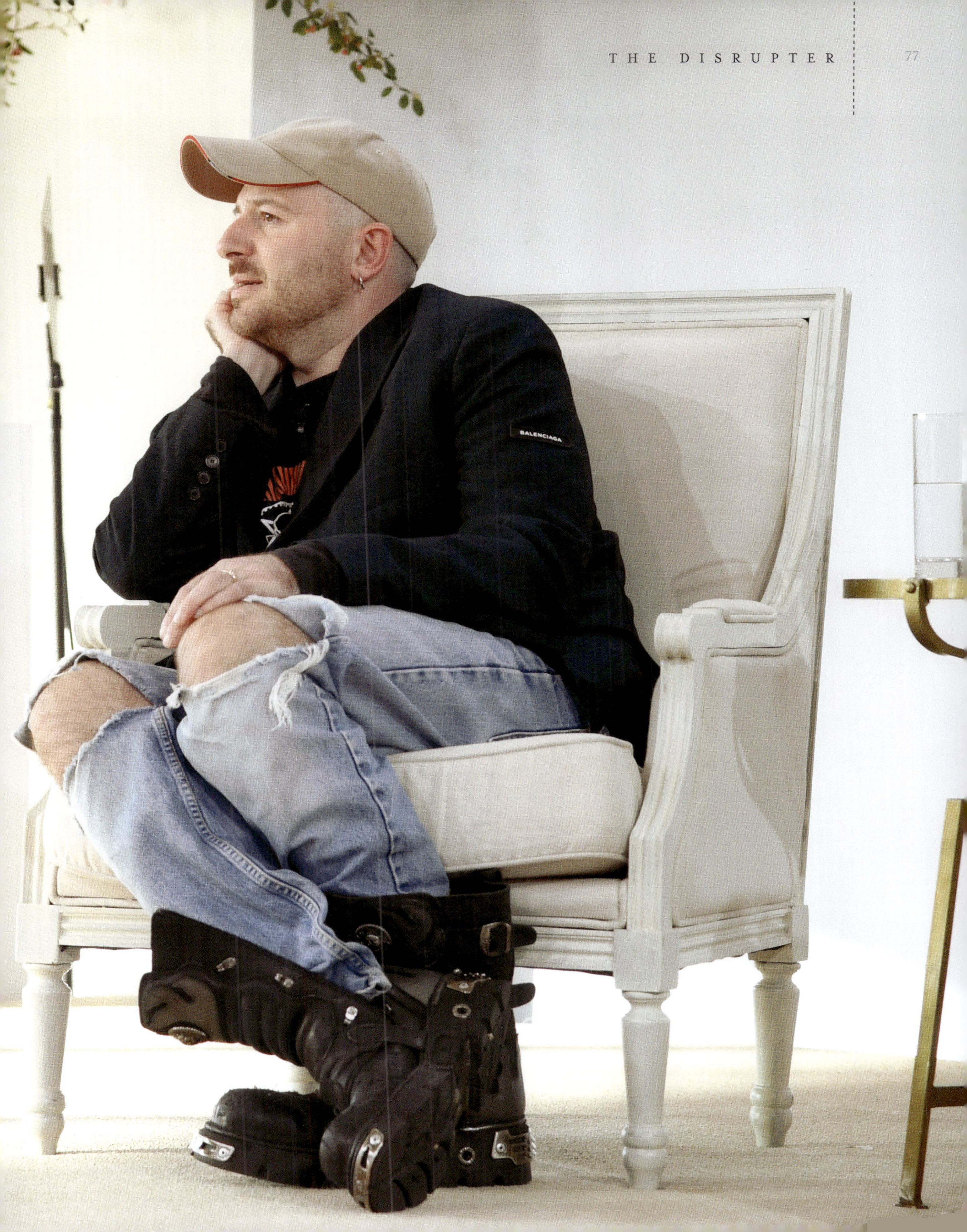

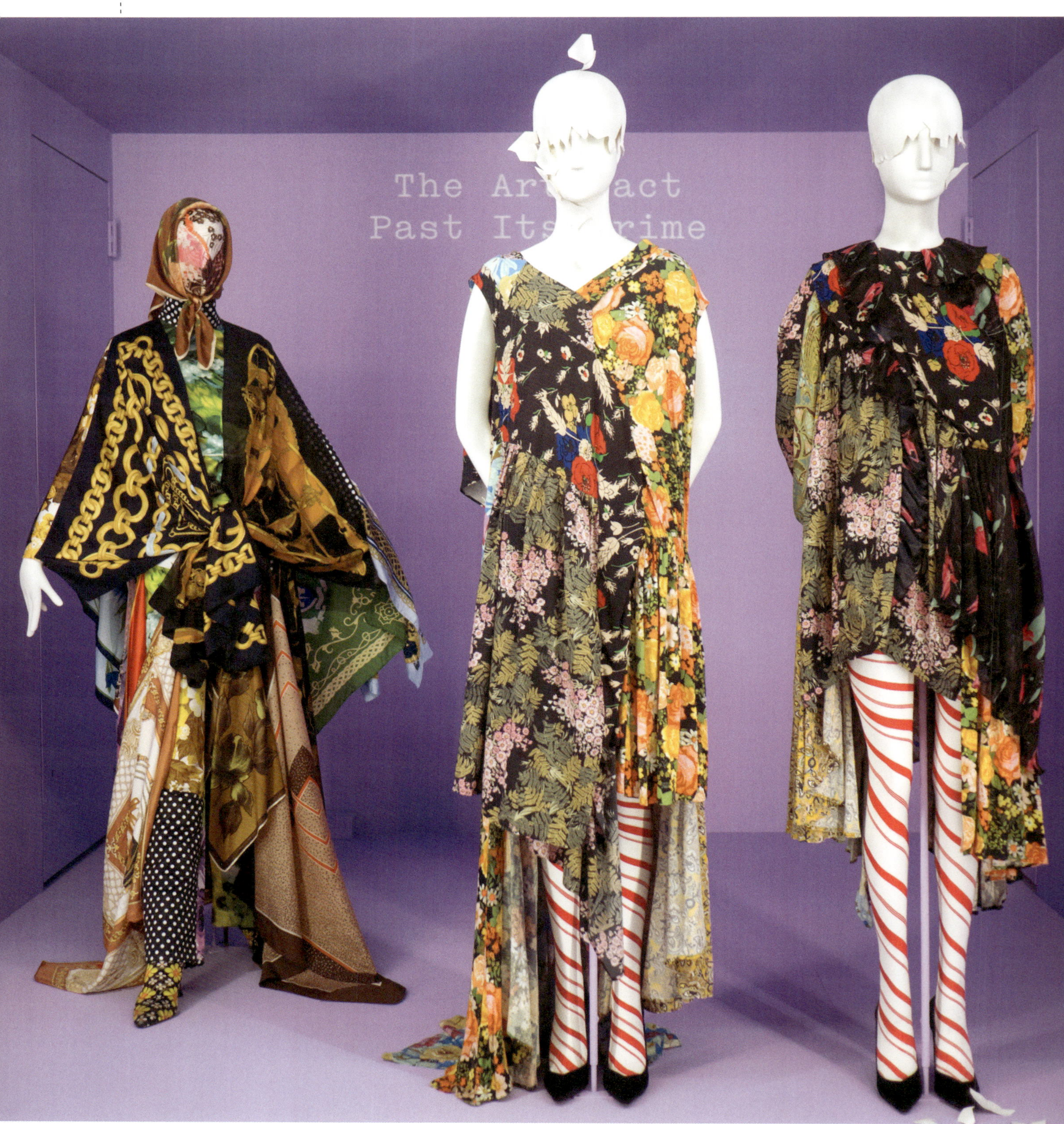

ABOVE: Demna Gvasalia for Balenciaga, Autumn/Winter 2016–17, "Notes on Fashion" exhibit at The Met
OPP PAGE: Nicole Kidman wearing Balenciaga for *British GQ*

very first collection, the answer was unmistakably yes but not because Demna played it safe. He instinctively understood that the soul of Cristóbal's work lay in truth and daring. Balenciaga the Master had been a technical innovator, a fabric sculptor and a genius of redefinition. Demna would also redefine - employing new codes and new forms while relentlessly questioning what luxury meant in the 21st century.

The Fall/Winter 2016 debut was where Demna's vision took shape. The runway saw exaggerated silhouettes that seemed to both simultaneously mock and honour Cristóbal's original lines - tailored coats with ballooning hips, trench coats sliced with unexpected curves, floral prints twisted into what amounted to a beautiful pastiche, normcore and utilitarian garments morphed into high fashion. He elevated everyday pieces by infusing them with irony, social commentary or architectural tailoring. These were garments meant to provoke as well as flatter. In the years that followed, Demna pushed the envelope even further. Anti-fashion as high fashion was his ethos. Platform Crocs; hoodies in fine cashmere paired with opera gloves; and oversized puffers that engulfed the models... Each collection seemed to view the future as disruptive, uncomfortable and all too real.

However, it was not just aesthetics. Demna rewired the very DNA of the brand. At his Balenciaga, luxury was no longer only about exclusivity and exquisite craftsmanship. It became a cultural commentary.

A way to reflect - and sometimes ridicule - the absurdities of 21st century life. The infamous 'IKEA bag', the blue plastic shopping bag sold for peanuts, was remade in leather and dubbed the 'Frakta' with a £2000 price tag.

'The perfect example of ready-made', commented its creator.

GQ magazine noted that Demna was pushing the boundaries of what defined luxury by *'repackaging the banal'*. They saw the bag as *'a clever, fashion-world in-joke'*. While *Vogue* commented that it was *'normcore irony'*. Whatever it was, it was hugely successful. The bag sold out.

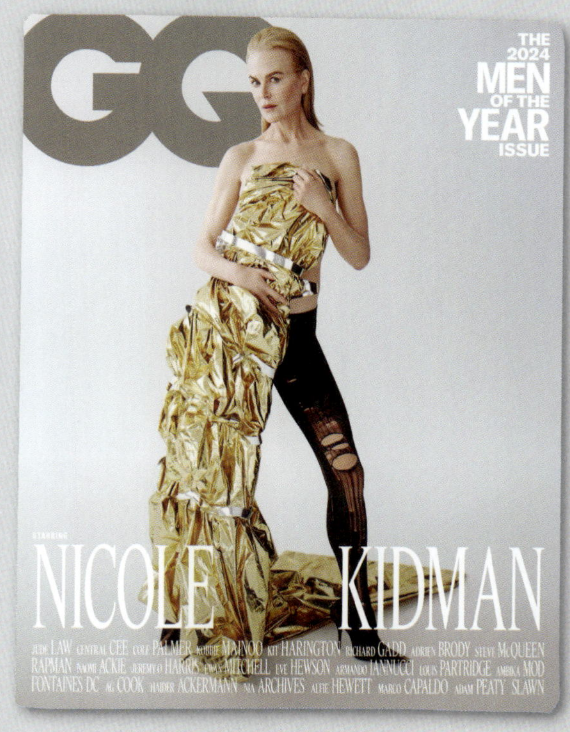

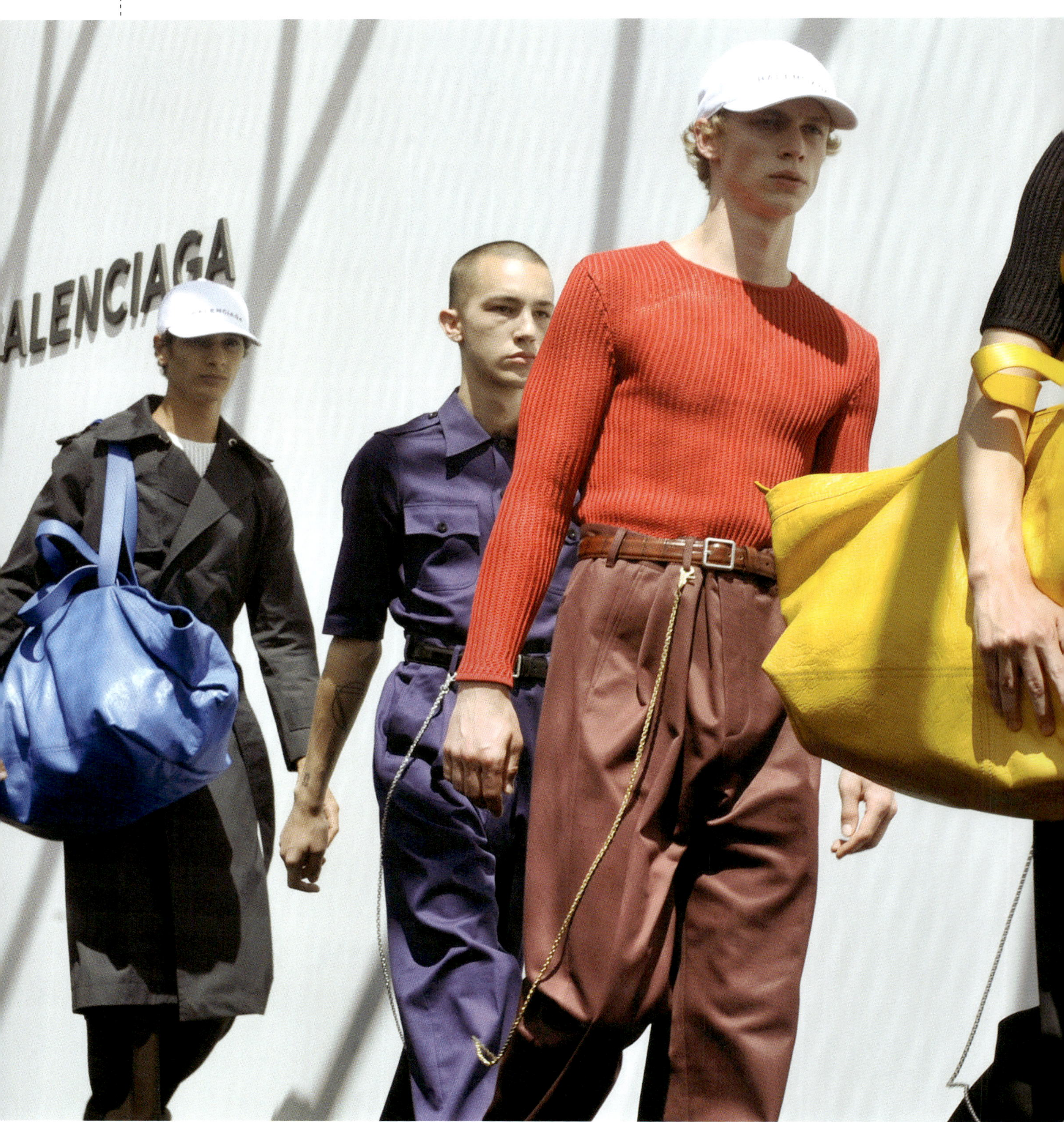

ABOVE: Balenciaga runway show at Paris Men's Fashion Week, Spring/Summer 2017 collection

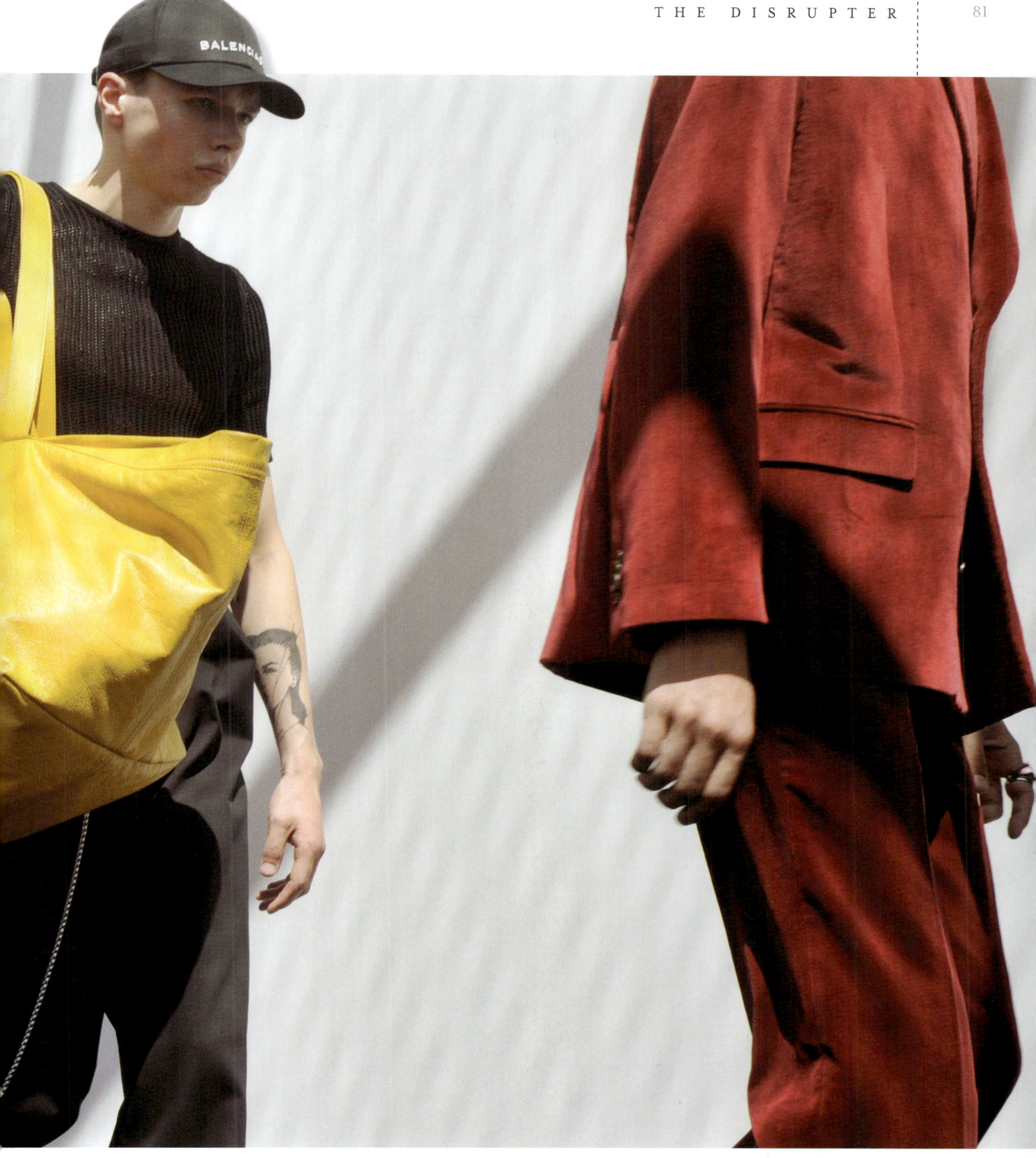

Demna also brought trainers to the forefront of the Balenciaga canon. The classic Triple S with its triple-stacked sole and quickly dubbed *'the dad shoe to end all dad shoes'* was launched in 2017; the best-selling, slip-on Speed Trainer (Sock Sneaker) with minimalist silhouette, the year before. His trail-runner inspired Track trainer with its complex design was launched in 2018 and became a cult favourite, ditto the Paris Sneaker unveiled in 2022 which was more of a fashion-art moment than a timeless staple trainer. The highly-conceptual Tyrex (2020) was too weird for most consumers while the prematurely-aged Runner trainer with its *'melted'* design was interesting as a concept but dismissed as a gimmick. Also hyper-niche was the Defender (2022) with its uber bold, Monster-truck aesthetic.

In yet another audacious move, Demna introduced a streetwear-centric aesthetic to Balenciaga, marking one of the most significant shifts in luxury fashion. This shift included hoodies, oversized T-shirts and distressed denim – often sporting controversial logos – which became status symbols. Balenciaga, driven by Demna's viral casualwear designs, became one of the most Google-searched and copied brands in the world.

Balenciaga under Demna was also theatrical. He staged runway shows that felt like installations, experiences, even challenges. The Fall 2018 show was set in a tunnel of mirrors with LED lights that glitched with political slogans and apocalyptic messages.

Another show took place in a simulated blizzard - a white-out through which models, wrapped in survivalist gear, trudged with stoic resolve. For Spring 2022, he collaborated with *The Simpsons*, premiering a short episode in which Homer, Marge, and Lisa walked the Balenciaga runway in Paris. The most controversial of all, however, was the Spring/Summer 2023 show which took place in a massive mud pit at Paris's Parc des Expositions and had Kanye West opening the runway sporting a dystopian, militaristic look. Demna described the setting as a metaphor for *'digging for truth and being down to earth'. British Vogue's* Anders Christian Madsen noted the eerie parallels between the mud-filled set and recent war imagery, writing that the show *'burst the escapist bubble of fashion week'.* The models navigated this muddy landscape wearing oversized, distressed garments, some carrying realistic-looking baby mannequins, and adorned with facial prosthetics and piercings. The footwear included platform heels and 3D-printed clogs, which added to the difficulty of walking through the sludge. Demna stated in his show notes that he would no longer explain his collections, emphasizing that fashion was a visual art meant to be seen and felt. This approach was evident in the show's immersive experience, which also included the scent of mud laced with antidepressants. The intention was to create a multisensory commentary on the human condition. While many praised the show's boldness and depth, some critics questioned its accessibility and commercial viability. *The Cut* observed that Demna's subsequent shows took a

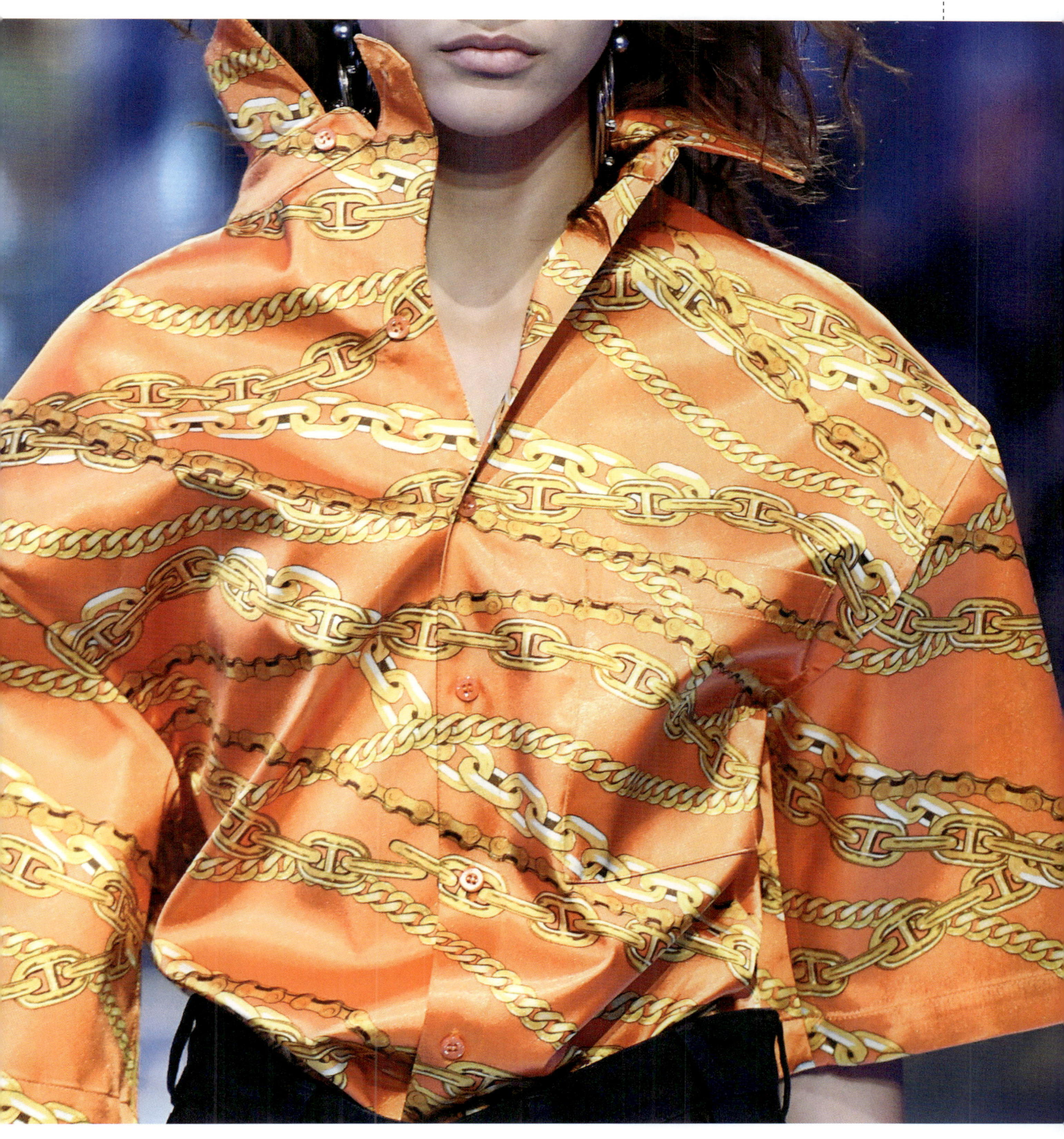

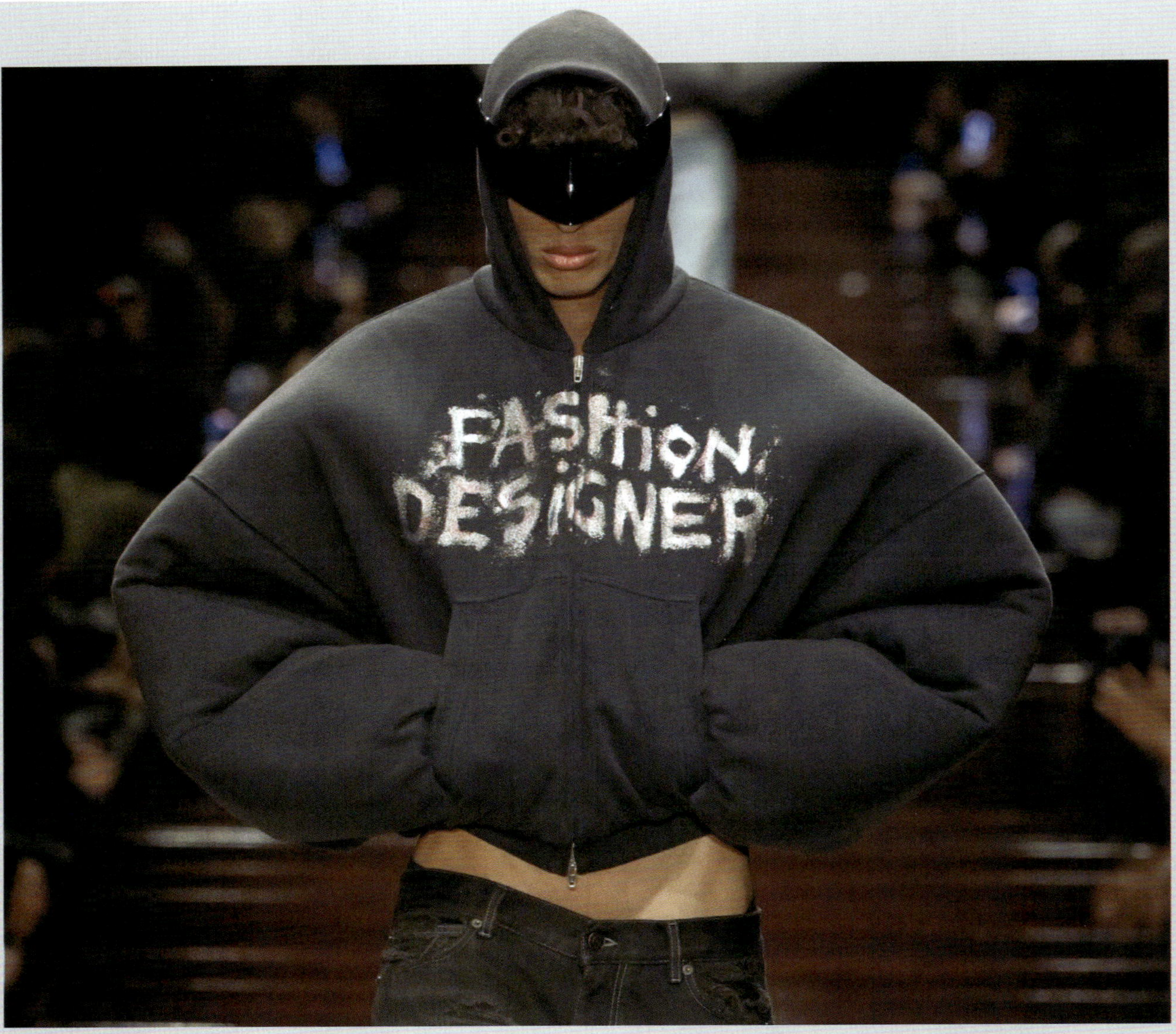

more restrained approach, suggesting a possible shift in strategy following the intense reactions to 'The Mud Show'.

Certainly, he had demonstrated a more conventional side two years earlier when he brought haute couture back to Balenciaga after a 53-year hiatus – an action that proved, despite the controversies that surrounded his collections, he was a worthy wearer of the Balenciaga crown. Couture, traditionally the most sacred realm of fashion where garments are constructed by hand with hundreds of hours of labour, was not a space many expected Demna to enter, let alone succeed in. Yet the collection stunned audiences. Held in Balenciaga's original salons on Avenue George V, the show was a masterclass

ABOVE: Streetwear takes centre stage in the Balenciaga Ready-to-Wear Spring 2025 collection
OPP PAGE: A look from the Balenciaga Spring 2025 Ready-to-Wear collection

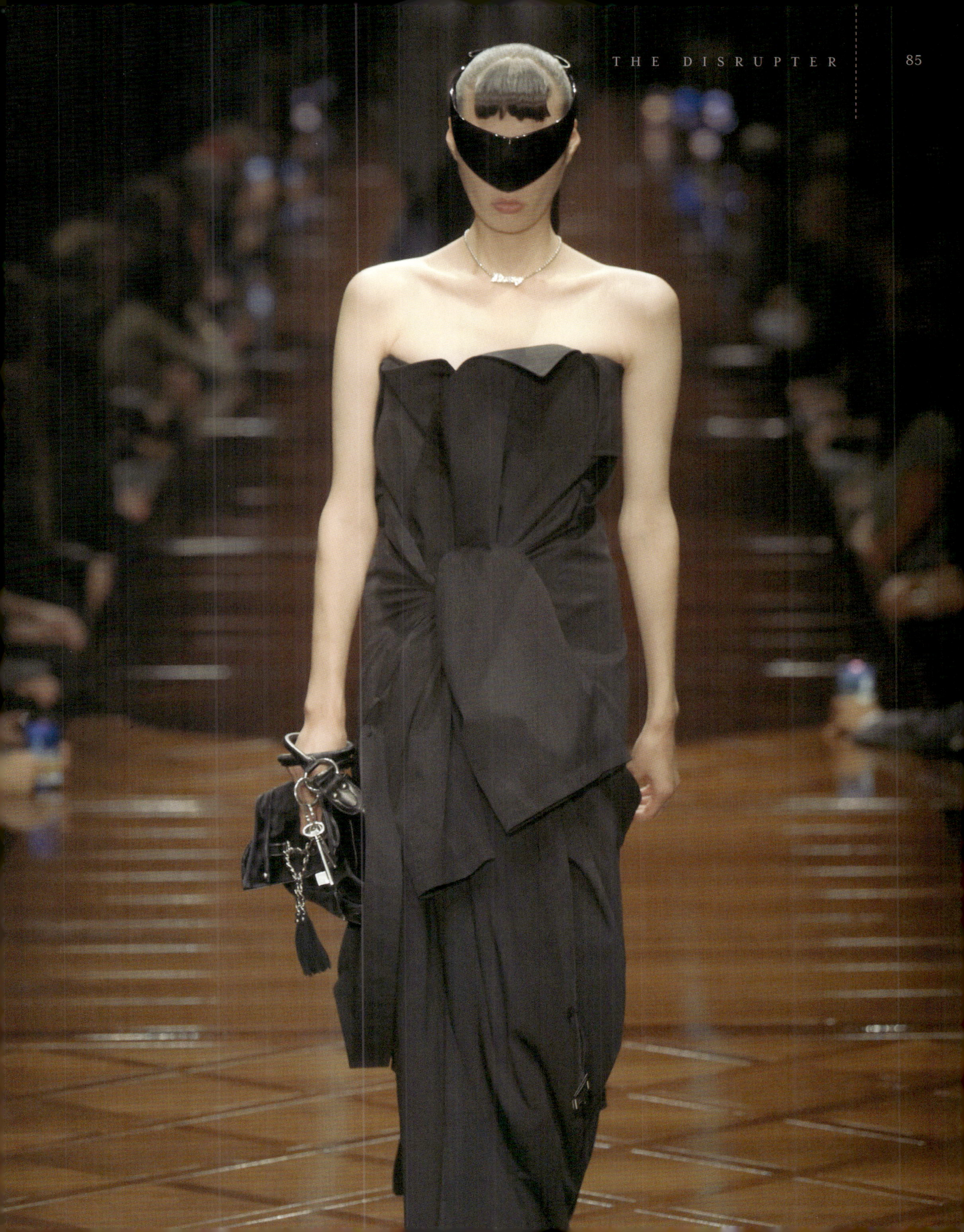

in reverence and rebellion. Classic tailoring was revived but filtered through a contemporary lens. The collection featured jeans crafted with the delicacy of silk, coats moulded from technical fabrics but finished with invisible hand-sewn seams, eveningwear that floated between elegance and industrial strength. This was couture that acknowledged the archive while rewriting it for a fragmented, fast-moving world.

For all his brilliance, Demna's time at Balenciaga was not without controversy. In 2022, the House released an ad campaign featuring children holding teddy bears dressed in BDSM-style harnesses. The backlash was swift and severe, with public outcry accusing the brand of inappropriate imagery. Demna issued a rare public apology, acknowledging that the campaign had crossed a line. It was a stark reminder of the razor's edge Demna walked - his art often relied on confrontation but in a digital world where images circulate instantly and context is easily lost, the price of miscalculation could be immense. The incident led to introspection both within Balenciaga and across the industry as a whole about the responsibilities of brands navigating the intersection of art, commerce and social ethics.

By the time Demna left Balenciaga in 2025 to assume the creative directorship at Gucci, he had already changed the blueprint for how fashion operates. He made Balenciaga the most talked-about, memed and dissected label of the decade - not just in fashion circles but in popular culture at large. Celebrities, tech moguls, artists and influencers all gravitated toward the

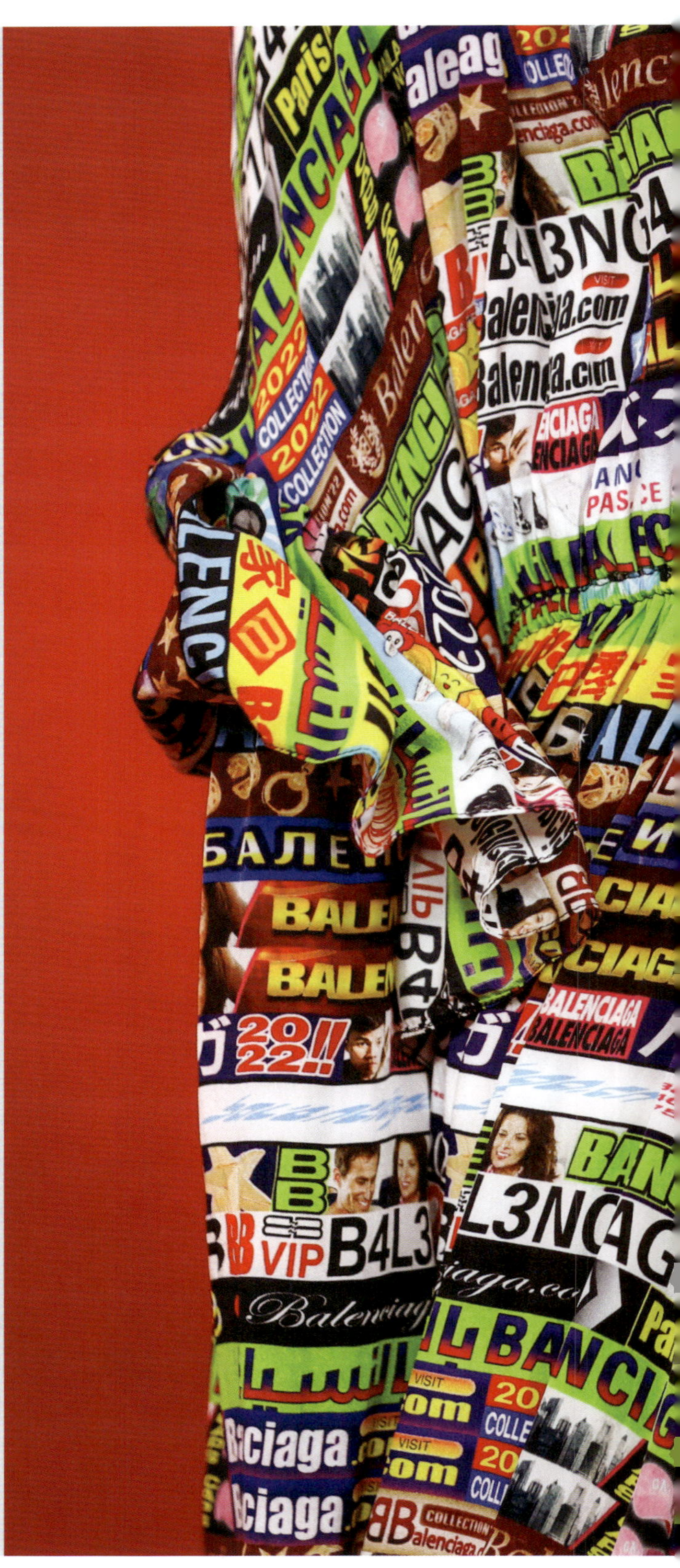

RIGHT: A bold piece from the Balenciaga Womenswear Spring/Summer 2022 collection

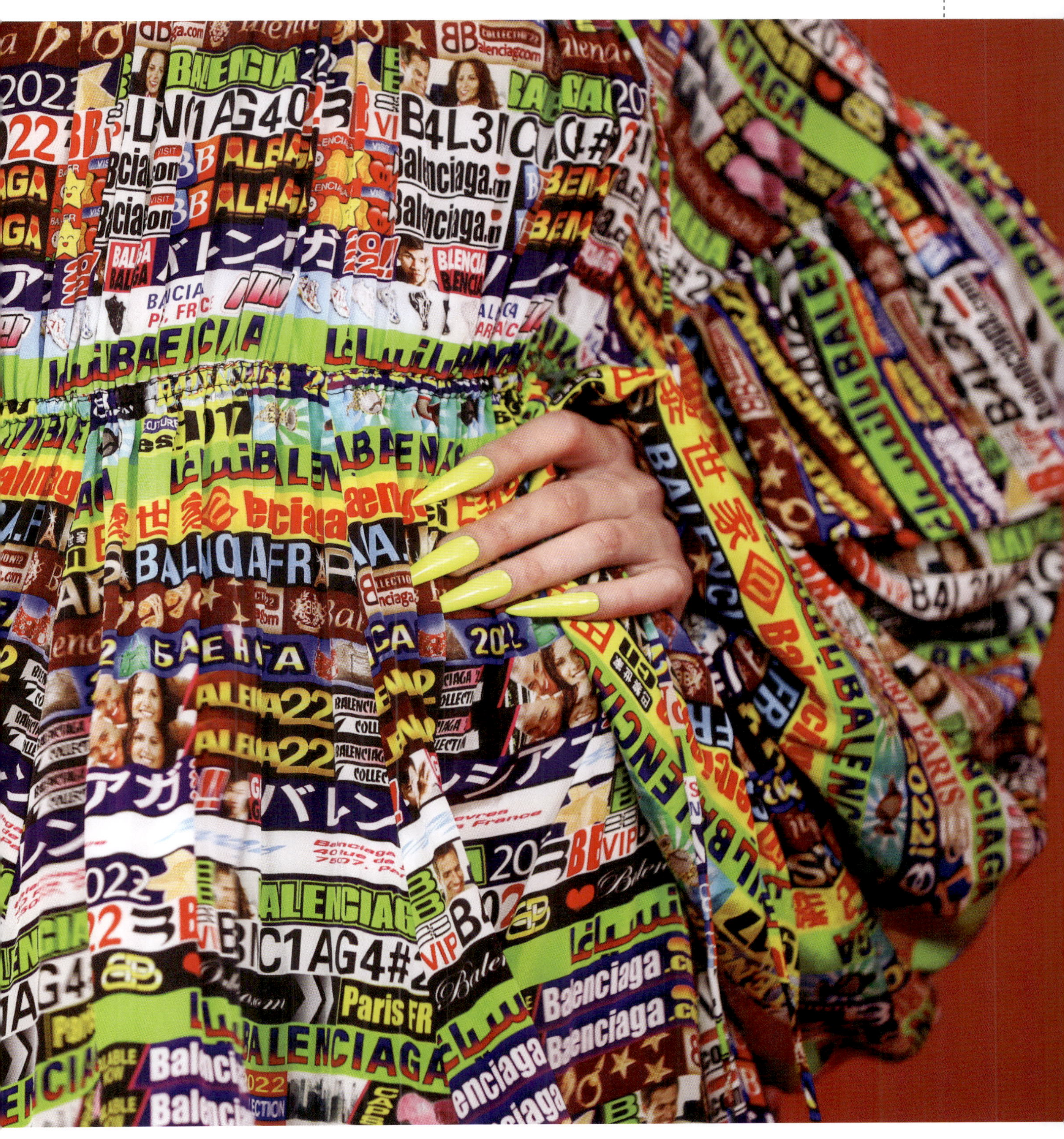

label's hybrid energy - where couture and streetwear, opulence and absurdity, past and future all collided. Under Demna, Balenciaga garments became not just statements of taste but vehicles of commentary.

In his place, Pierpaolo Piccioli, formerly of Valentino, stepped in with a markedly different tone - romantic, emotionally expressive and rooted in the belief that beauty itself could be revolutionary. Where Demna saw fragmentation and irony, Piccioli saw the potential for softness and soul. Yet even as Balenciaga entered a new chapter, it remained undeniably shaped by Demna's imprint - the bold proportions, the challenging silhouettes, the willingness to court discomfort in pursuit of something authentic.

Demna's time at Balenciaga was not about fashion in the narrow sense - it was about redefining the role of the designer in a turbulent world. He brought with him the sensibility of the outsider, the urgency of the refugee and the craft of the master tailor. He showed that fashion could speak, loudly and clearly, about power, politics, identity and, yes, absurdity. And while not every message was universally received or celebrated, his impact was undeniable. Balenciaga, under Demna, was not just a brand - it was a barometer for the anxieties and aspirations of its era. As fashion continues to evolve, his legacy remains a challenge to others - to be bold, to be disruptive and, above all, to make fashion matter.

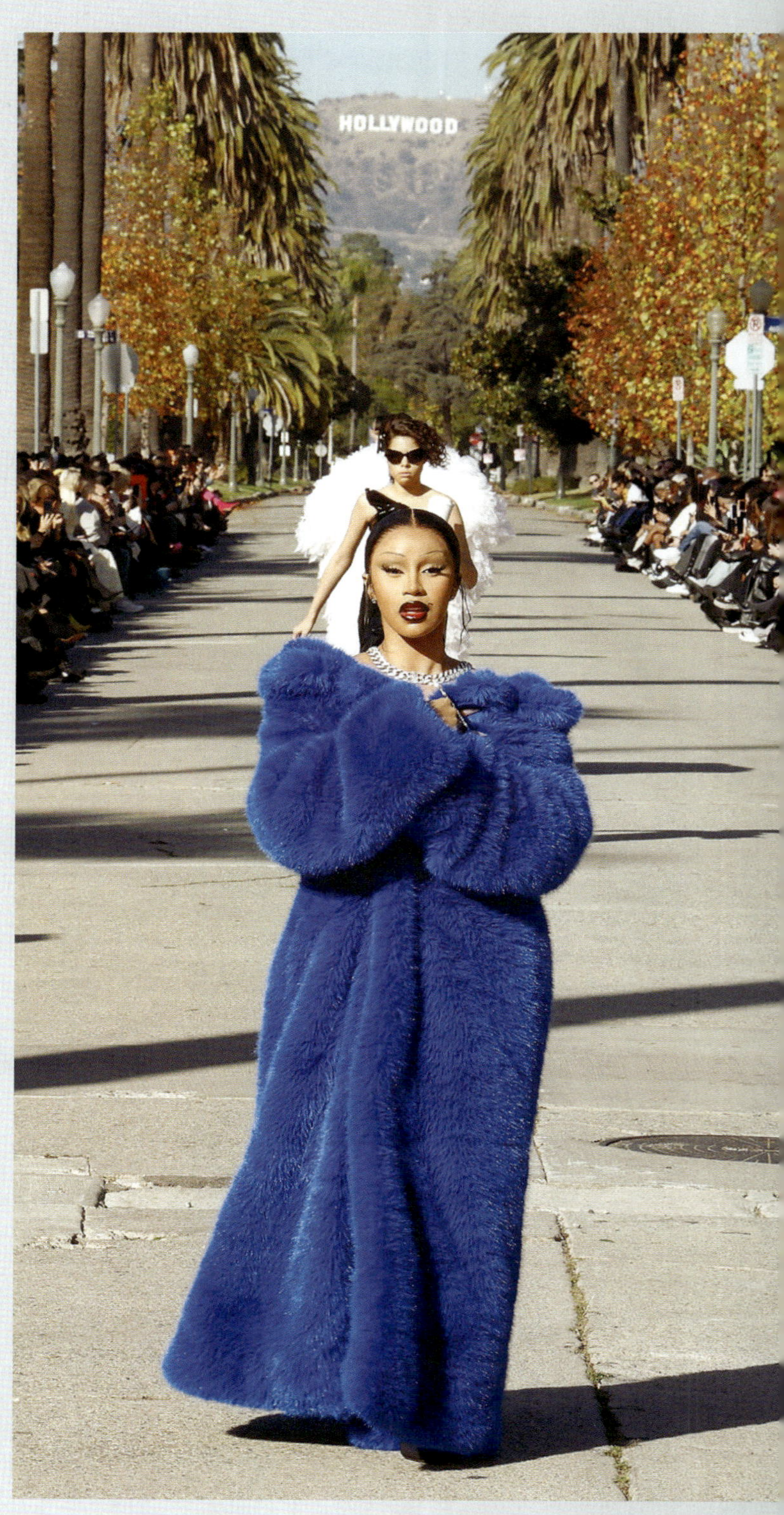

RIGHT: Cardi B walks down South Windsor Boulevard during the Balenciaga Fall 2024 fashion show
OPP PAGE: Another look in the Balenciaga Fall 2024 show

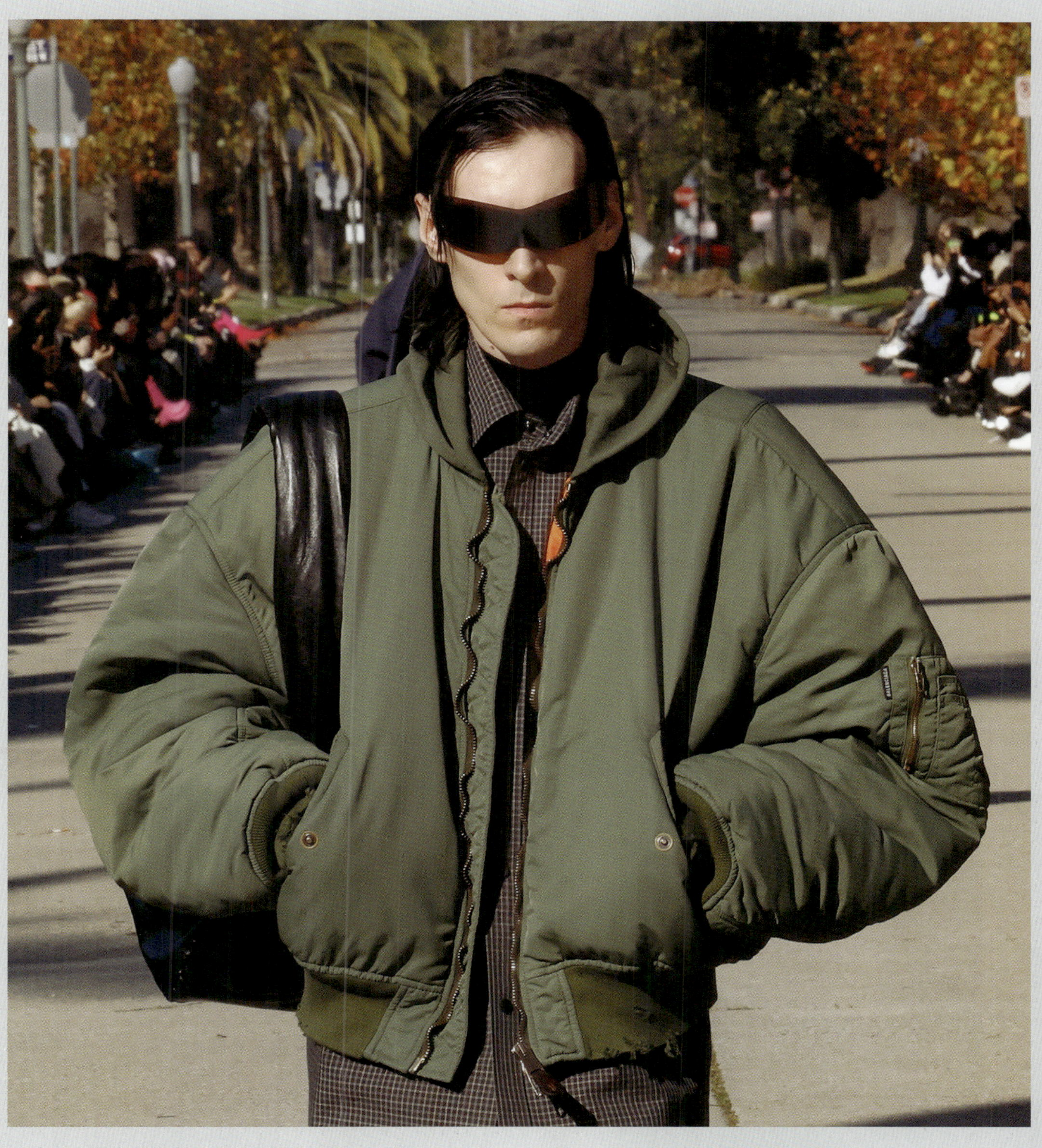

MODEL MUSES

All fashion houses have favourite model muses. Here are some of Balenciaga's most beloved...

ELIZA DOUGLAS

Eliza Douglas is the definitive face of Demna's Balenciaga. She debuted for the brand in 2016 and went on to appear in nearly every one of his shows - from ready-to-wear to couture. With her androgynous features, intellectual aura and unflinching charisma, she perfectly embodied the brand's anti-glamour, post-ironic identity. Often styled in exaggerated silhouettes or stark minimalism, Douglas didn't just model the clothes - she became part of the performance. Her background in fine art strengthened her role as a collaborator. Whether walking alone in a silent showroom or flanked by politicians and celebrities in an immersive set, Douglas has remained Balenciaga's constant. However now Demna has departed, her reign as the model muse queen of the brand, may have come to an end.

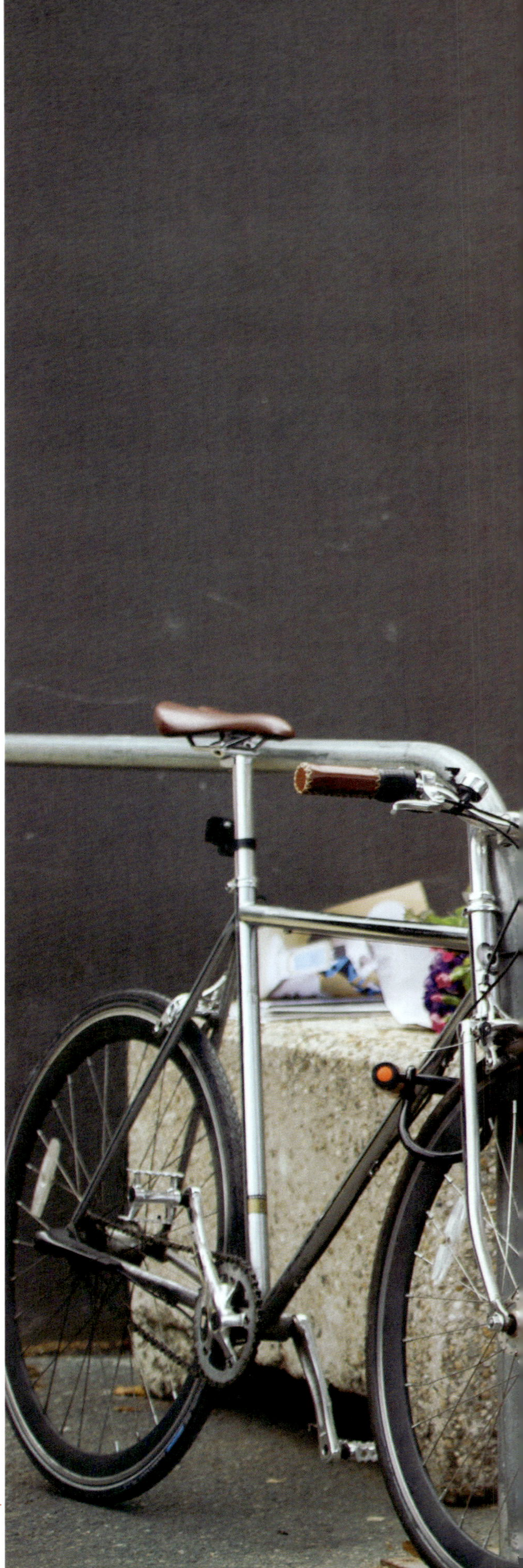

RIGHT: Model Eliza Douglas after the Balenciaga show at Paris Fashion Week Spring/Summer 2017

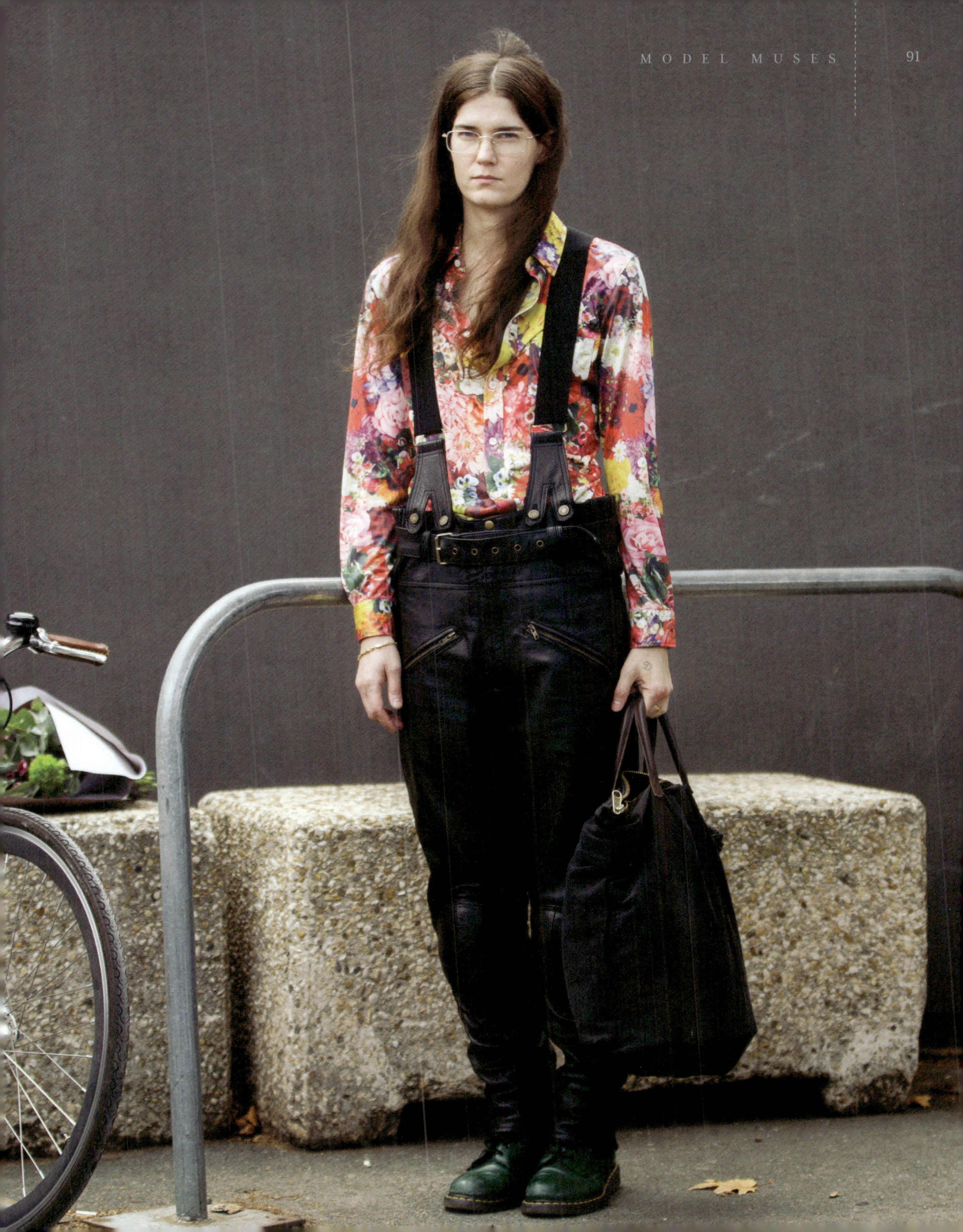

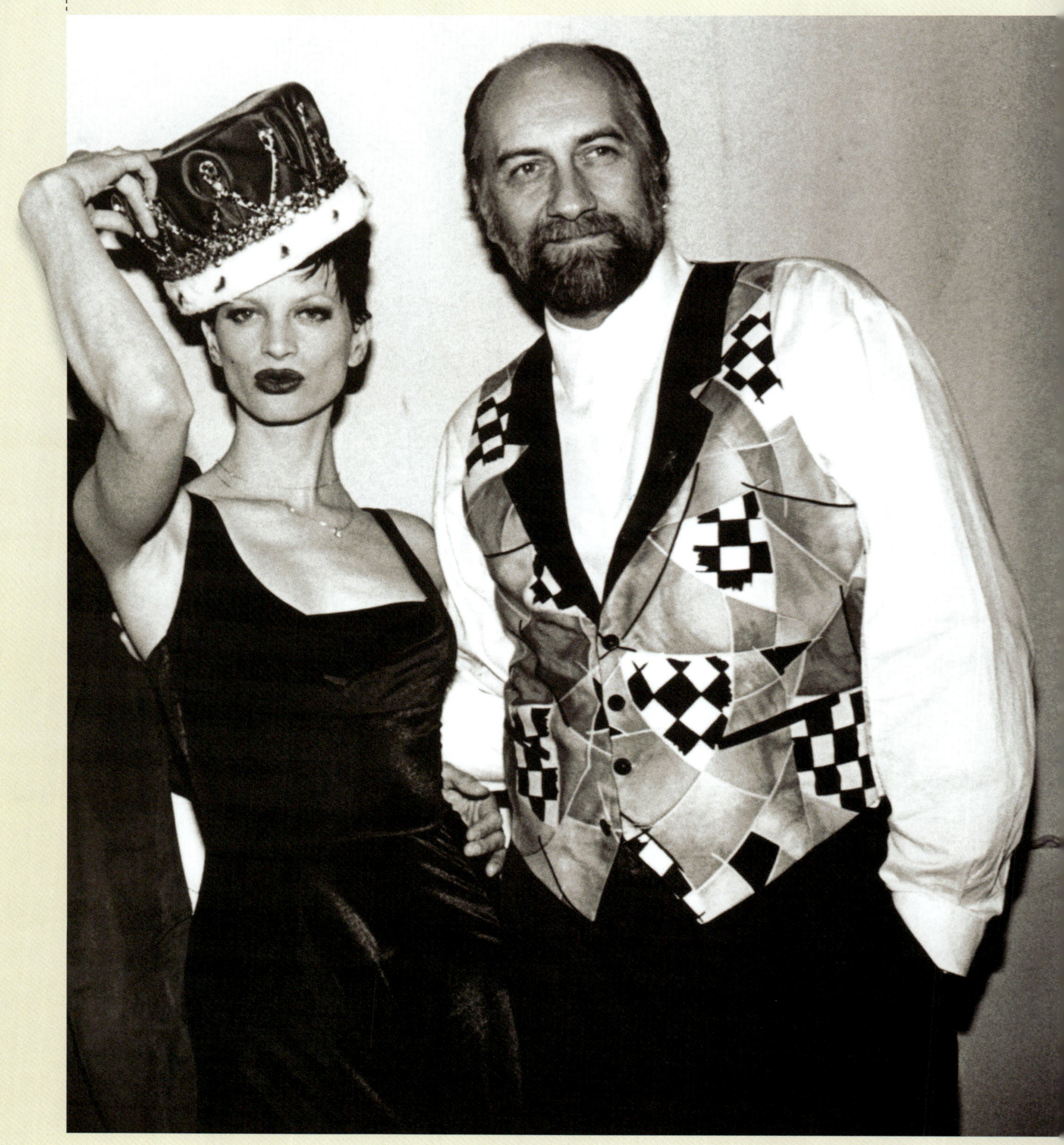

ABOVE: Kristen McMenamy poses for a photo with Mick Fleetwood, New York, 1993
OPP PAGE: Bella Hadid on the runway at the Balenciaga Spring/Summer 2020 Show, Paris Fashion Week

KRISTEN MCMENAMY

McMenamy's appearances for Balenciaga perfectly merged legacy with avant-garde reinvention. A '90s supermodel known for her radical beauty and boundary-pushing attitude, McMenamy returned to the runway for Balenciaga's Haute Couture collections under Demna - often in surreal, sculptural silhouettes. With her signature silver hair and statuesque presence, she brought a haunting elegance to the brand's dystopian glamour. Whether cloaked in velvet or latex, McMenamy is capable of transforming the runway into fashion theatre.

BELLA HADID

Though not a core muse, Bella Hadid has played a prominent role in Balenciaga's global presence. Known for her ability to shift between high glamour and edgy futurism, she's appeared in several Balenciaga campaigns and shows that emphasize the brand's darker, cyberpunk sensibility. Hadid's sculptural features and expressive walk make her an ideal vessel for the brand's couture and streetwear fusion. She's worn Balenciaga off the runway, too, and is often snapped in oversized coats, pointed pantaboots and structured tailoring that highlight her personal alignment with the House aesthetic.

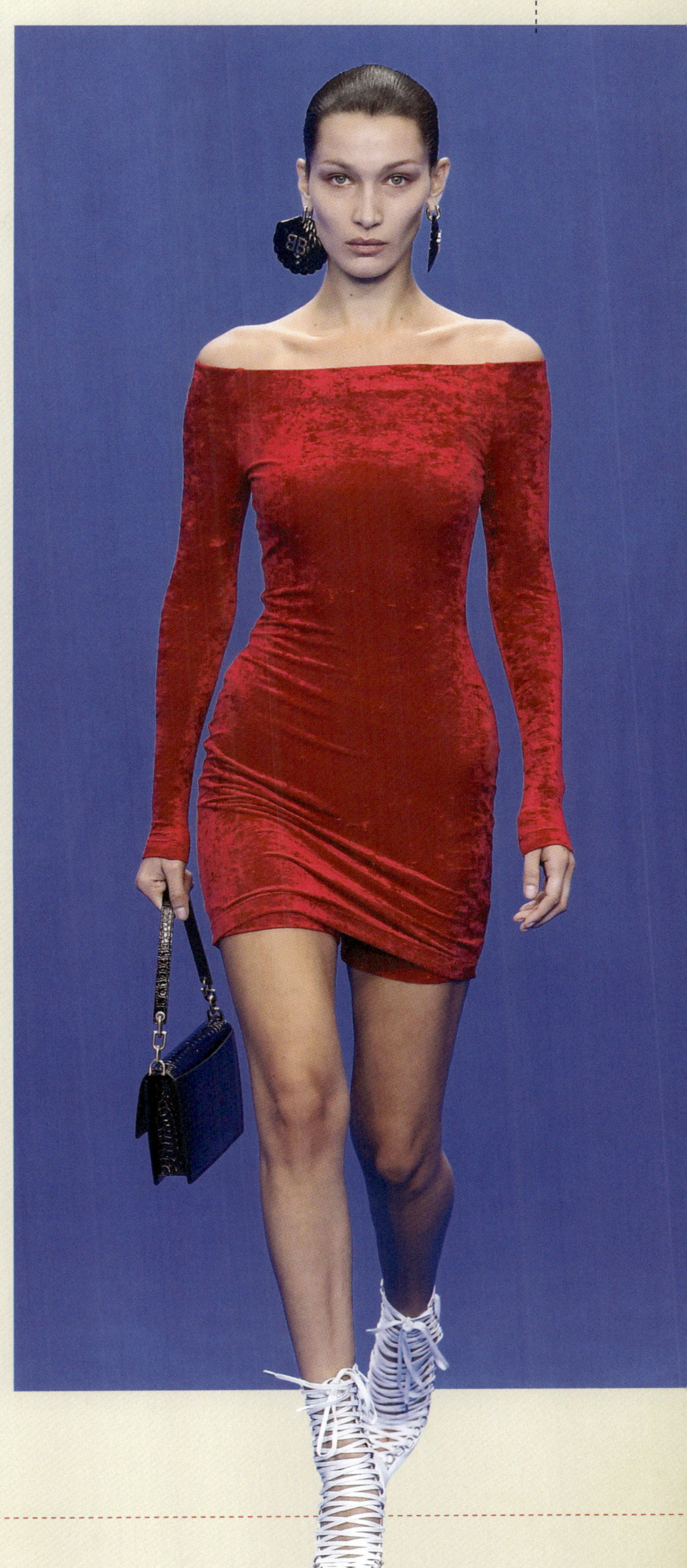

NAOMI CAMPBELL

Naomi Campbell's relationship with Balenciaga is one of legacy and spectacle. Campbell walked in the Fall 2021 Couture show - Balenciaga's first haute couture collection in over 50 years - in a voluminous, architectural black gown, closing the show with dramatic flair. Naomi's regal strut and

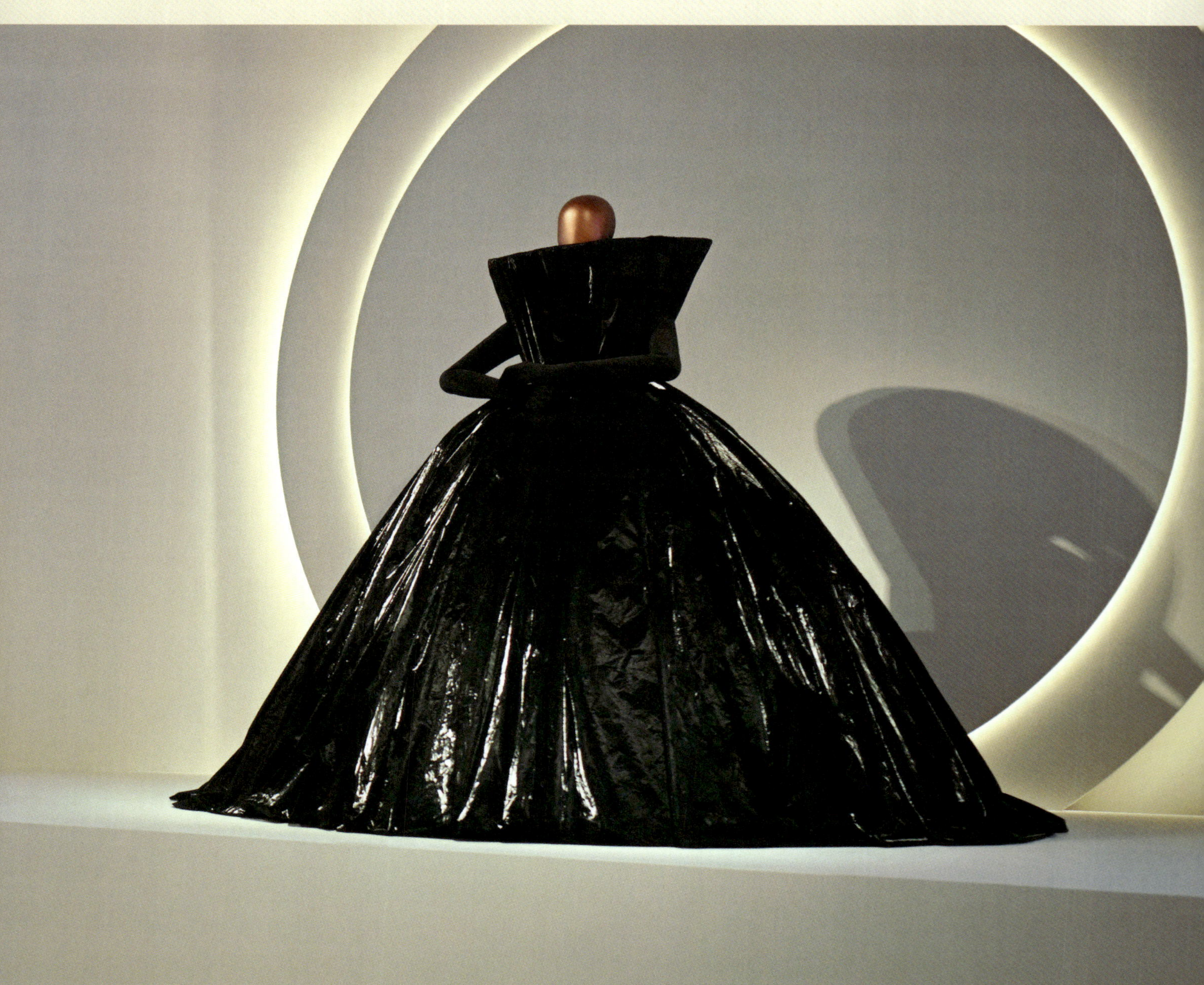

ABOVE: The gown Naomi Campbell wore in the Balenciaga Fall 2021 couture show, on display at London's Victoria and Albert Museum
OPPOSITE: Naomi Campbell at the Balenciaga Spring/Summer 2022 Red Carpet Collection event

commanding stage presence brought gravitas and timeless beauty to Balenciaga's experimental world. Her unforgettable appearances demonstrate how the brand blends old-world prestige with contemporary fashion codes. Campbell doesn't just wear Balenciaga - she owns it.

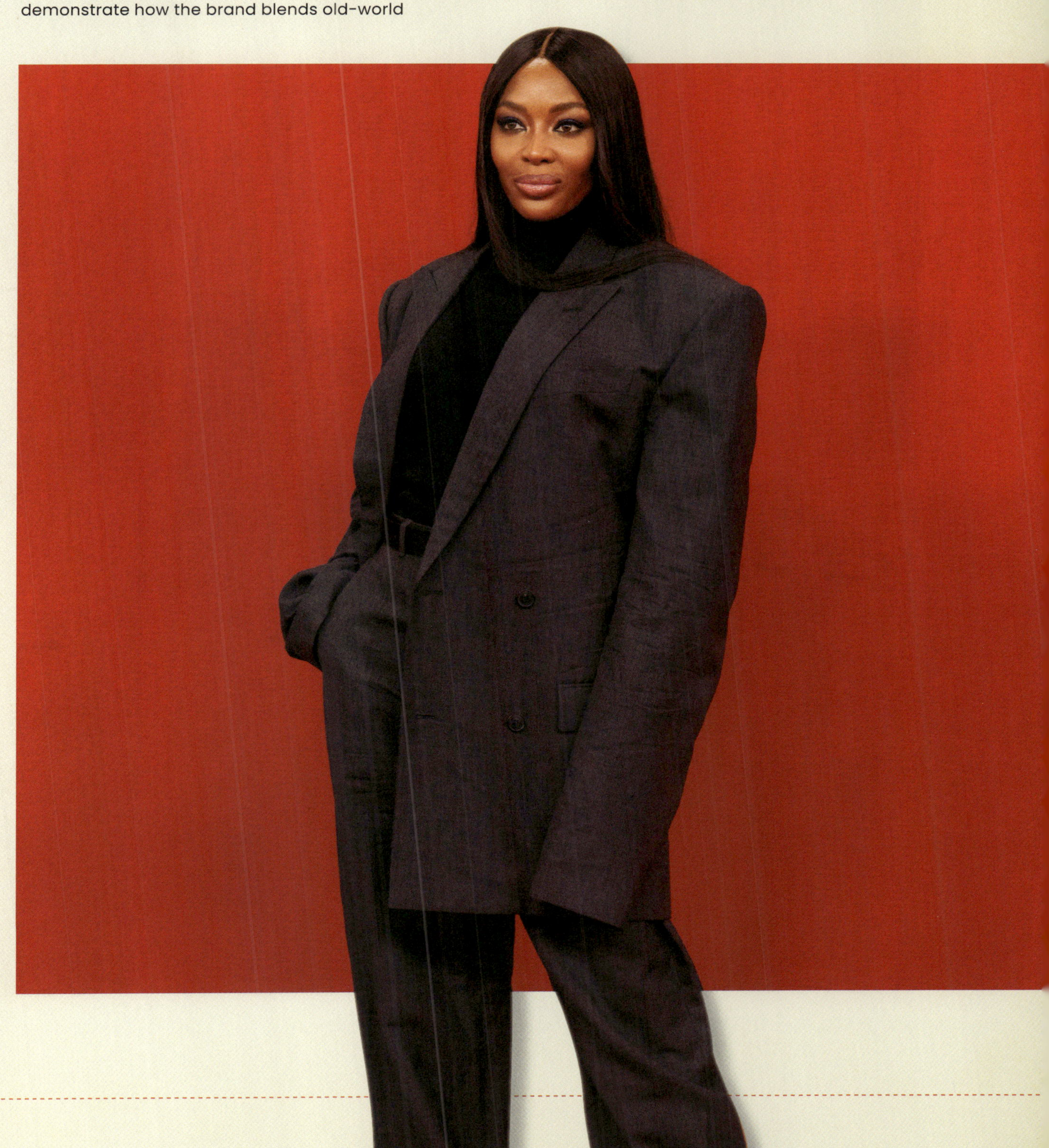

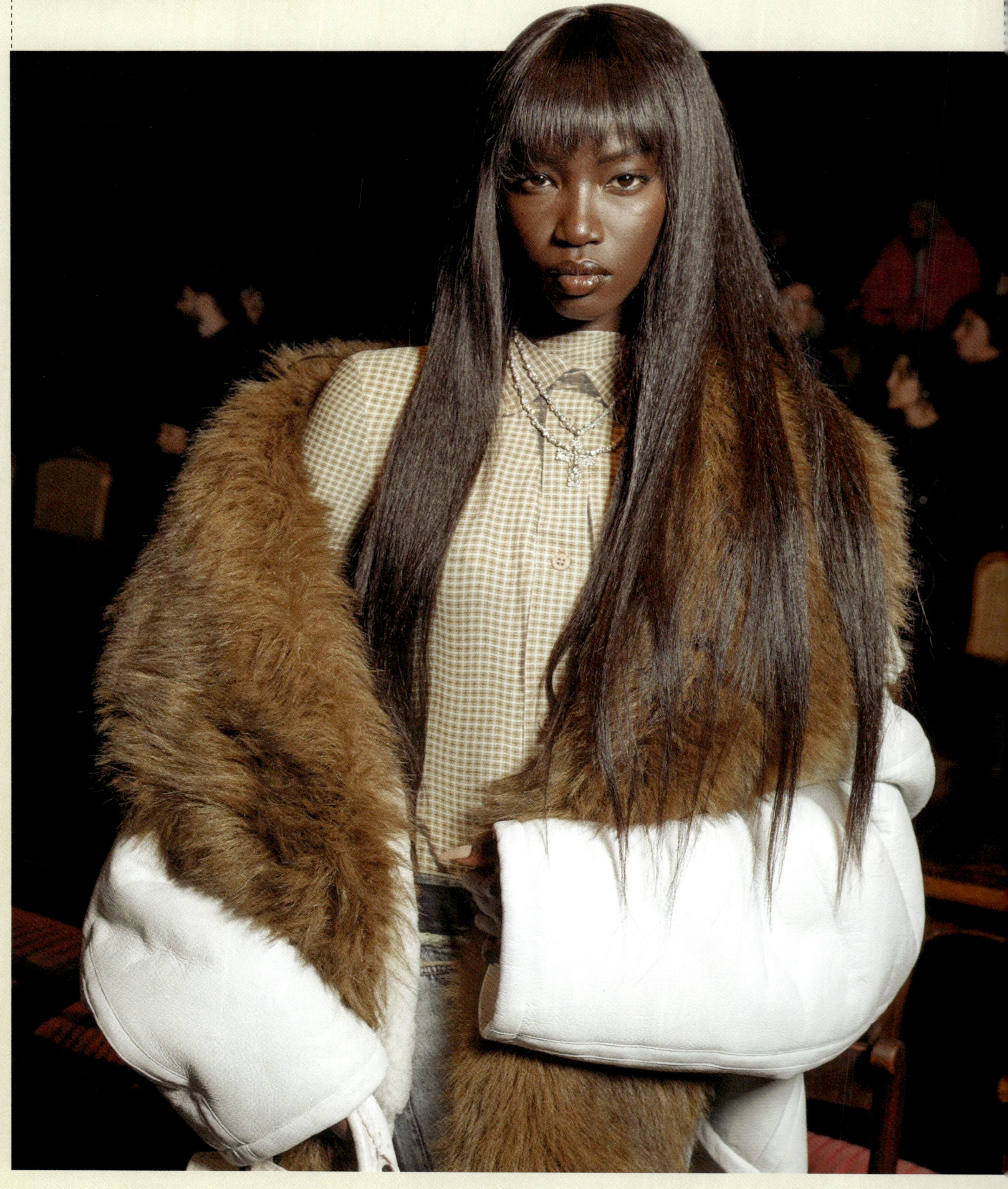

ABOVE: Anok Yai at the Balenciaga Ready-to-Wear
Spring 2025 show during Paris Fashion Week
OPP PAGE: Awar Odhiang walks the runway during the
Balenciaga Ready-to-Wear Spring/Summer 2026 show

ANOK YAI

Known for her striking symmetry, commanding walk, unconventional beauty and aura of cool detachment, Yai is a powerful fixture in Balenciaga's modern casting, frequently walking in shows and starring in key campaigns. Her ability to exude both quiet elegance and razor-sharp presence makes her an ideal model for Balenciaga's structured tailoring, dystopian silhouettes and sometimes brutalist styling. She has walked in multiple seasons, from ready-to-wear to couture, often opening or closing the show.

AWAR ODHIANG

Odhiang has emerged as one of Balenciaga's runway powerhouses. Her statuesque frame, fierce walk and natural elegance make her a perfect match for the brand's imposing, structured silhouettes. Odhiang has walked in several of Demna's Balenciaga shows, often wearing the most extreme or high-concept pieces - from exaggerated shoulders to full-body looks that challenge conventional form. Her presence brings grace to even the most experimental garments. While less publicly recognized than Bella Hadid or Naomi Campbell within the fashion industry, Awar is respected for her ability to deliver consistent, emotionally detached, almost otherworldly performances. Whether in head-to-toe latex, padded armour-like suits, or tailored floor-length coats, she embodies the brand's commitment to pushing silhouette and identity.

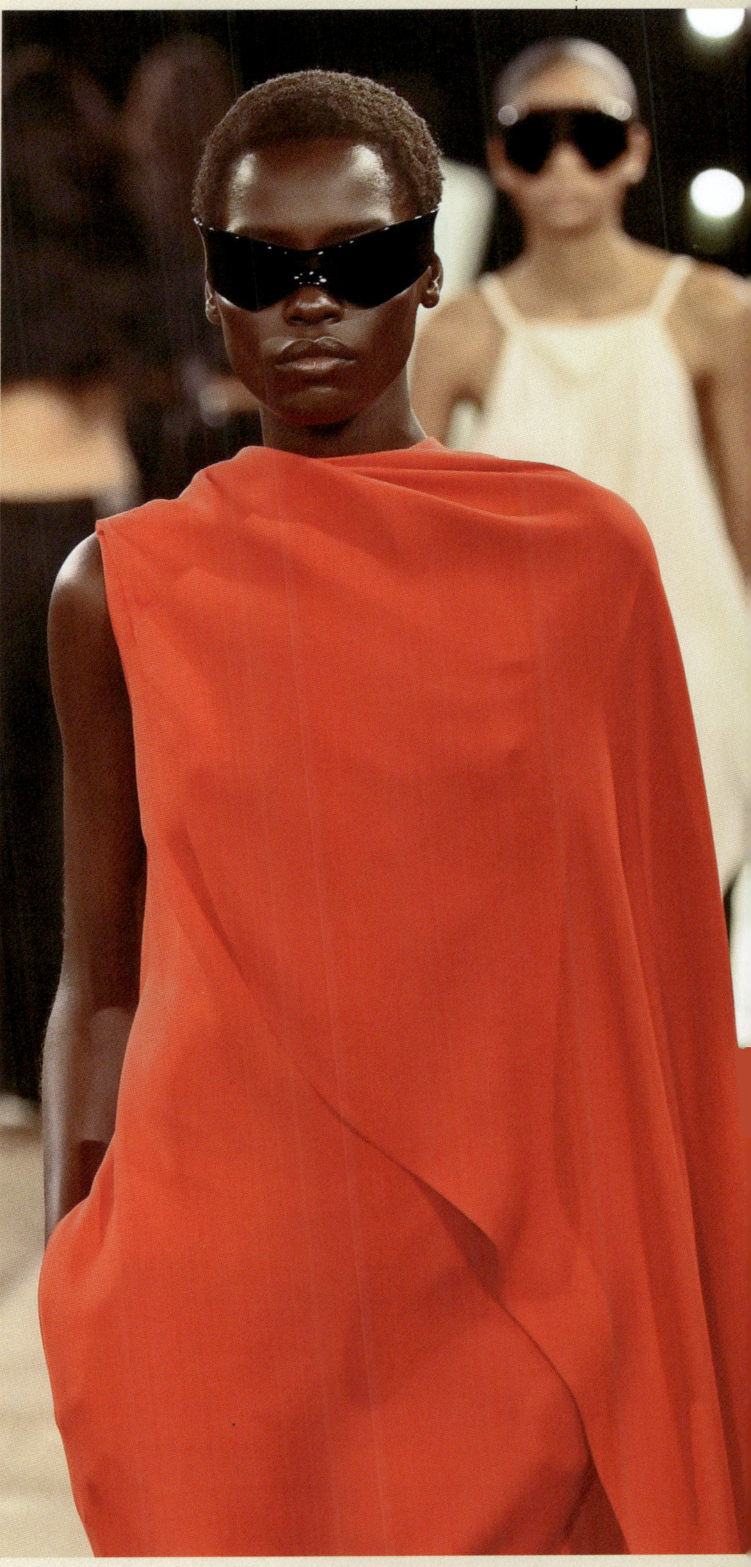

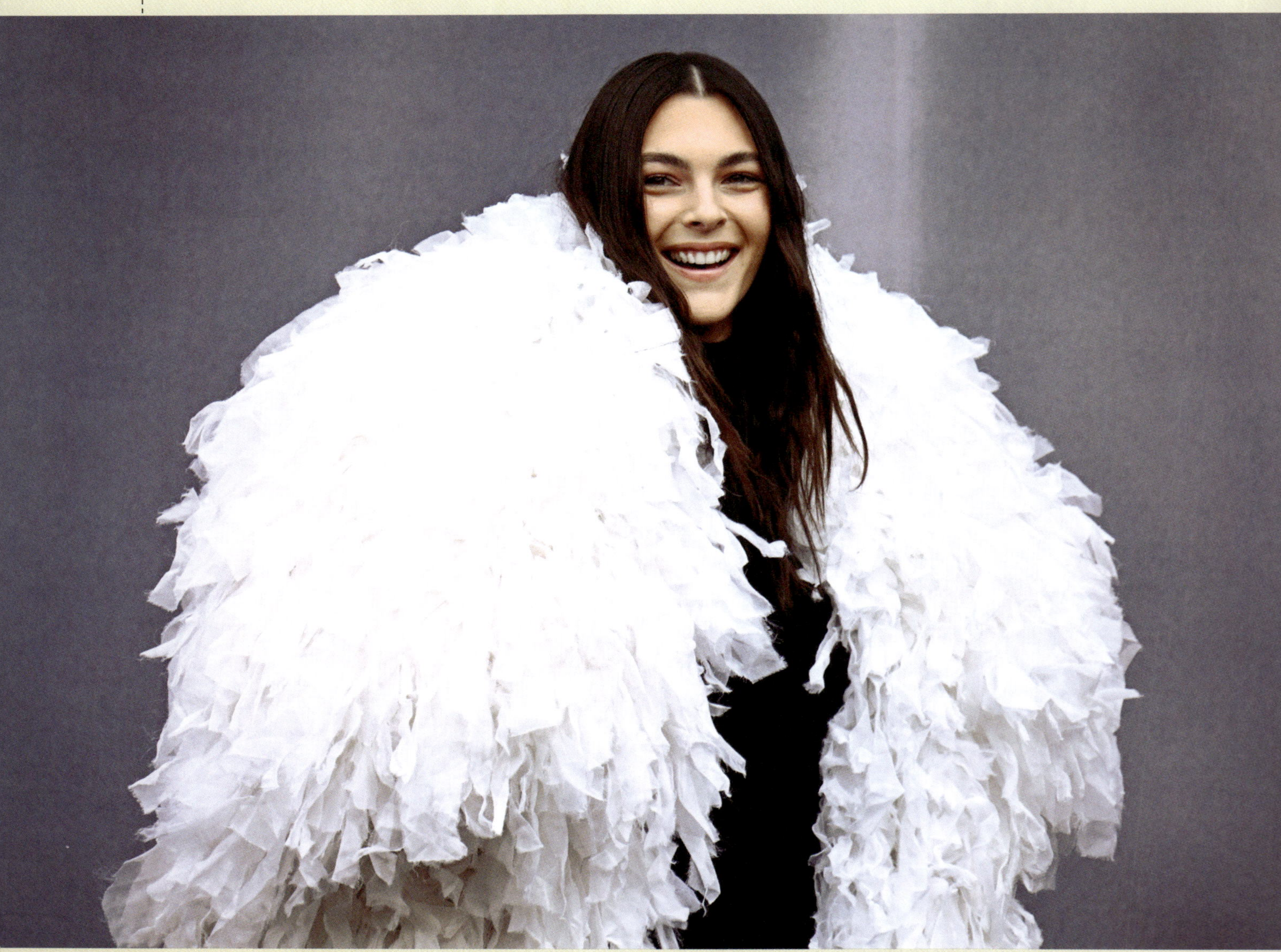

VITTORIA CERETTI

Vittoria Ceretti brings classic beauty with a modern edge to Balenciaga's runway and campaigns. As one of the most versatile models of her generation, Ceretti can shift from soft and romantic to stark and architectural - qualities that Balenciaga under Demna used to full effect. She has appeared in editorial campaigns and walked in numerous shows – on the runway bringing a calm confidence to the sometimes chaotic parade of oversized silhouettes, bizarre materials and experimental staging. By merging her classic Italian elegance with the brand's stark futurism, Vittoria Ceretti became a key figure during Demna's tenure at Balenciaga.

ABOVE: Vittoria Ceretti arrives for Balenciaga's Autumn/ Winter 2024/2025 Ready-to-Wear show
OPP PAGE: Vittoria Ceretti wears a custom all-black, strapless Balenciaga gown to the 2023 Met Gala celebrating "Karl Lagerfeld: A Line of Beauty."

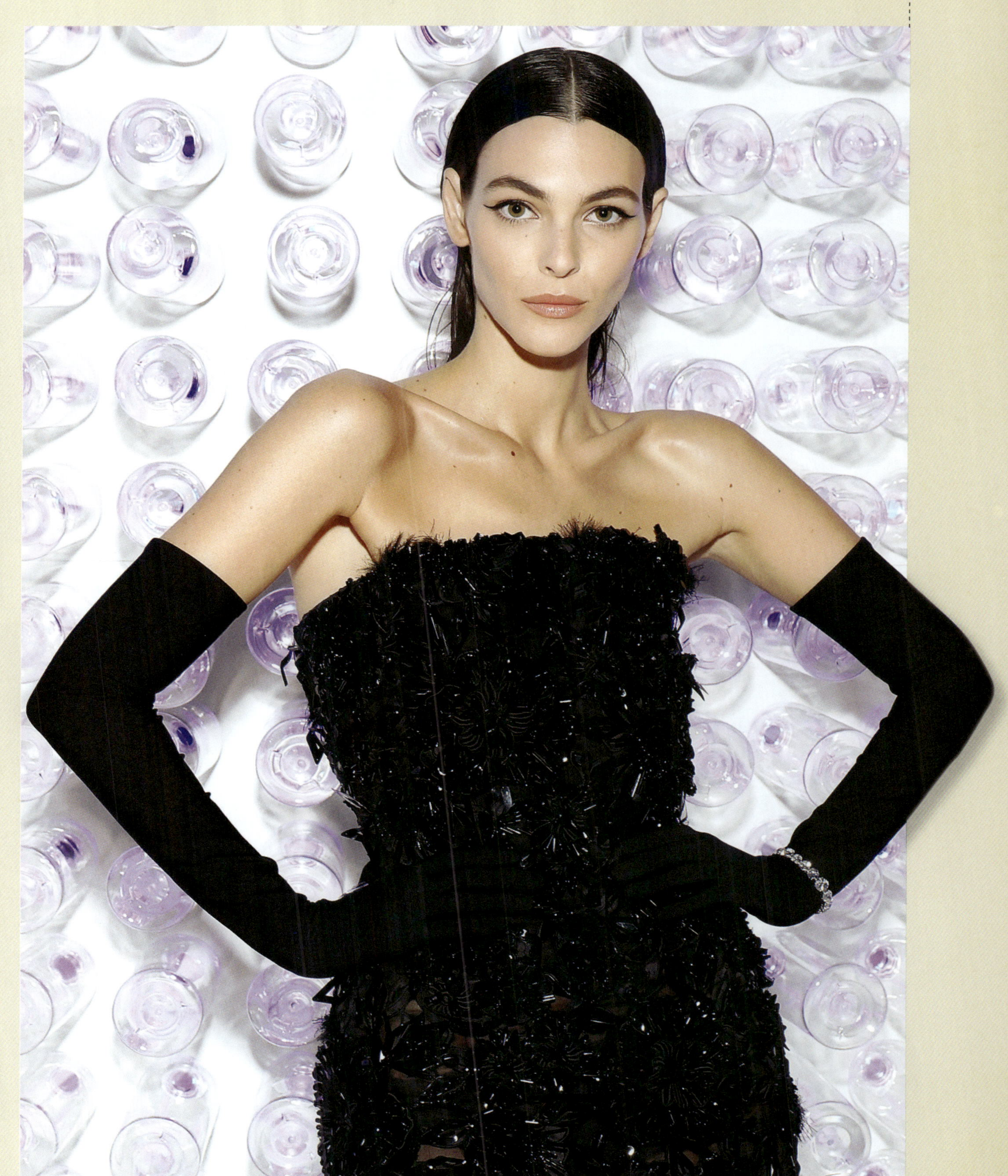

KATE MOSS

'Mossy' has had a longstanding and influential relationship with Balenciaga, playing a pivotal role in popularising some of the brand's most iconic designs. In the early 2000s, Moss was instrumental in catapulting Balenciaga's Le City bag to It-bag status. After spotting a prototype, she requested one, leading to its limited production and subsequent popularity. Her frequent appearances with the bag contributed significantly to its cult following. In 2024, Balenciaga reintroduced the Le City bag, and Moss was once again at the forefront, starring in the campaign alongside Nicole Kidman and Amelia Gray. Photographed by Mario Sorrenti, the campaign paid homage to the bag's legacy while presenting it to a new generation. Later in 2024, Moss featured in Balenciaga's Bel Air handbag campaign. Through these collaborations, Kate Moss continues to embody Balenciaga's fusion of timeless style and modern innovation, reinforcing her status as a fashion icon and muse for the brand.

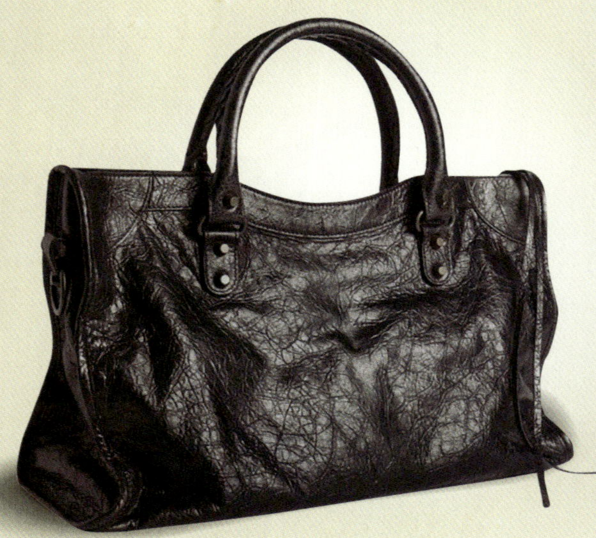

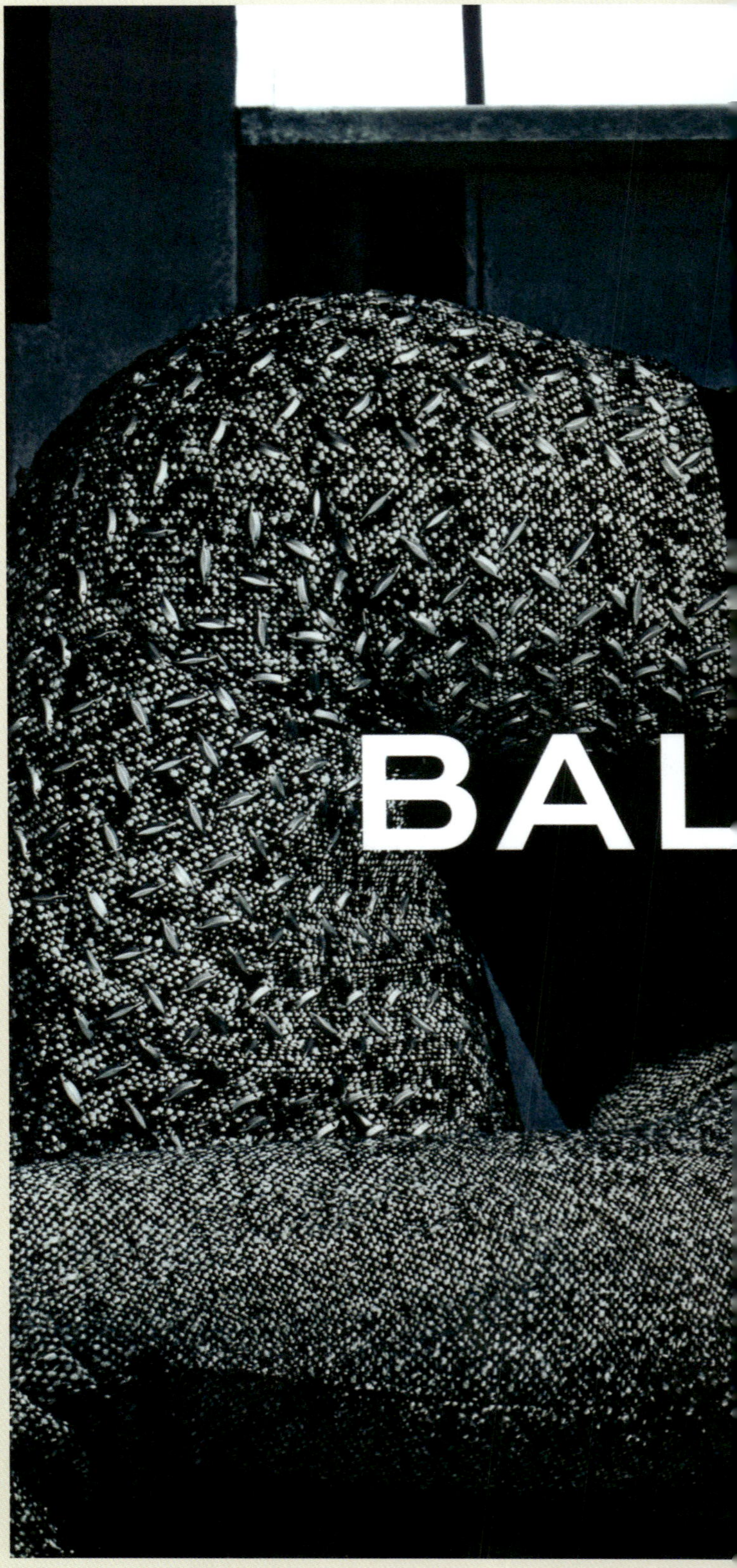

ABOVE: Balenciaga's Le City bag
RIGHT: 2010s Balenciaga advertising campaign featuring Kate Moss

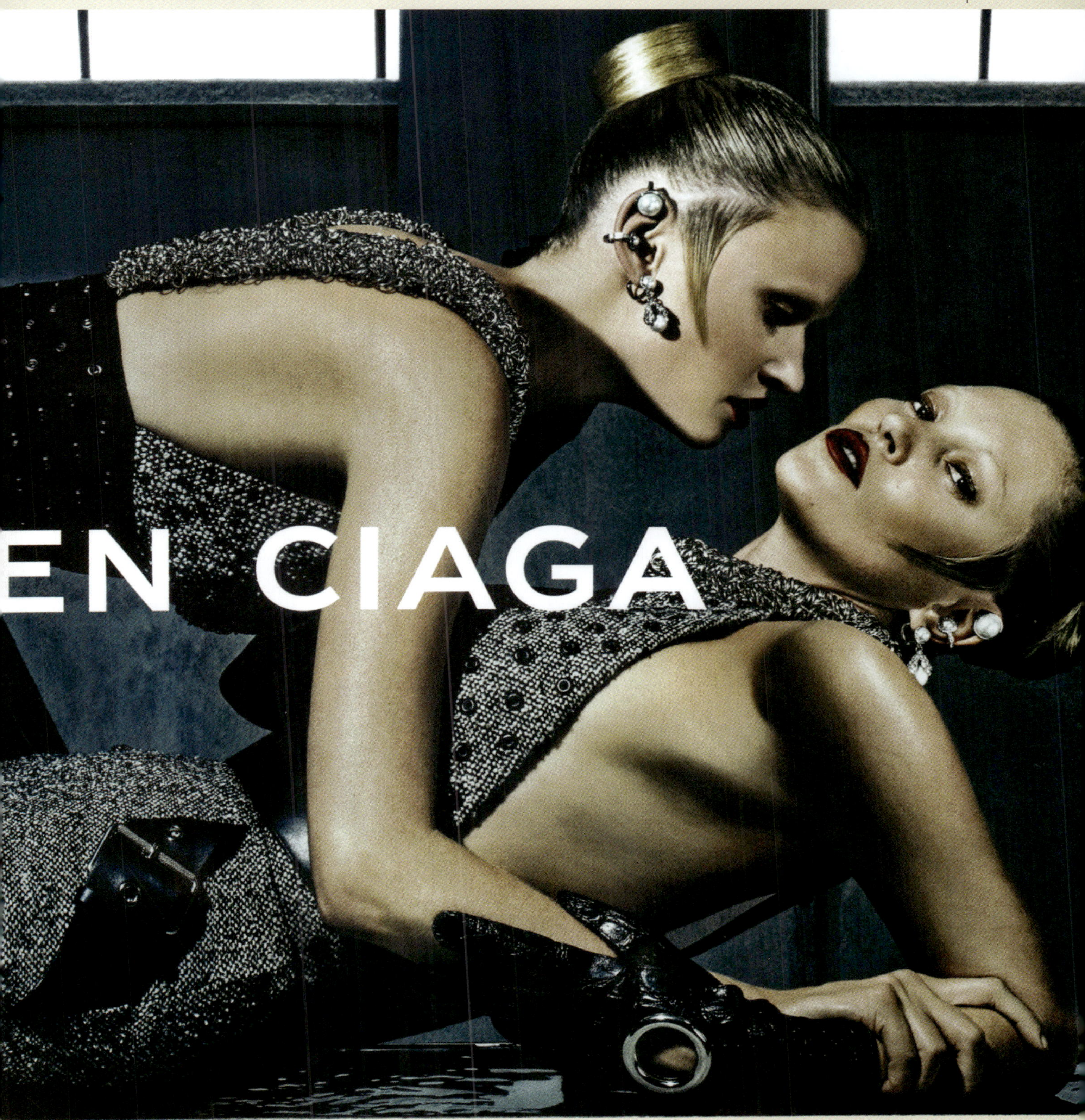
EN CIAGA

CLASSIC ACCESSORIES

"It's not a bag, it's a Balenciaga"

Widely quoted in memes & fashion forums

Balenciaga has long been revered not only for its ground-breaking couture but also for its distinctive accessories. The house has been through many transitions yet, throughout all these transformations, Balenciaga's accessories - particularly its bags, shoes and eyewear - have maintained a unique identity rooted in both functional minimalism and avant-garde aesthetics. Tradition merged with modernity, iconic and enduring, Balenciaga's accessories are never just add-ons. They are integral to the narrative of the brand, each telling a story of fashion rebellion, architectural precision or futuristic vision. In a world saturated with fleeting trends, Balenciaga accessories endure not because they follow the rules of classicism but because they rewrite them. This, ultimately, is what makes them timeless.

BAGS

THE MOTORCYCLE BAG - A CULT CLASSIC

Perhaps the most iconic item in Balenciaga's accessory canon is the Motorcycle Bag, also known as the City Bag. First introduced in 2001 under the creative direction of Nicolas Ghesquière, the Motorcycle Bag broke conventional handbag norms of the early

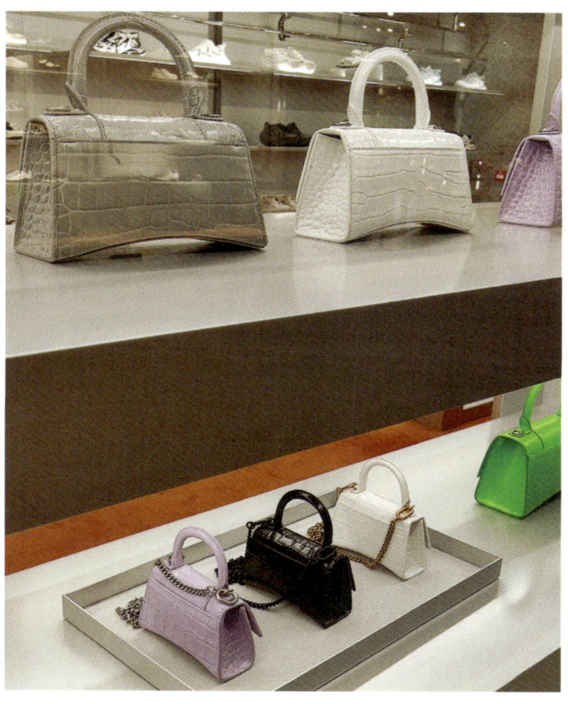

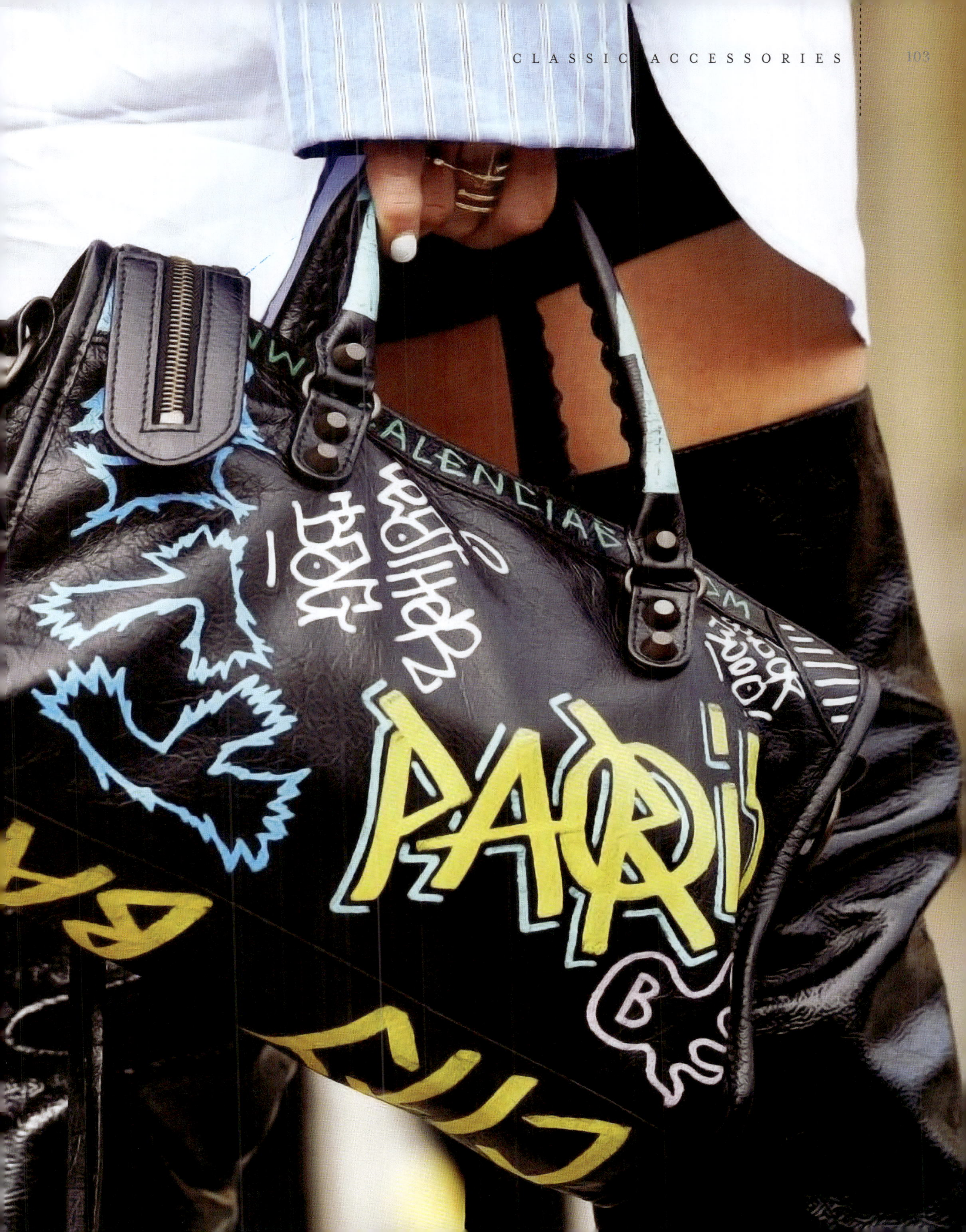
BALENCIAB
PARIS

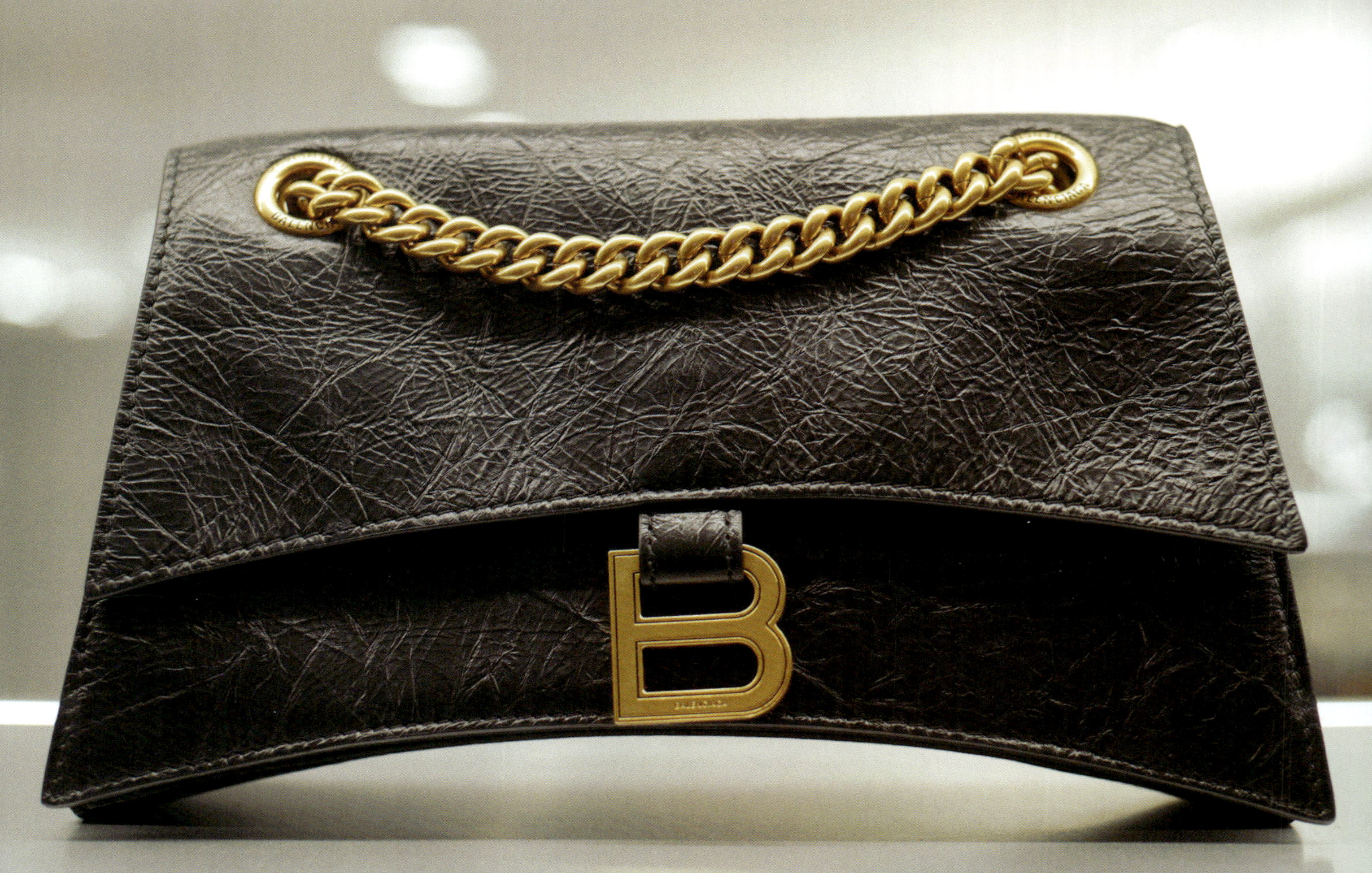

2000s. At a time when structured, logo-heavy bags dominated, Balenciaga offered something different - a slouchy, distressed-leather tote with aged brass hardware, signature tasselled zippers and a casual attitude. The City Bag became an instant favourite among fashion editors, models and celebrities - from Kate Moss to the Olsen twins. Its worn-in aesthetic gave it a rebellious charm that contrasted sharply with the polished designs of rival luxury houses. Lightweight, practical and available in a wide colour spectrum, the bag attained cult status. Today, the Motorcycle Bag is considered a quintessential Balenciaga accessory.

THE HOURGLASS BAG - A MODERN NOD TO HERITAGE

The Hourglass Bag, introduced in recent years, is another essential piece in the line-up of classic Balenciaga accessories. Its sharply curved silhouette is a modern reinterpretation of the dramatic, cinched waists that defined many of Cristóbal Balenciaga's original couture designs. The structured top-handle bag features a distinctive 'B' logo clasp and comes in a variety of sizes - from mini to medium. Despite being a newer release, the Hourglass Bag has quickly gained iconic status due to its blend of historical homage and contemporary appeal. It's equally popular among influencers and luxury consumers, proving that Balenciaga still understands how to make accessories that resonate across generations.

THE EVERYDAY TOTE AND CANVAS PIECES

While Balenciaga excels in high-concept design, it also offers more understated accessories like the the Everyday Tote and canvas bags. These pieces reflect a quieter luxury and are appreciated for their functionality and minimalist branding. The Everyday Tote, for example, is a simple leather bag embossed with the Balenciaga logo, available in both neutral tones or bold colours. Its clean lines and unassuming style make it a go-to for those who prefer subtlety in their luxury purchases. Canvas accessories - often in the form of shopping totes or belt bags - carry the same DNA. They often feature logo-heavy prints but are grounded in utility, aligning with the modern consumer's desire for both fashion and function. These pieces prove that Balenciaga's classic accessories are not just about visual impact but also about practicality and everyday usage.

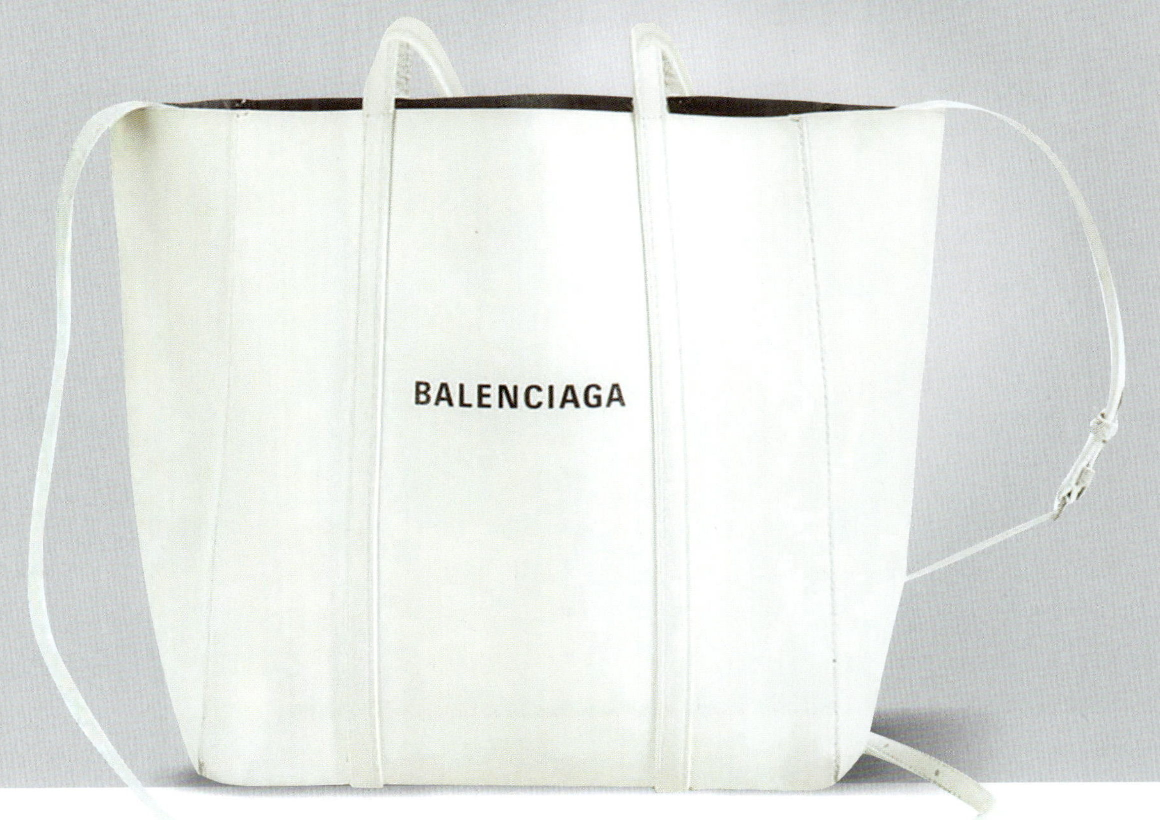

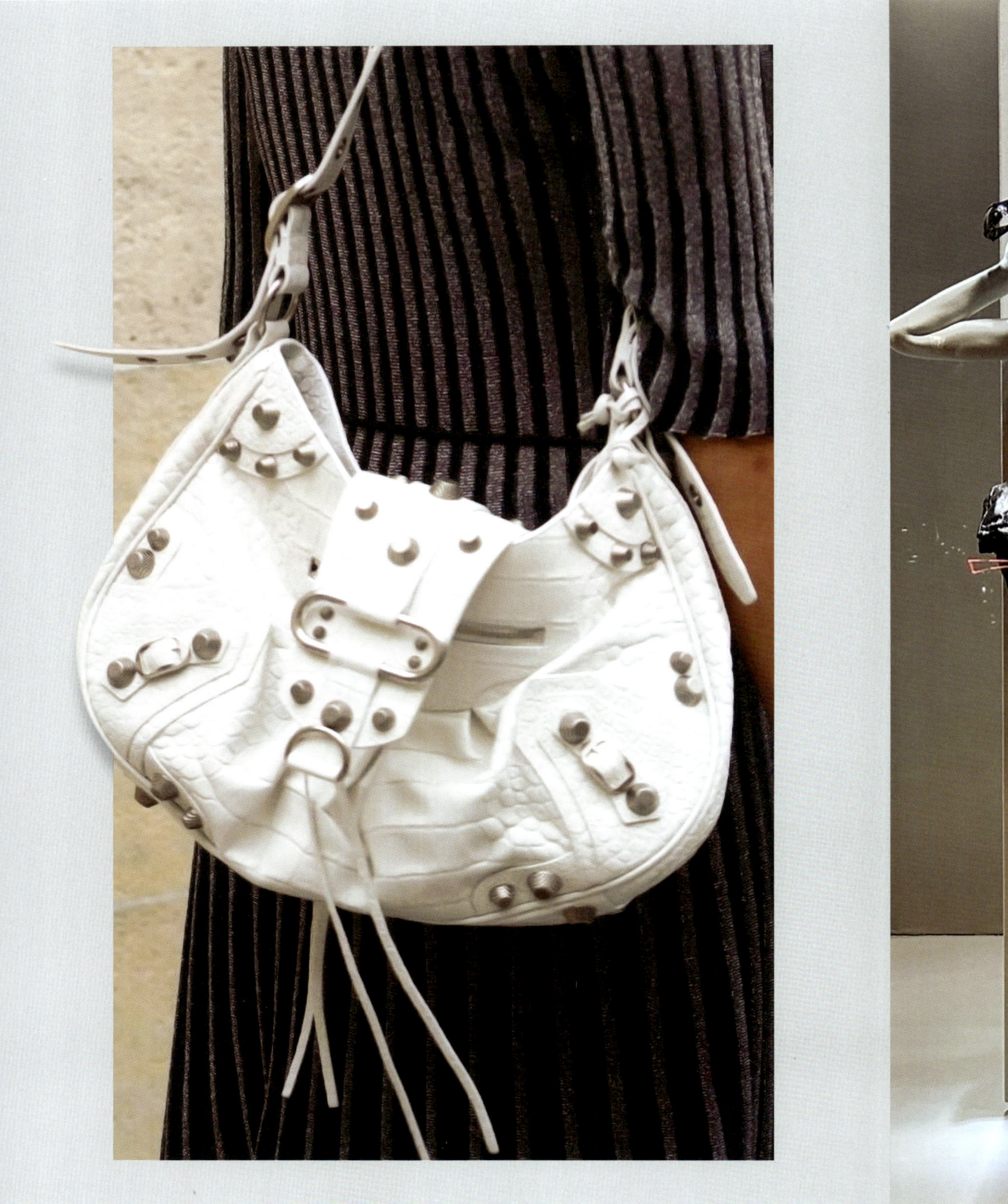

ABOVE: White Le Cagole embossed shoulder bag from Balenciaga
RIGHT: Balenciaga handbags on display at the Galeries Lafayette in Paris

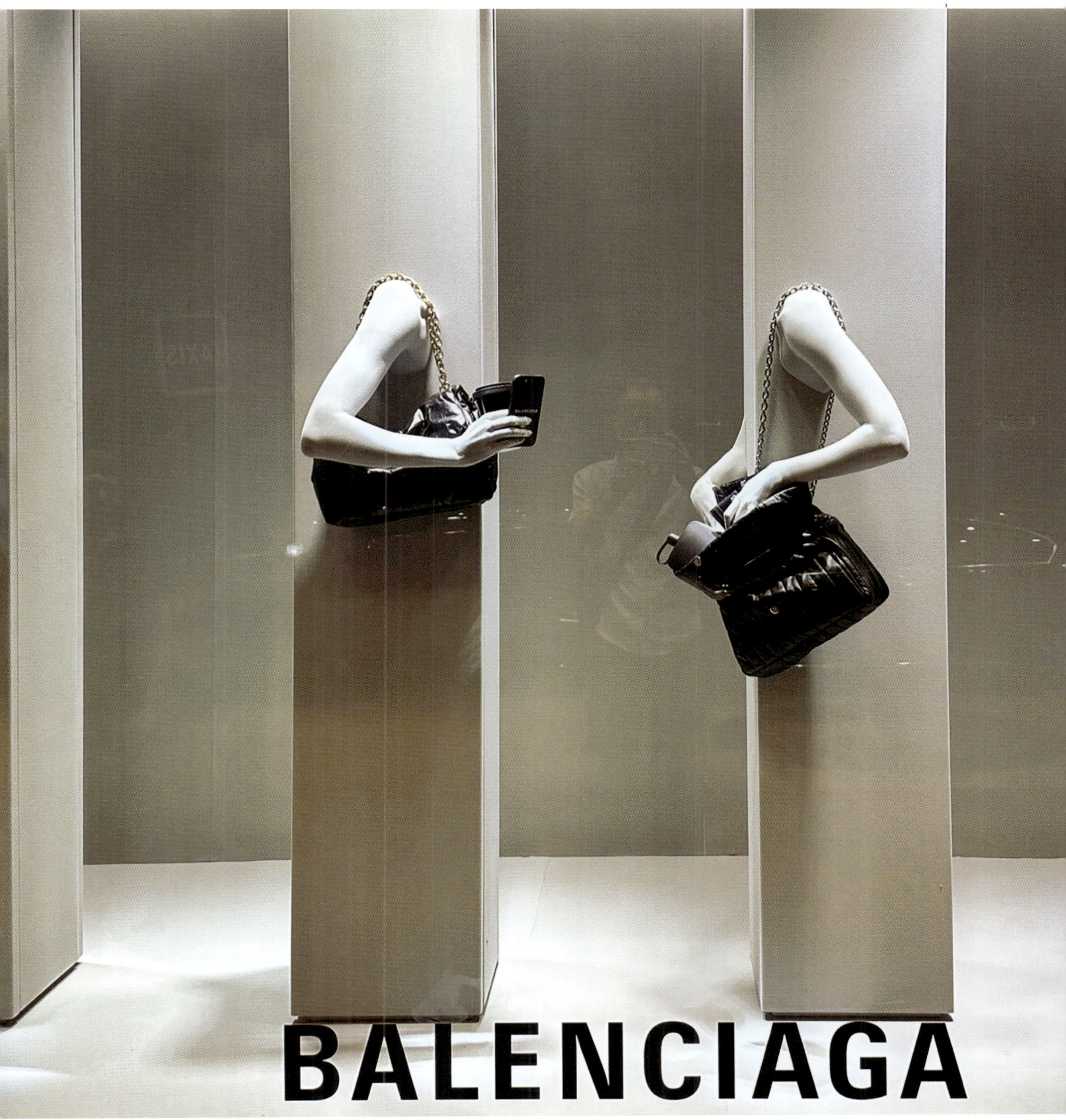
BALENCIAGA

FOOTWEAR

KNIFE BOOTS

Another classic in Balenciaga's accessory arsenal is its footwear, especially the Knife Boot. Introduced during Demna's tenure as creative director, the Knife Boot quickly became a fashion favourite. With its exaggerated pointed toe, second-skin fit and sock-like construction, the design challenged traditional ideas of elegance and comfort. Named for its razor-sharp silhouette, the Knife Boot draws from both fetish-wear and high fashion, blending provocative styling with minimalist execution. It often comes in bright colours, metallic finishes or patterned fabrics - pushing the boundaries of what high-fashion footwear can be. Bold, uncompromising and rooted in conceptual design.

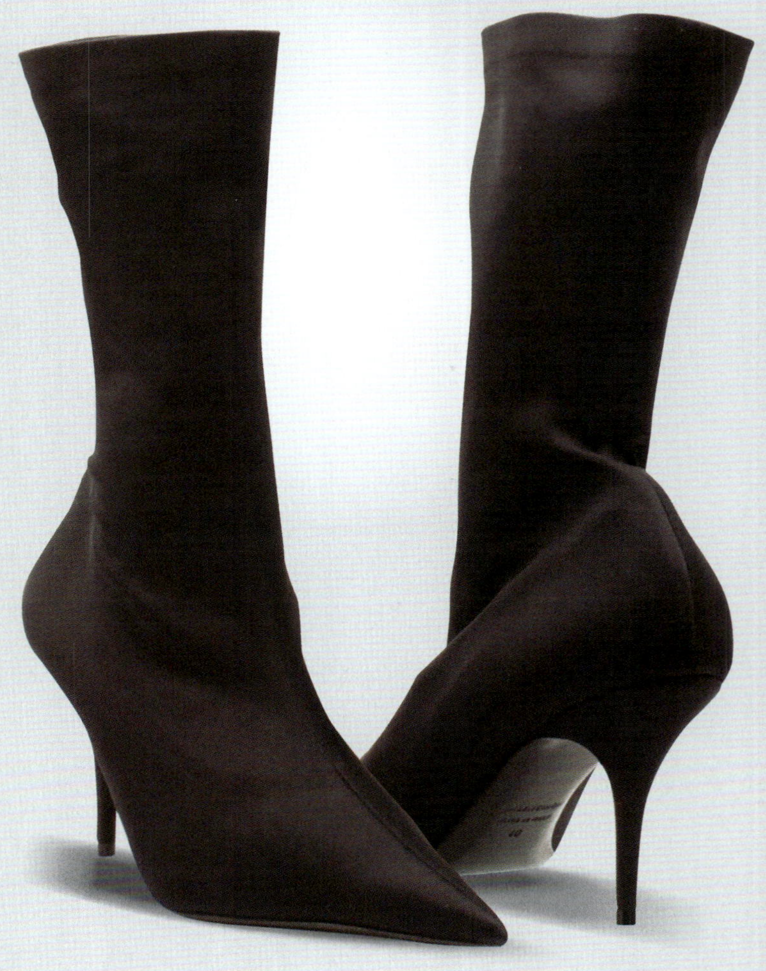

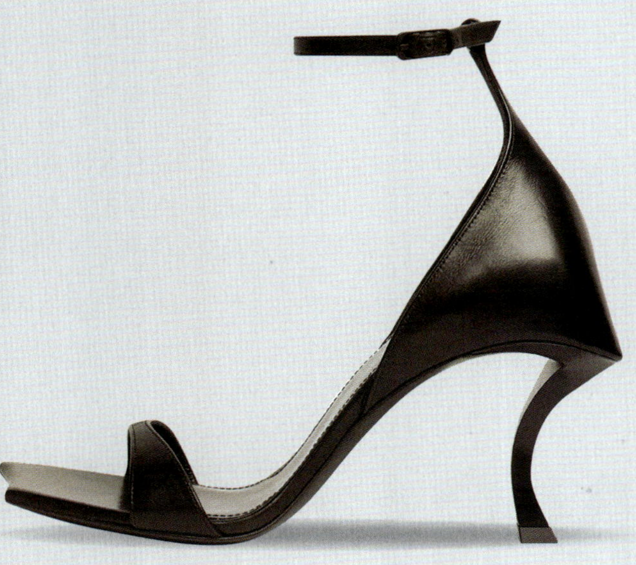

HEELS

Similarly, Balenciaga's heels - including the hourglass-shaped heel and sculptural soles - have been celebrated for their artistic flair. Rather than simply functional pieces, these shoes operate as wearable art, often incorporating unexpected materials or surrealistic forms. They resonate with the brand's architectural heritage.

ABOVE: The iconic Knife boots and Hourglass heels
OPPOSITE: (TOP) Sarah Posch wearing Balenciaga black Speed Trainers, 3 August, 2021, Berlin, Germany
(BOTTOM) Influencer Mar Mayorga wearing the Balenciaga Triple S sneakers in 2019

SPEED TRAINER

The Balenciaga Speed Trainer, introduced in 2016, revolutionized luxury trainers with its minimalist, sock-like design. Composed of a single-piece knit upper and a lightweight sculptural sole, it was a bold departure from traditional sneaker construction. The look is sleek and futuristic. Its slip-on design offers comfort and ease, while the high-top silhouette gives it an athletic yet refined edge. The Speed Trainer became a go-to shoe for fashion minimalists and was quickly adopted by celebrities and stylists alike. It also triggered a wave of imitators, influencing everything from streetwear to designer runways. Years after its launch, the trainer remains a core element of Balenciaga's line-up of classics.

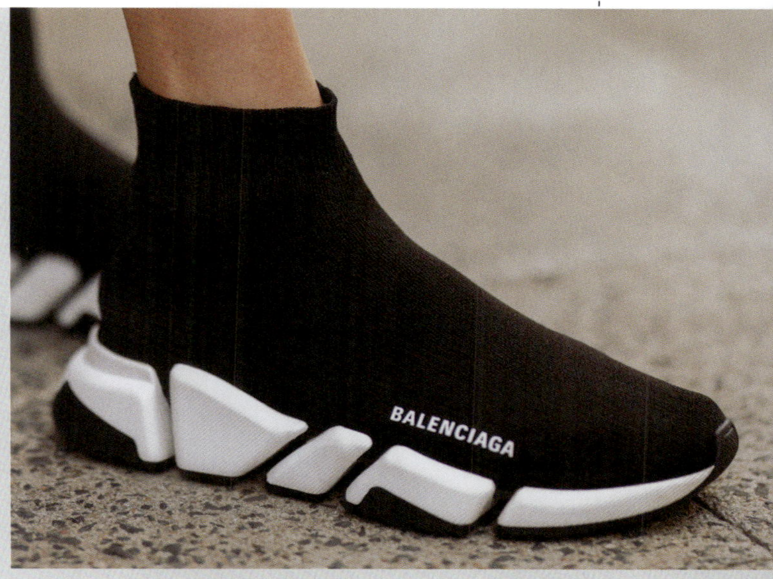

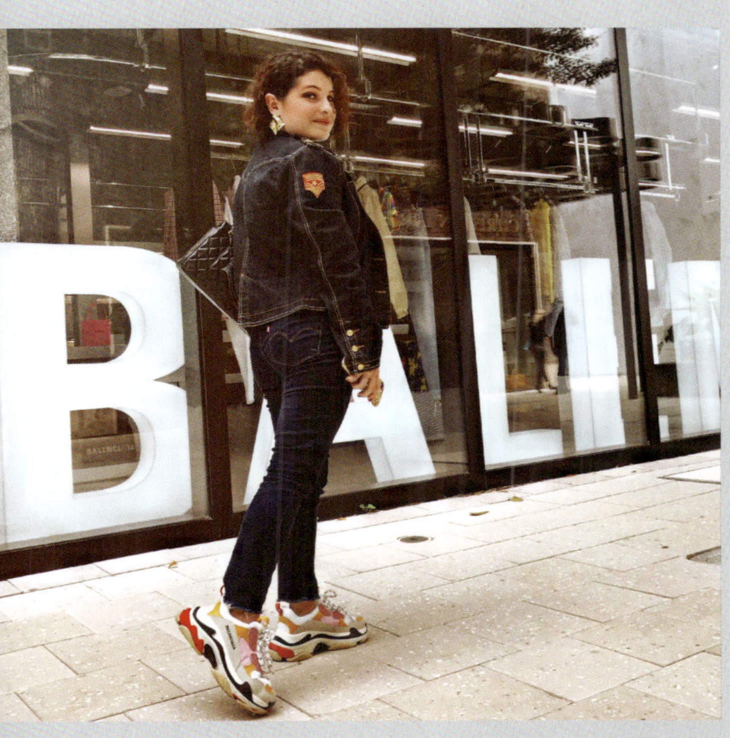

TRIPLE S

The Balenciaga Triple S, launched in 2017, redefined trainer culture with its oversized, multi-layered sole and intentionally 'ugly' aesthetic. Named for its triple-stacked sole derived from track, basketball and running shoes, it sparked the luxury 'dad sneaker' trend and became something of a fashion disruptor. Designed by Demna (who else?), the shoe was both loved and mocked but its impact was undeniable. Its bulky silhouette, embroidered sizing on the toe and vintage-style colourways challenged traditional trainer design. It quickly became a streetwear icon, spawning countless imitations and cementing Balenciaga's position at the intersection of irony and luxury.

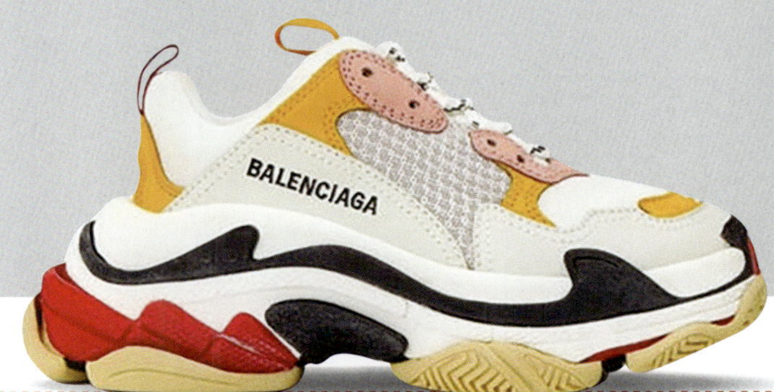

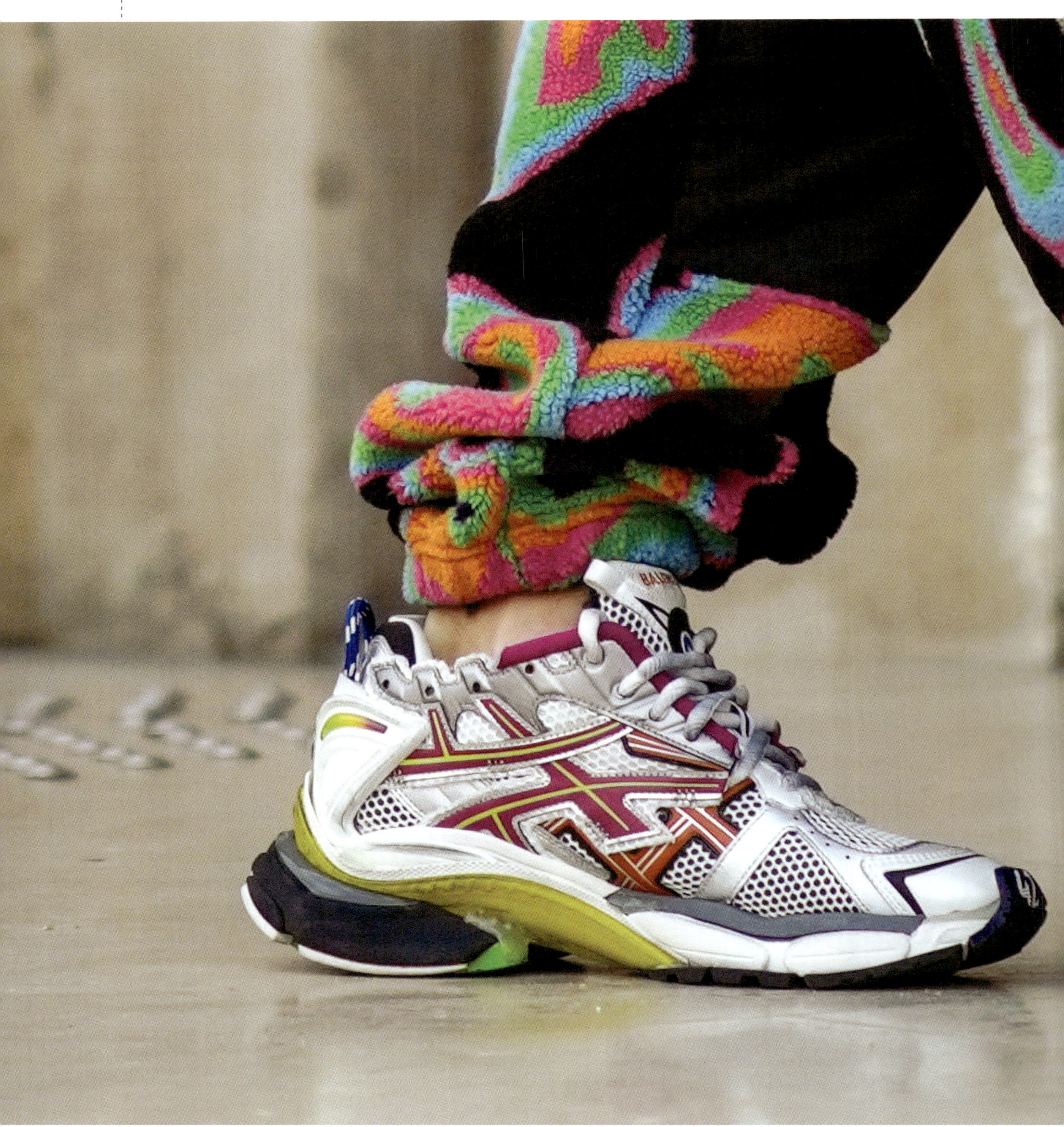

ABOVE: Multicolour Balenciaga Runner Sneakers at Paris Fashion Week, 2022, Paris, France

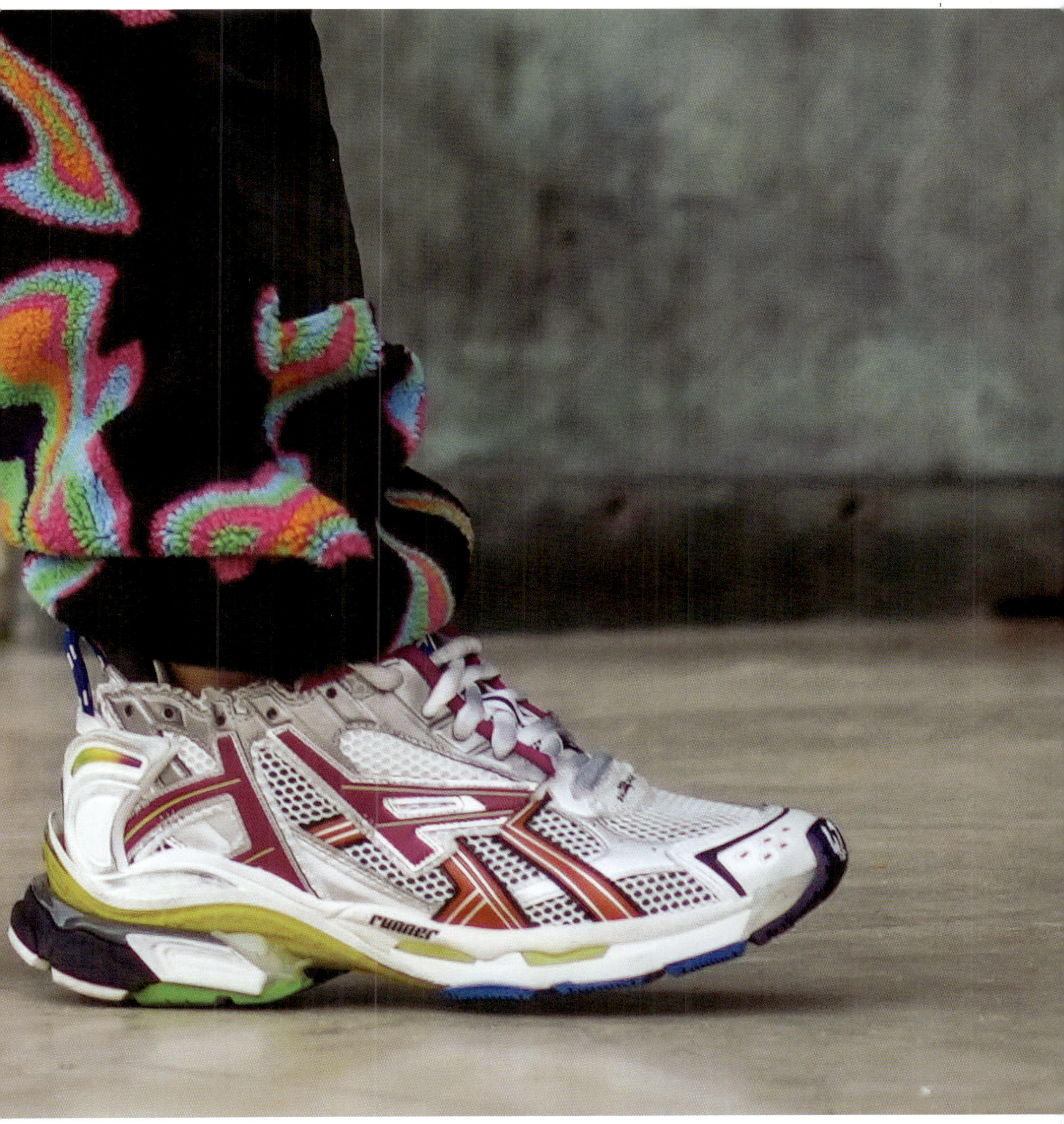

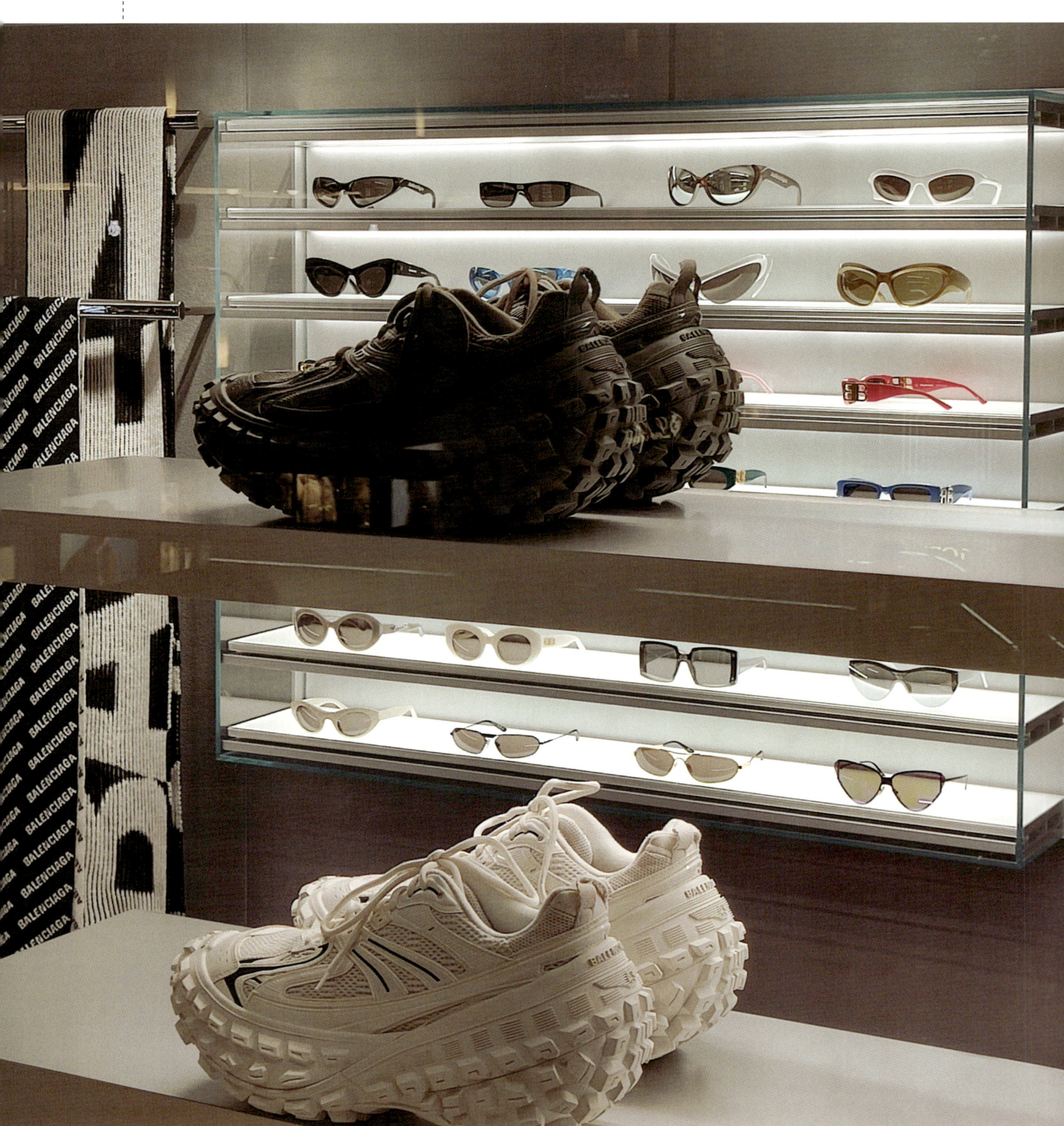

ABOVE: Balenciaga sneakers and sunglasses showcased at the Landmark Mall store on Des Voeux Road, Hong Kong
OPP PAGE: A model walks the runway at the Balenciaga Ready-to-Wear fashion show, 2019

SUNGLASSES

Balenciaga's eyewear offerings are also deserving of classic status, especially the oversized and futuristic shield sunglasses. These accessories reflect the house's commitment to bold silhouettes and experimental materials. Often inspired by sportswear or cyberpunk aesthetics, Balenciaga sunglasses are both functional and fashion-forward. Designs like the Dynasty or BB Shield sunglasses feature wraparound frames and reflective lenses, offering a modern armour-like look that complements the brand's more avant-garde ready-to-wear pieces. They've become staples on runways and red carpets alike, highlighting the House's talent in taking utilitarian objects and elevating them into statement-making fashion pieces.

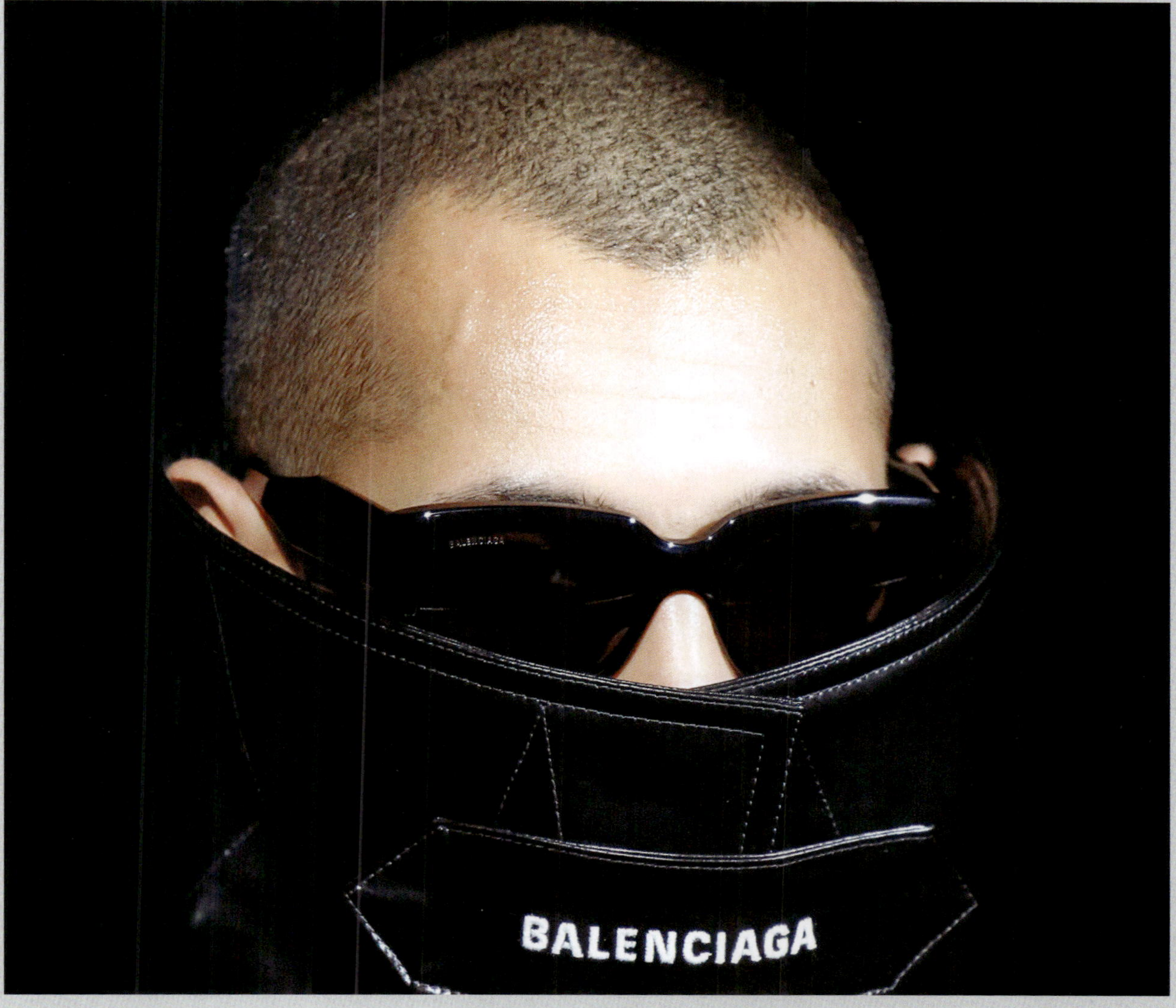

FRAGRANCE

Balenciaga's fragrance history is relatively selective compared to other fashion houses but a few standout scents are widely regarded as classics.

LE DIX

Named after Balenciaga's original Paris address (10 Avenue George V) and unveiled in 1947, Le Dix was the brand's first perfume - in the same vein as Chanel No. 5 but more powdery and sophisticated with notes of lilac, rose, sandalwood.

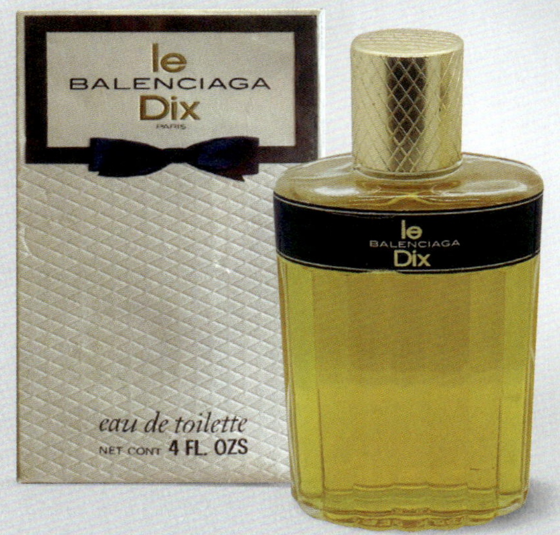

RUMBA (1988)

Launched in 1988 Rumba is a bold, loud, dramatic fragrance – both spicy and sweet with notes of plum, leather, patchouli, jasmine and amber. Often overlooked, it's now beloved by fans of vintage, powerhouse fragrances.

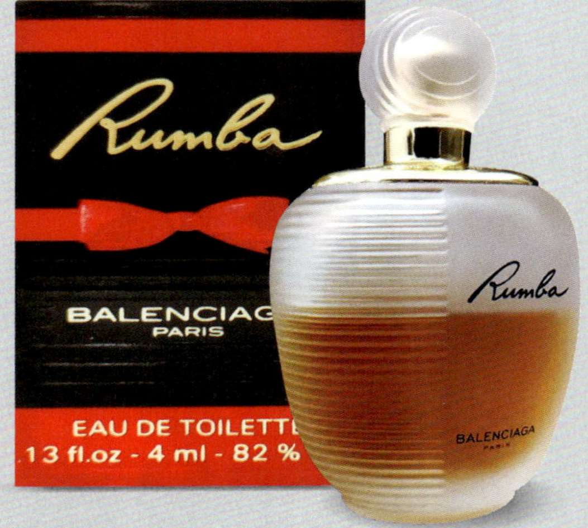

BALENCIAGA PARIS

Launched in 2010, Balenciaga Paris is arguably the House's most recognized modern fragrance. Airy yet structured, floral but woody with notes of violet leaf, cedarwood, patchouli, pepper, the scent reflects the brand's intellectual femininity. The bottle design, inspired by couture silhouettes, adds to its refined legacy. It is now discontinued, which has only added to its cult status.

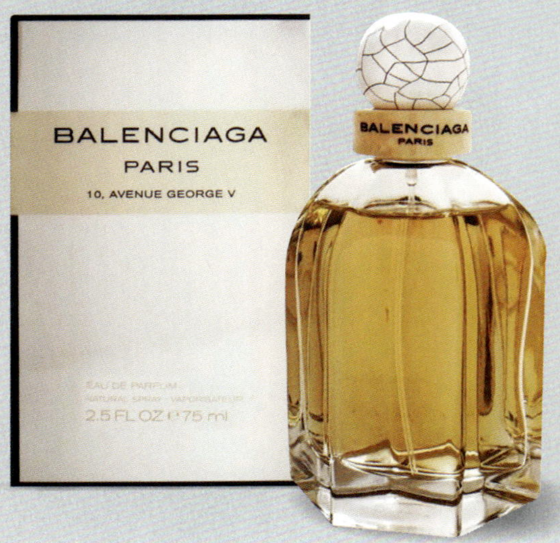

ABOVE: Le Dix, Rumba and Balenciaga Paris fragrances
OPP PAGE: 2010s UK Balenciaga Florabotanica fragrance advertisement featuring Kristen Stewart

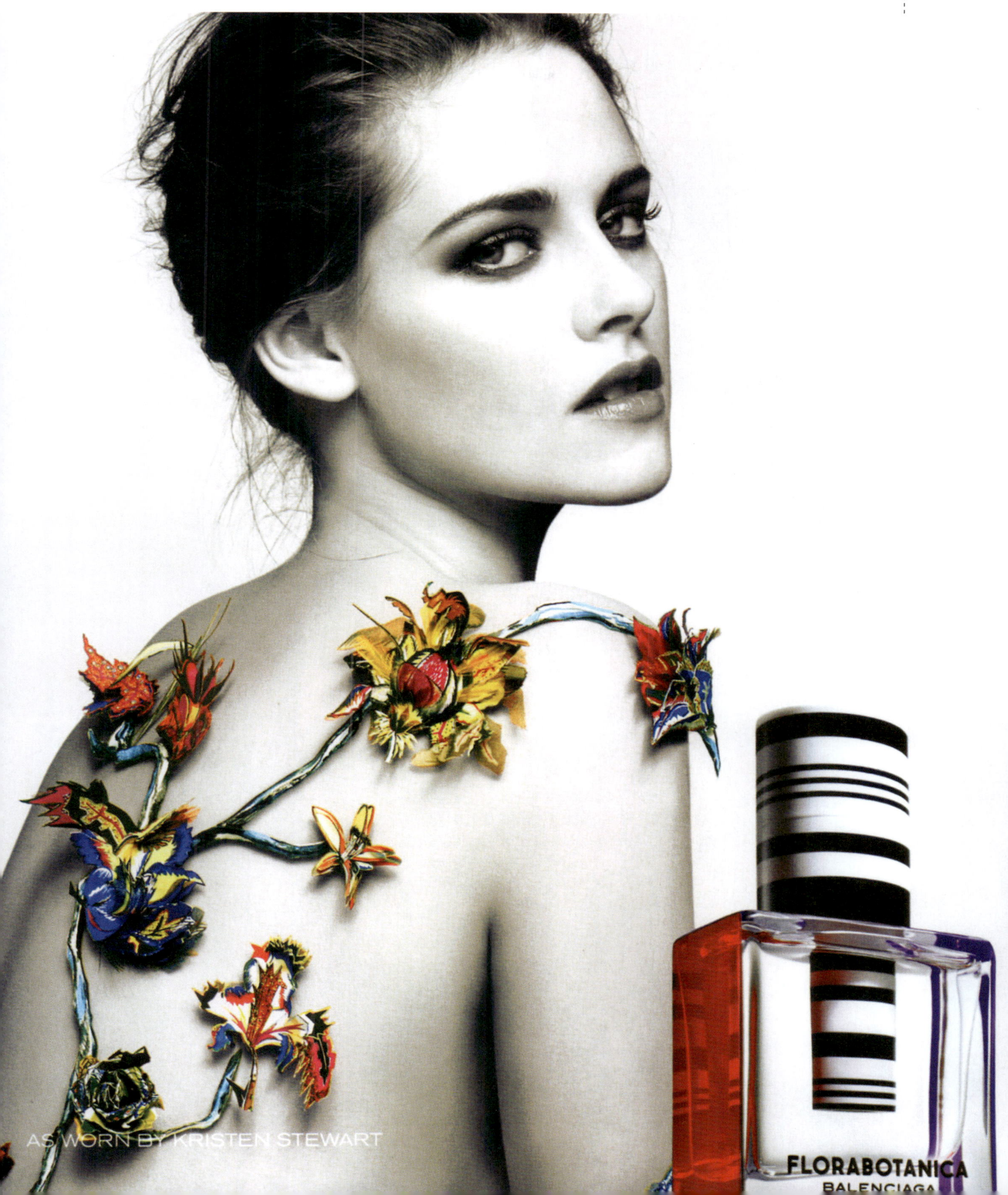
AS WORN BY KRISTEN STEWART
FLORABOTANICA
BALENCIAGA

BALENCIAGA BY NUMBERS

Go figure…

1

The number of times Christian Dior called Balenciaga 'the master of us all'

1.2

How quickly the Crocs collaboration sold out in seconds!

3

The number of key cities that shaped Cristóbal Balenciaga – San Sebastián, Madrid and Paris

1

The number of 'Caution: Slippery When Wet' signs accidentally mistaken for Balenciaga runway props

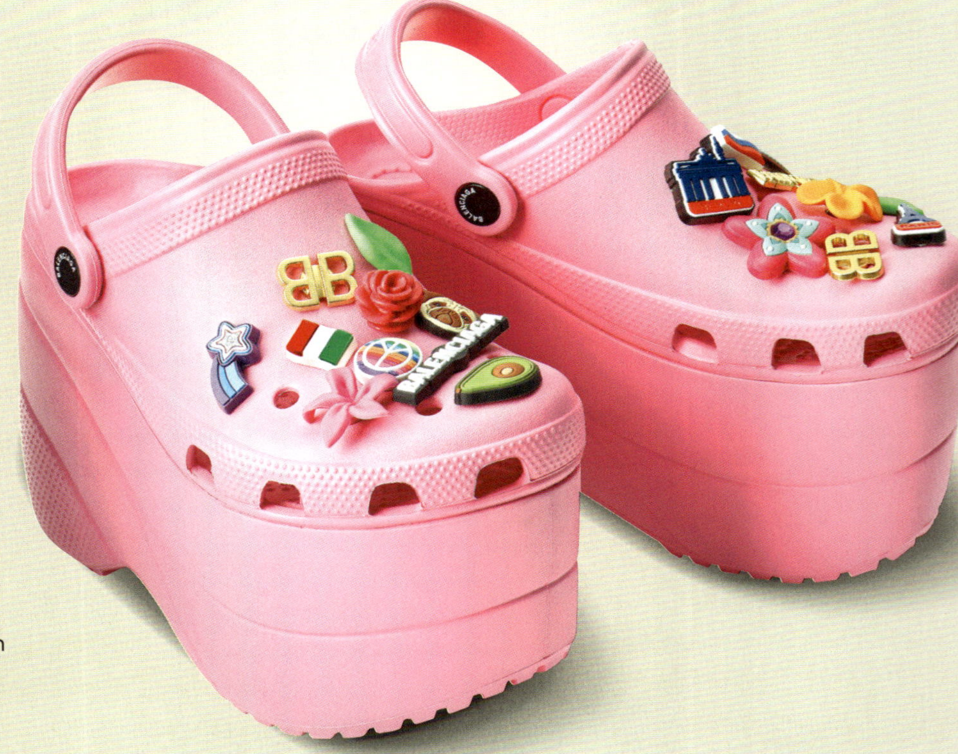

ABOVE: Balenciaga crocs
OPP PAGE: Exhibition of Balenciaga haute couture in Barcelona

3

*T*he number of seamstresses needed to construct a single cocoon coat.

3.5

The height of the Speed Trainer sole in inches

10

The hours it can take to hand-sew just one hem on a Balenciaga haute couture gown

5

The average number of oversized layers worn in a single Demna outfit

6

The number of original Balenciaga silhouettes that revolutionized mid-century fashion - Sack, Balloon, Cocoon, Baby Doll, Tunic and Empire

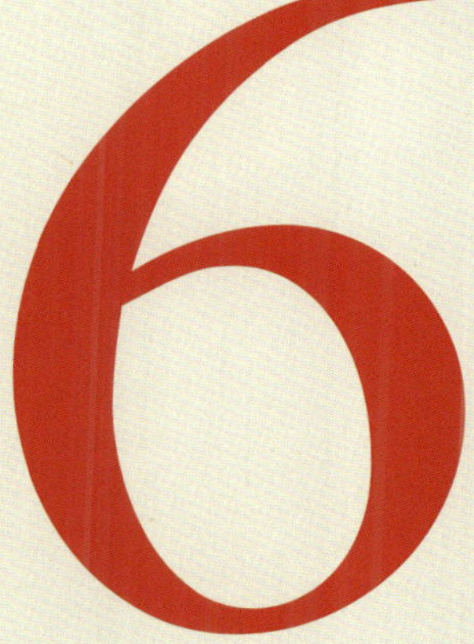

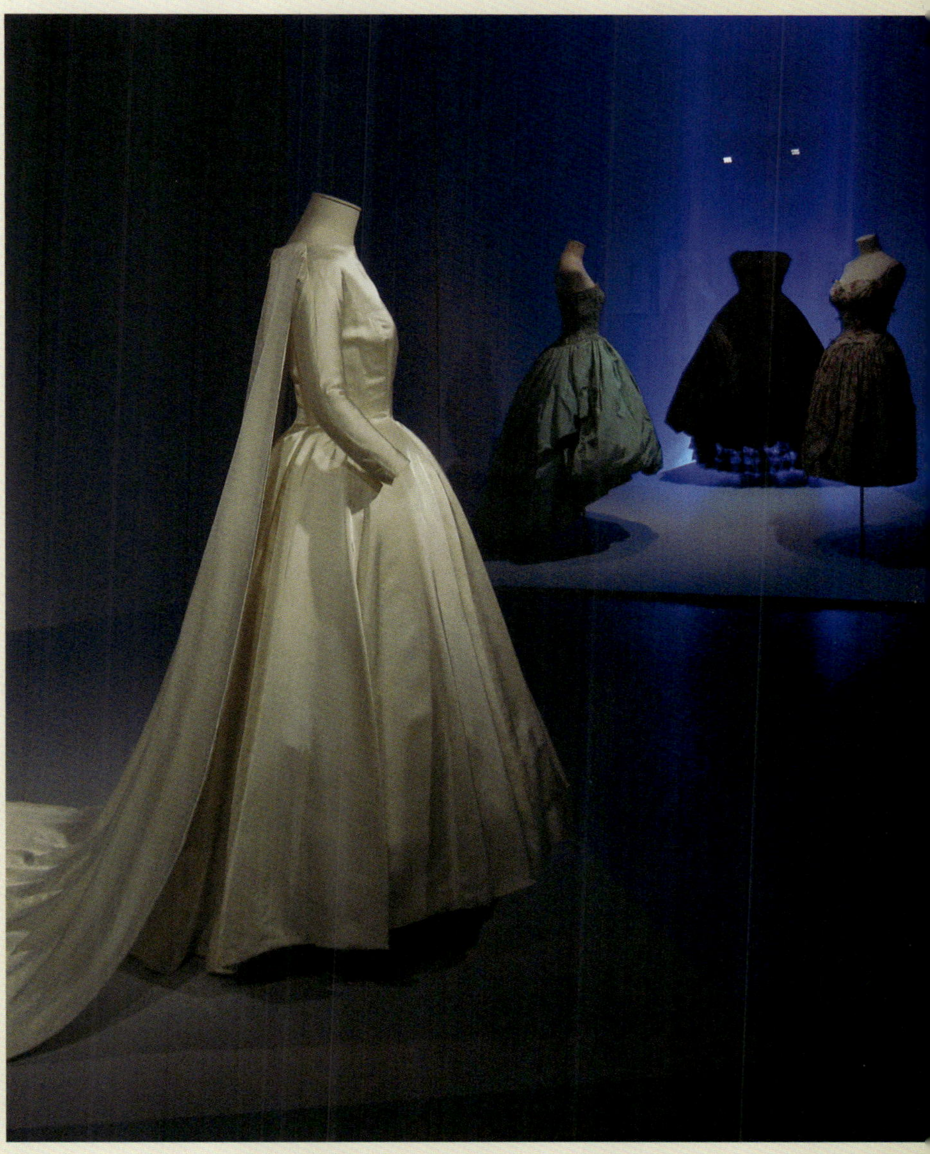

11

The number of minutes 2021 The Simpsons/Balenciaga fashion film ran for

10+

High-profile brand collaborations, including Gucci, Fortnite, and Adidas

12

The approximate number of shades of black used in a single collection

27

In pounds, the weight of a 2021 couture gown made entirely of silver sequins and hand-embroidered by artisans

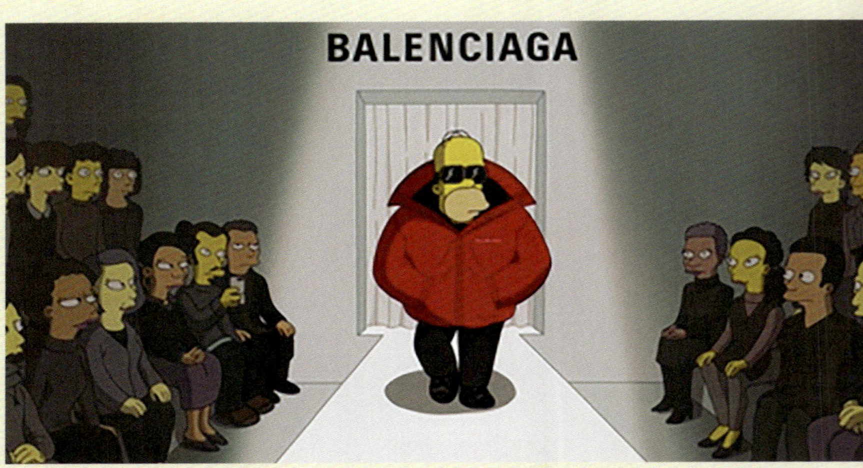

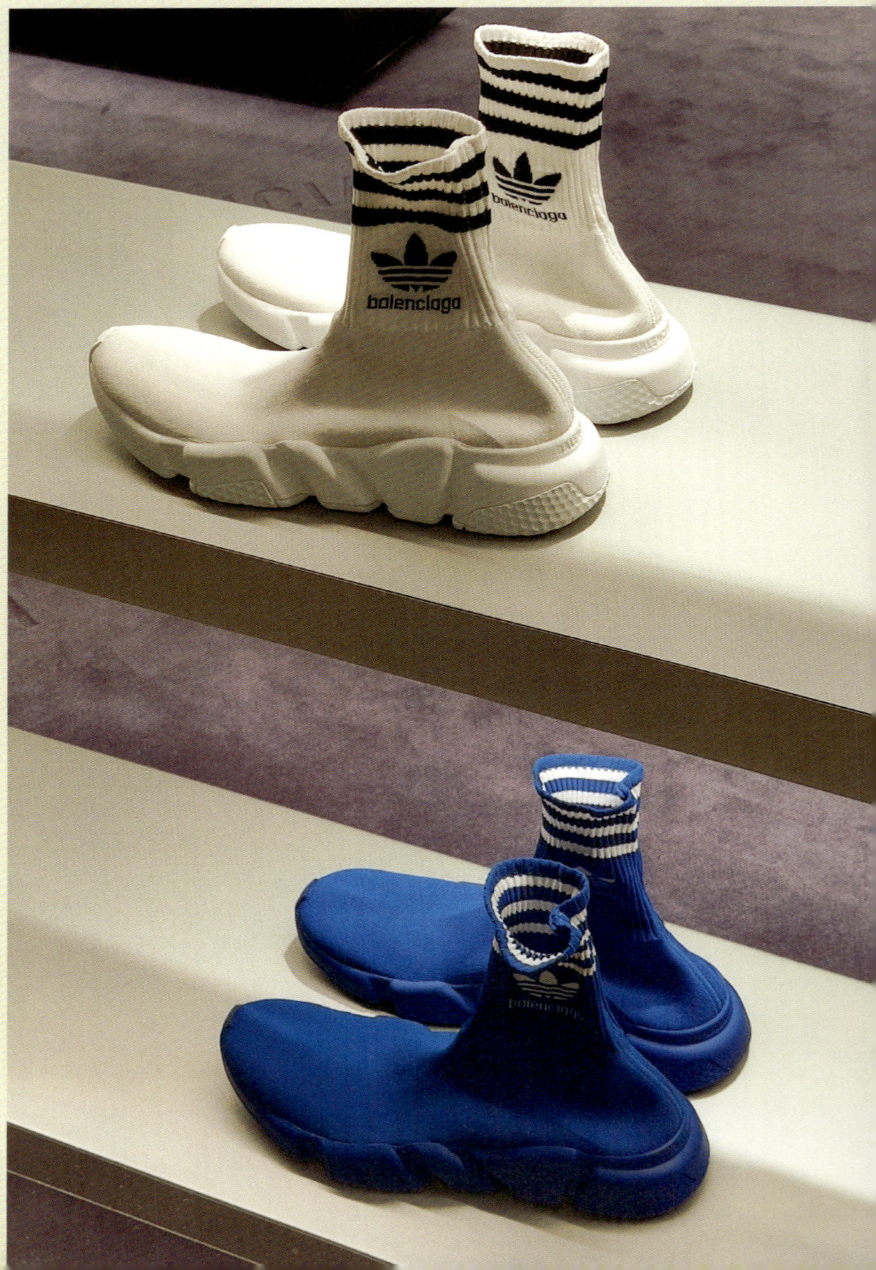

TOP: The Simpsons | Balenciaga 2021 animated short film
RIGHT: Balenciaga X Adidas collaboration

40

In kg, the approximate weight of a custom Balenciaga coat worn by Kanye West

24

Calories in the complimentary 'runway air' scented water served to VIP guests

60

In cm, the height of the ultra-platform Balenciaga X Crocs boots

6

The number of times he's mentioned in the Pet Shop Boys' 1986 single "Paninaro"

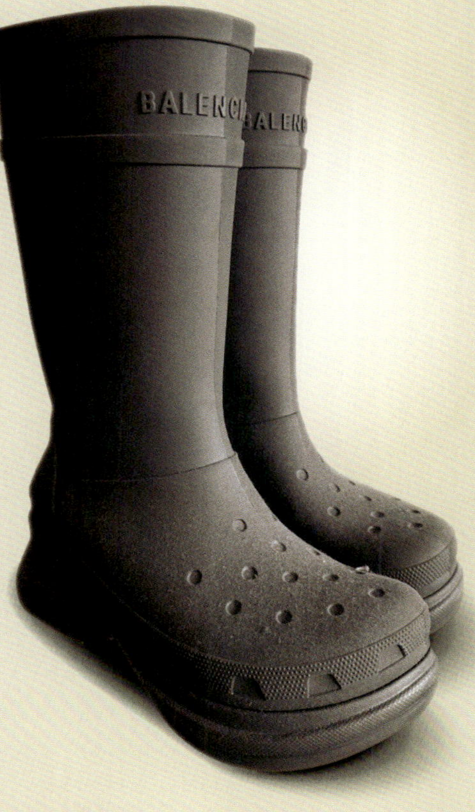

20

The centimetres of invisible structure sometimes hidden under a seemingly 'effortless' silhouette

33

The number of times *Vogue* has called Balenciaga a 'master of modern volume'

10,000+

Crystals on a single pair of Knife Boots

ABOVE: Balenciaga X Crocs Rubber Rain Boots
LEFT: 1957 Balenciaga collections Vogue cover

60+

The number of stores located in China, making it the brand's largest market

108

The number of hours artisans may spend hand-embroidering a Balenciaga couture look

77

The rumoured maximum weight (in pounds) of a full-layered Demna-era look including accessories

180+

The number of Balenciaga stores worldwide

666

The style code of a limited bag

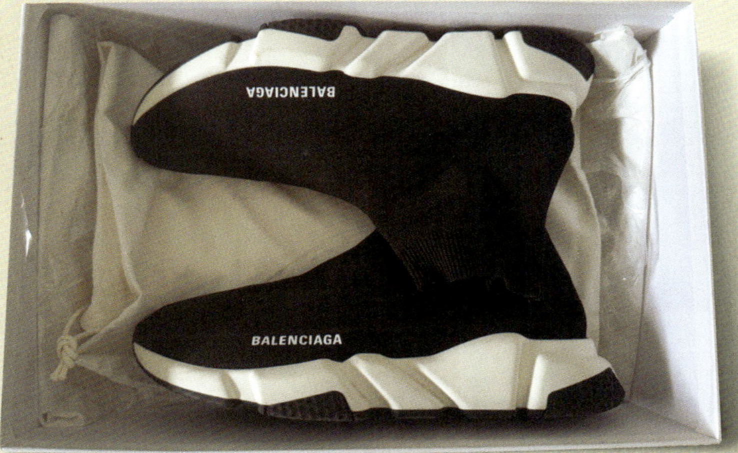

1000+

The number of knockoffs spawned by a single Balenciaga trainer drop

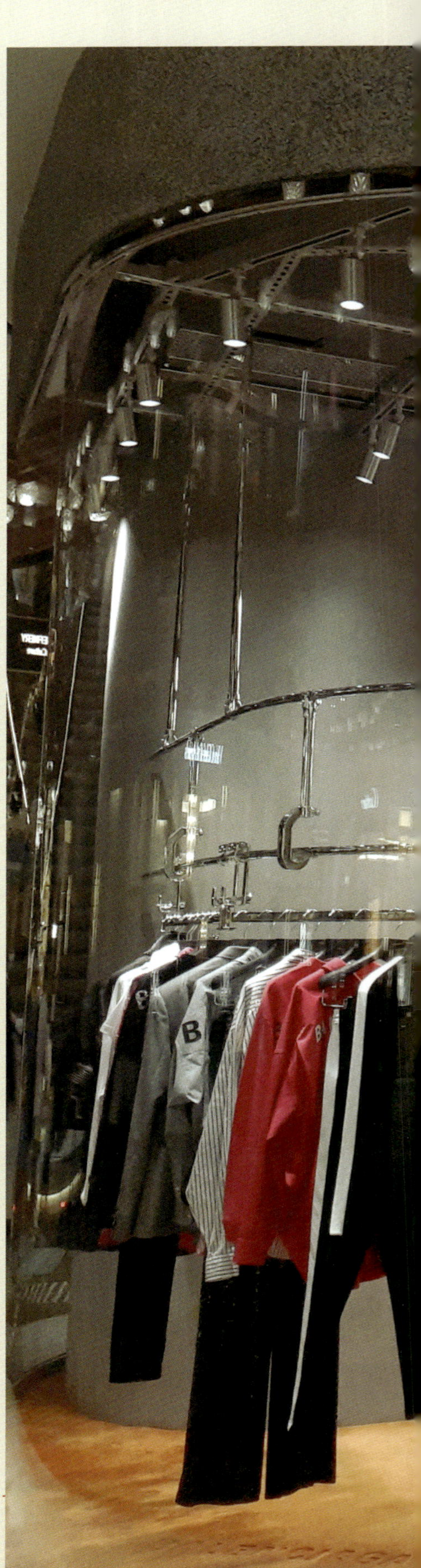

ABOVE: Real or fake? Balenciaga knockoff shoes often feature poor-quality materials, inconsistent logos
RIGHT: A Balenciaga store in Hong Kong

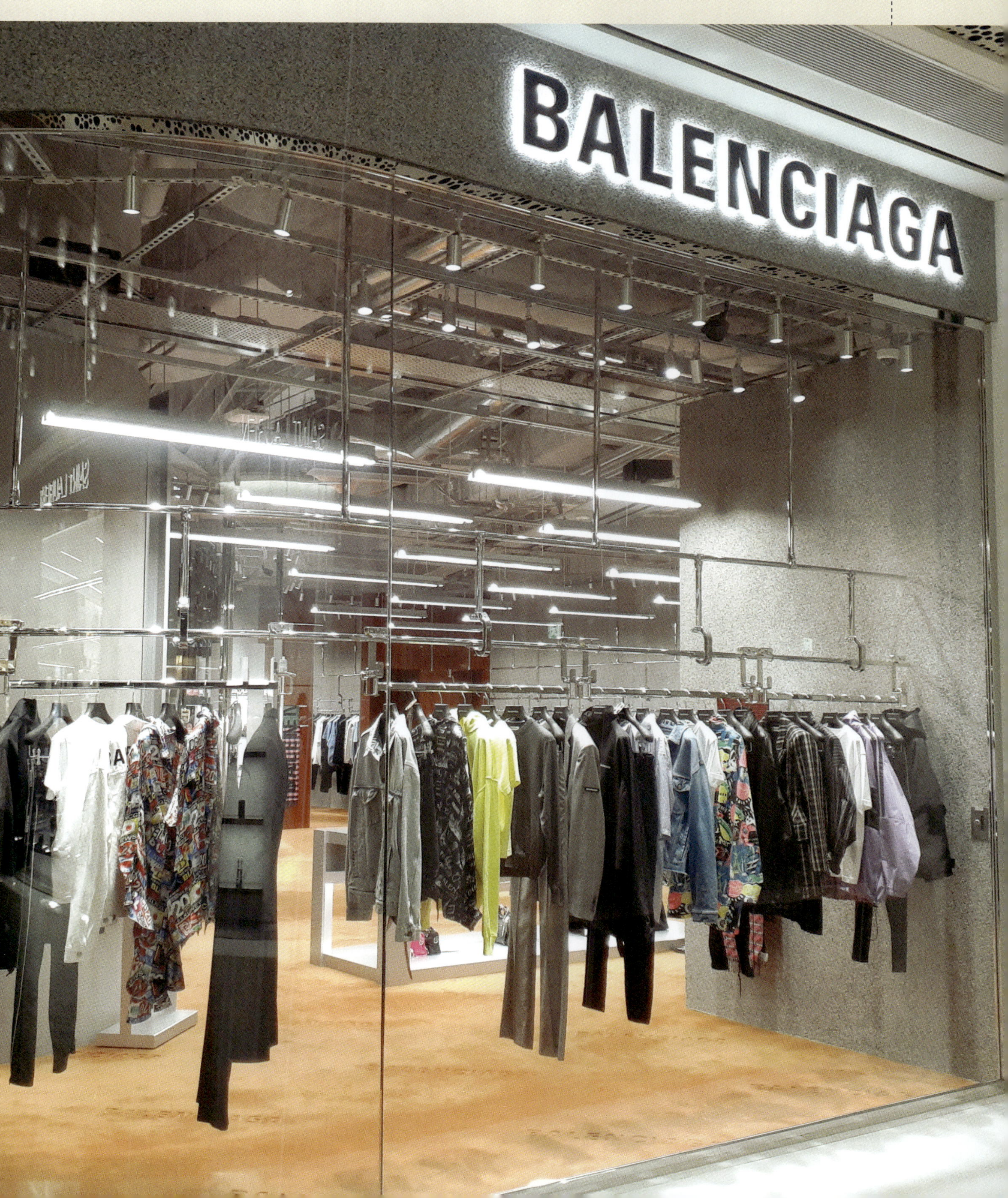

15 MILLION

Instagram followers

42

The steps involved in crafting a
single pair of Balenciaga Knife boots

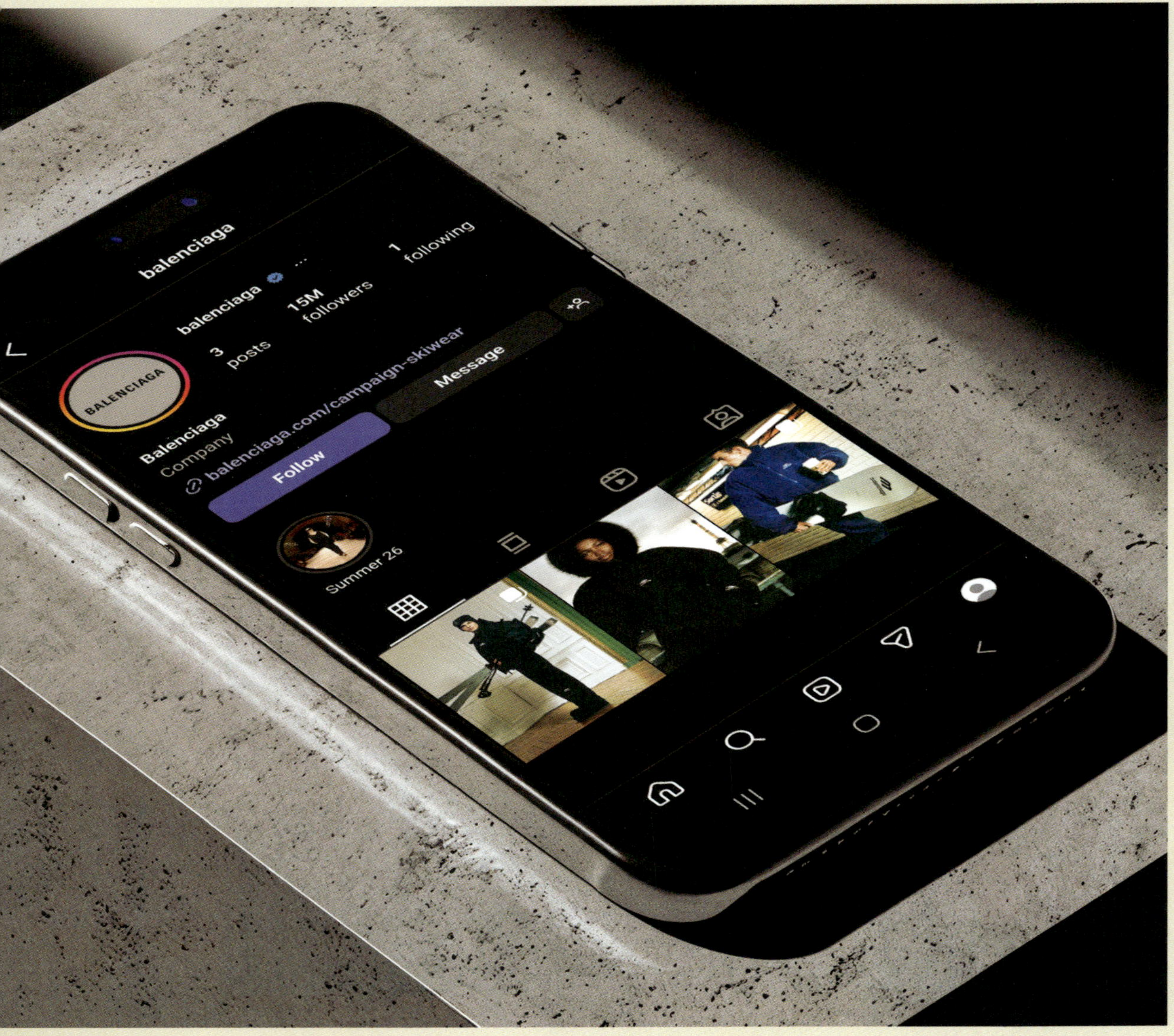

ABOVE: Balenciaga have a huge social media following
RIGHT: Lisa Hahnbueck wearing red Balenciaga X
Colette Knife boots

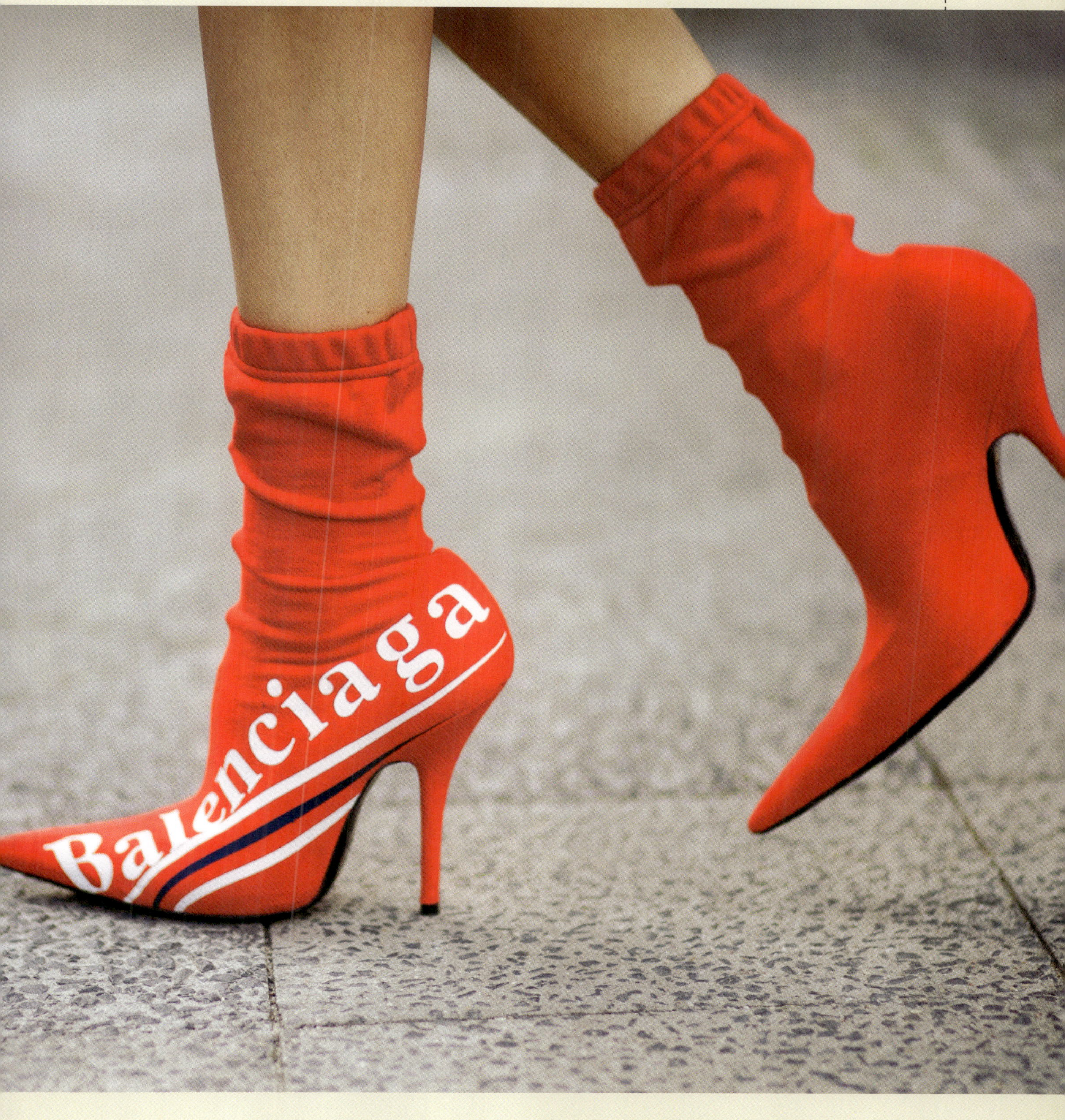
Balenciaga

THE FUTURE

"I'm excited to begin this new era at Balenciaga with Pierpaolo. His creative vision will thrive and he will perfectly interpret the legacy of Cristóbal Balenciaga, building on the House's bold creativity, rich heritage and strong culture"

Balenciaga CEO Gianfranco Gianangeli

When Balenciaga announced Pierpaolo Piccioli as its new creative director in May 2025, it was more than a fashion headline - it marked the beginning of a new chapter for one of the most scrutinised and talked-about luxury houses in the world. It was, in many ways, a surprising appointment. For nearly a decade, Balenciaga lived at the edge of the fashion conversation – a dialogue that was often loud, disruptive, fearless and provocative. Now it has welcomed a designer whose name has become synonymous with elegance, emotion and refinement. This contrast is precisely what makes the future of Balenciaga so intriguing.

RIGHT: Designer Pierpaolo Piccioli is seen on the catwalk at the Balenciaga fashion show during Paris Fashion Week Spring/Summer 2026 season

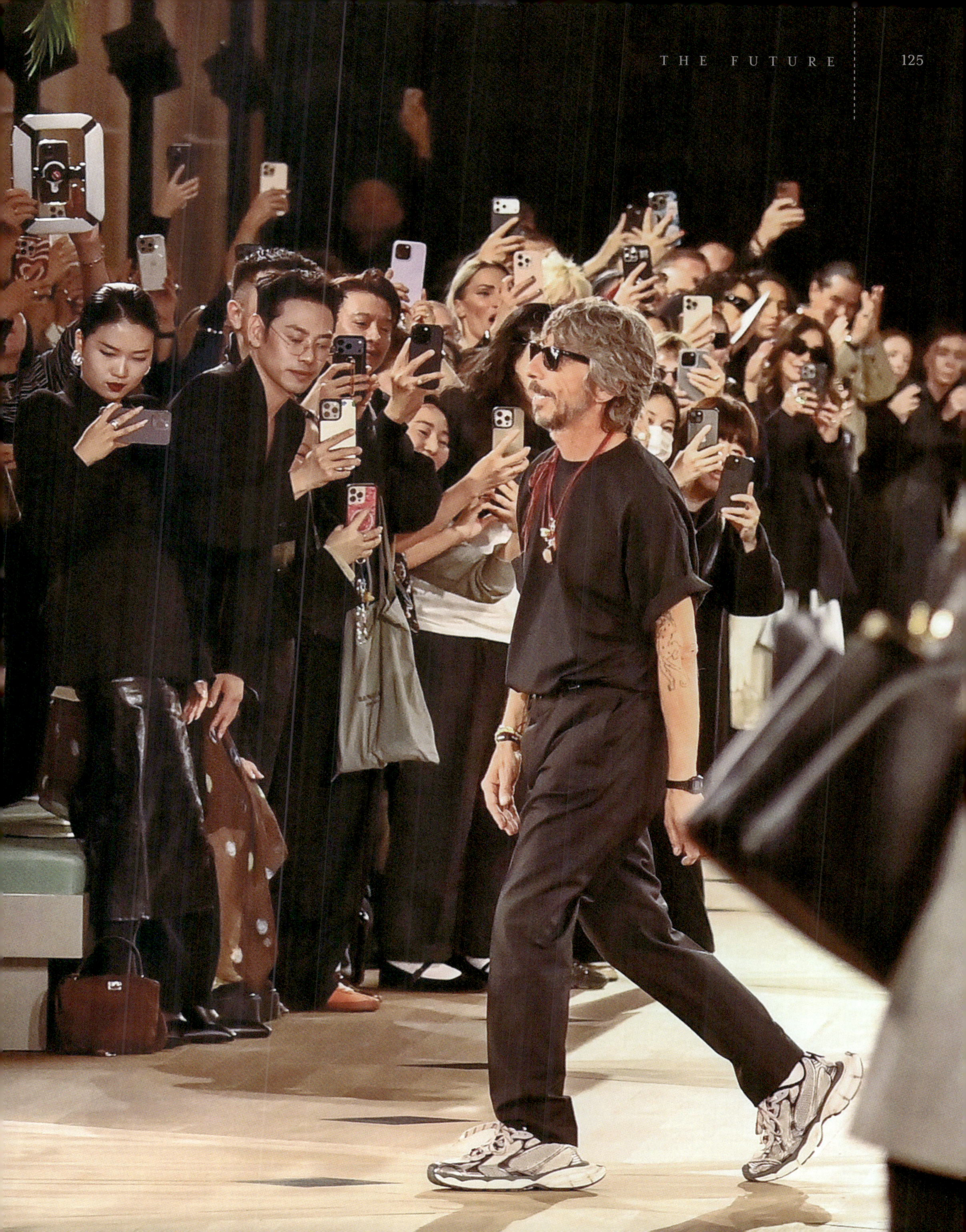

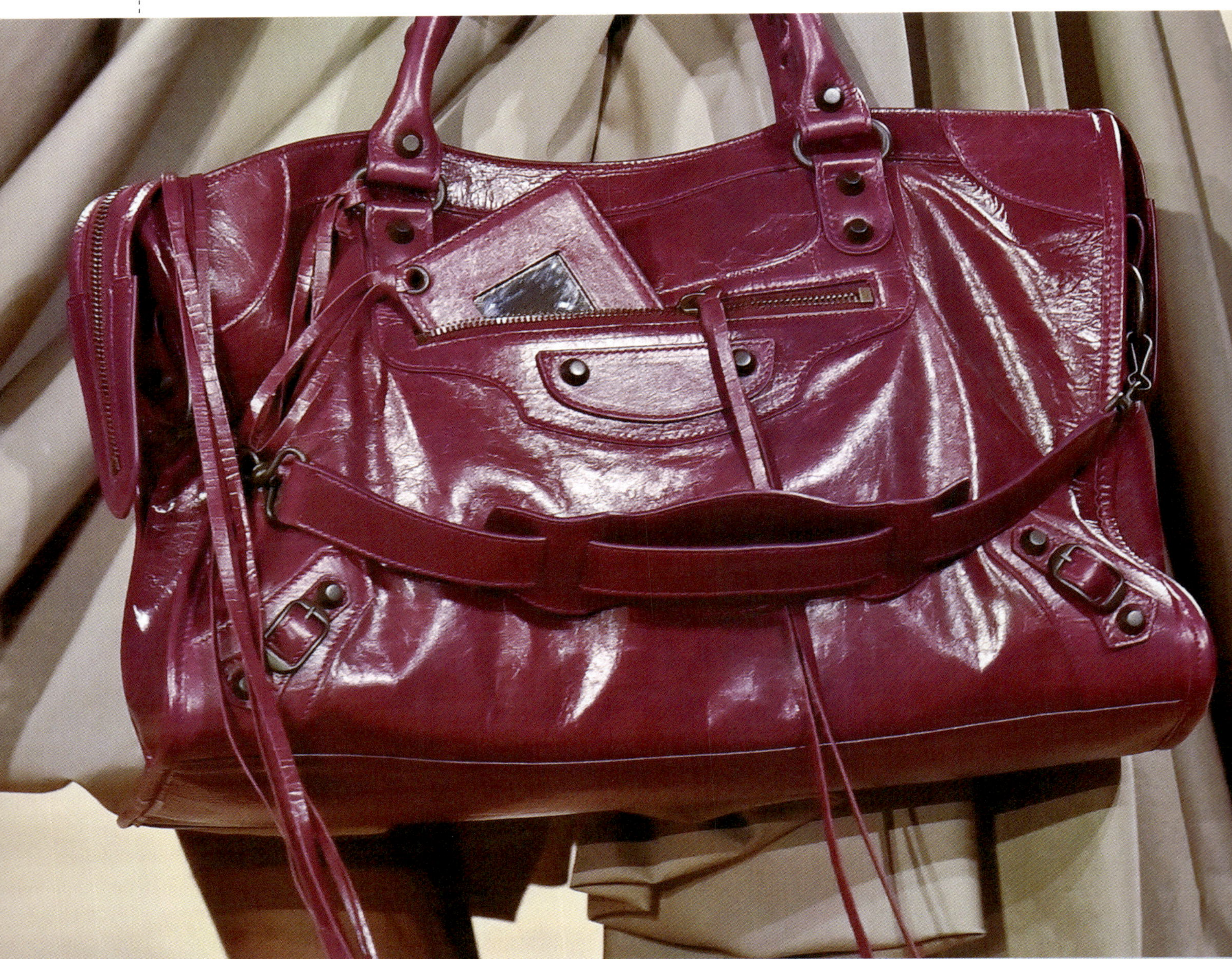

Piccioli is no stranger to pressure or prestige. He spent over two decades at Valentino where he helped transform the brand from a formal, tradition-bound house into a global symbol of modern beauty and expressive, inclusive luxury. Starting in accessories, he went on to become co-creative director and, eventually, the sole visionary behind the brand's creative renaissance. He built a reputation as a skilled designer and a deeply humanistic one, at that - someone who viewed fashion not just as product but as a form of cultural language. Under his leadership, Valentino became known for its powerful silhouettes, emotionally charged runway shows and sincere celebration of individuality. His collections often

ABOVE: Balenciaga bag. Spring/Summer 2026 collection, Paris Fashion Week

moved people through connection rather than shock.

Now Piccioli has stepped into a role that couldn't be more different in tone. Balenciaga, particularly under the direction of Demna, evolved into fashion's enfant terrible - a House that thrived on irony, subversion and confrontation. From oversized silhouettes to dystopian campaign aesthetics, from high-concept digital rollouts to controversial advertisements, Balenciaga became a mirror – at times a distorted one - reflecting the anxieties, absurdities and contradictions of modern life. It was, and remains, a brand that sparked discussion far beyond fashion circles. But after years of walking the fine line between commentary and provocation, and following a series of public controversies that strained even its most loyal supporters, Balenciaga appears ready for a tonal reset.

Piccioli's appointment signals exactly that - a conscious shift from irony to sincerity, from noise to nuance. While his first collection has not yet been revealed, anticipation is already stirring across the industry. What will Balenciaga look like under his tenure? What happens when you place one of fashion's most soulful designers at the helm of one of its most confrontational brands? If history offers any indication, Piccioli won't be looking to replicate Demna's formula or, for that matter, to outdo his predecessor in shock value. That's not his style. He doesn't trade in spectacle for its own sake. Instead, his creative voice tends to unfold with a quiet

confidence. At Valentino, he showed that fashion can still be modern without being cynical, that it can be emotional without being sentimental. He reinvented the notion of romance not as escapism but as a form of resilience - a position that may prove especially resonant in Balenciaga's next era. But don't expect a simple return to Cristóbal-type classicism either. Piccioli is too contemporary for that. He understands the power of strong lines, bold statements and cultural relevance. His skill lies in weaving these elements together with care and grace. His design language is precise but poetic. What's likely to emerge from his first Balenciaga collection is not a total aesthetic overhaul but a redirection of energy - from provocation to presence, from commentary to composition.

One area where Piccioli is almost certain to make an impact is in representation. Throughout his tenure at Valentino, he championed inclusion not as a trend but as a creative principle. He cast models of all sizes, ages and identities, and consistently pushed for a broader definition of beauty. Under his direction, the Balenciaga runway and campaigns may begin to reflect a different kind of diversity - less performative and more integrated. The same goes for his fashion storytelling. Balenciaga has long leaned into visual ambiguity – at times to the point of confusion. With Piccioli we may see a more emotionally legible narrative emerge - one that still embraces complexity but also invites audiences in rather than pushing them away.

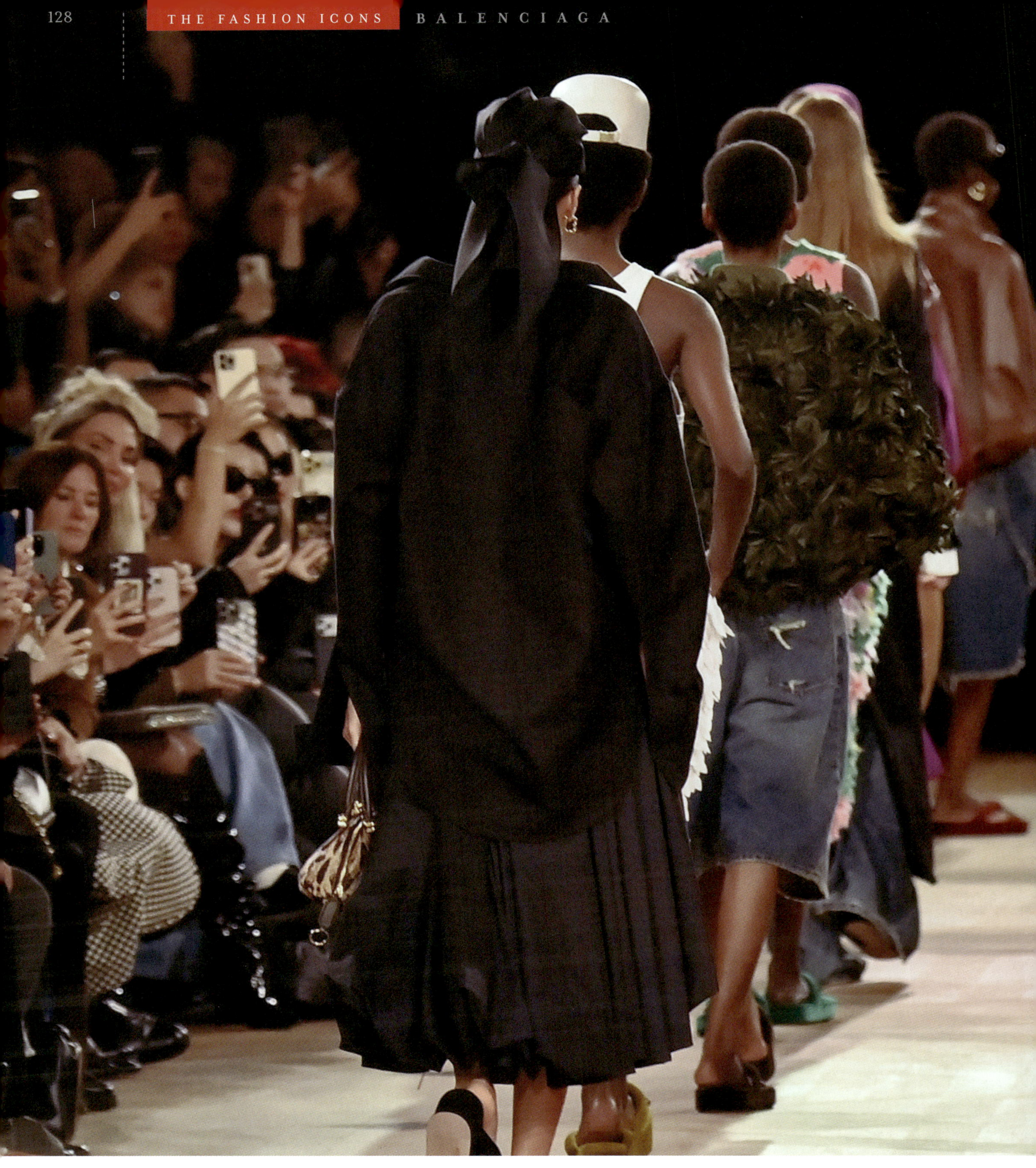

ABOVE: Balenciaga Ready-to-Wear Spring/Summer 2026
fashion show, Paris Fashion Week, 4 October 2025

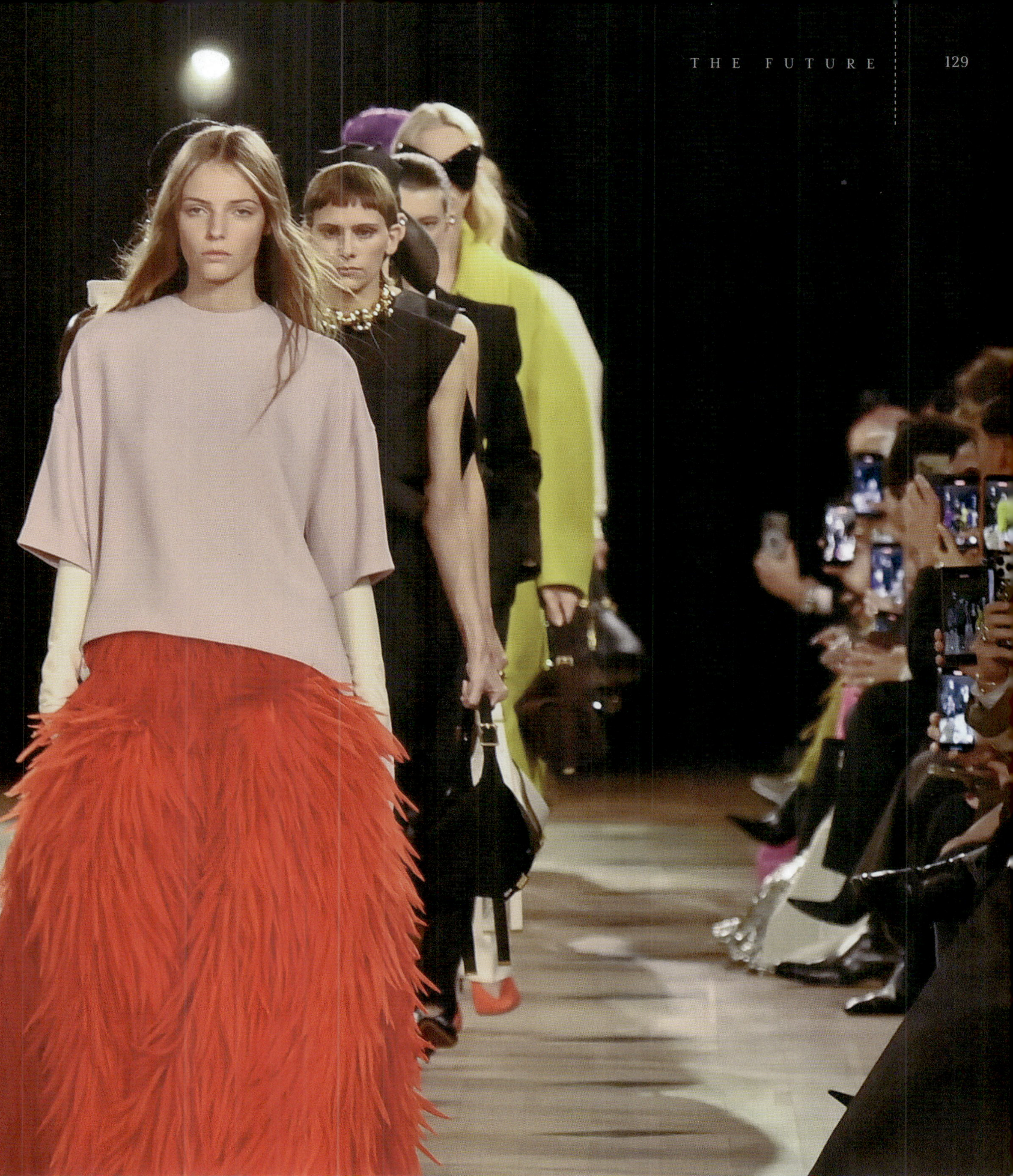

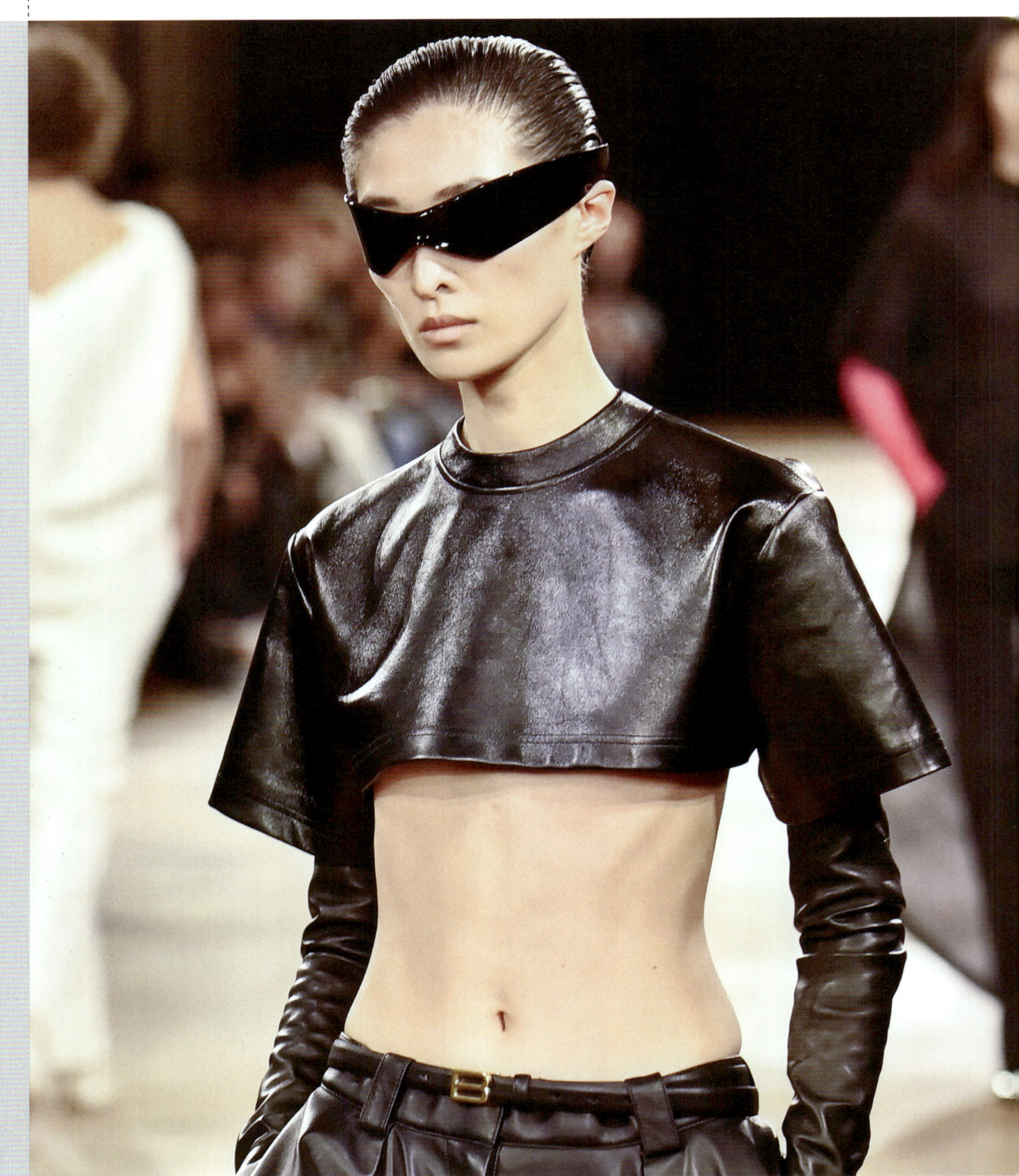

ABOVE: Balenciaga Ready-to-Wear Spring/Summer 2026 fashion show

Another key dimension of this upcoming era will likely be sustainability. The fashion industry is increasingly confronting its environmental impact and luxury brands are under particular pressure to lead by example. At Valentino, Piccioli began implementing more responsible practices in sourcing, production and design. While no major house is without challenges in this space, he has shown an ability to incorporate sustainability as part of his creative vision. That philosophy is expected to carry over to Balenciaga. Already there are signs of a shift. Insiders suggest that Piccioli is working closely with Balenciaga's teams to reassess material sourcing, reduce waste and develop pieces that are both luxurious and lasting. Rather than chasing seasonal novelty, he appears interested in cultivating timelessness – clothes that are not just of the moment but made to outlast it. The move fits with a broader mood in fashion right now – a desire for design that is slower, more intentional and less disposable. As consumers increasingly turn toward brands that reflect sustainable values alongside aesthetics, this could be a meaningful point of differentiation for Balenciaga in a crowded market.

The virtual side of fashion is also likely to evolve under Piccioli's leadership. Balenciaga has previously been a pioneer in the digital space, experimenting with video game shows, virtual influencers and immersive online environments. Those efforts, often provocative and unconventional under Demna, became a signature part of the brand's appeal. The question now is how

Piccioli – who tends to favour emotional depth over visual tricks – will integrate these tools into his own way of working. Early indications suggest he won't abandon digital platforms but will use them differently. Rather than chasing attention through spectacle, he may use virtual spaces to deepen his fashion and design narrative. What emerges could be a more thoughtful digital strategy – one that enhances the message of the collection rather than distracting from it. Virtual experiences could become spaces of exploration rather than just consumption. In that sense, Piccioli has the opportunity to redefine what digital fashion can be.

The fashion industry loves elements of transformation and Balenciaga under Piccioli offers just that. But what makes this moment feel significant isn't just the promise of aesthetic change. It's the feeling that something deeper might be underway – a reconsideration of what fashion really is for. For nearly a decade, Balenciaga has been the brand asking hard questions – often with a cynical voice. Under Piccioli, it may begin to ask different ones –quieter, perhaps, but no less urgent. What does it mean to make something beautiful now? What does luxury look like when it values emotion over irony, craft over social commentary? None of this is guaranteed, of course. Fashion is fickle and change – even carefully planned change – is never simple. Piccioli inherits not just a brand but a legacy of expectations, controversies and contradictions. But he also inherits a golden opportunity with the chance to lead one of fashion's most watched houses into a new and exciting era.

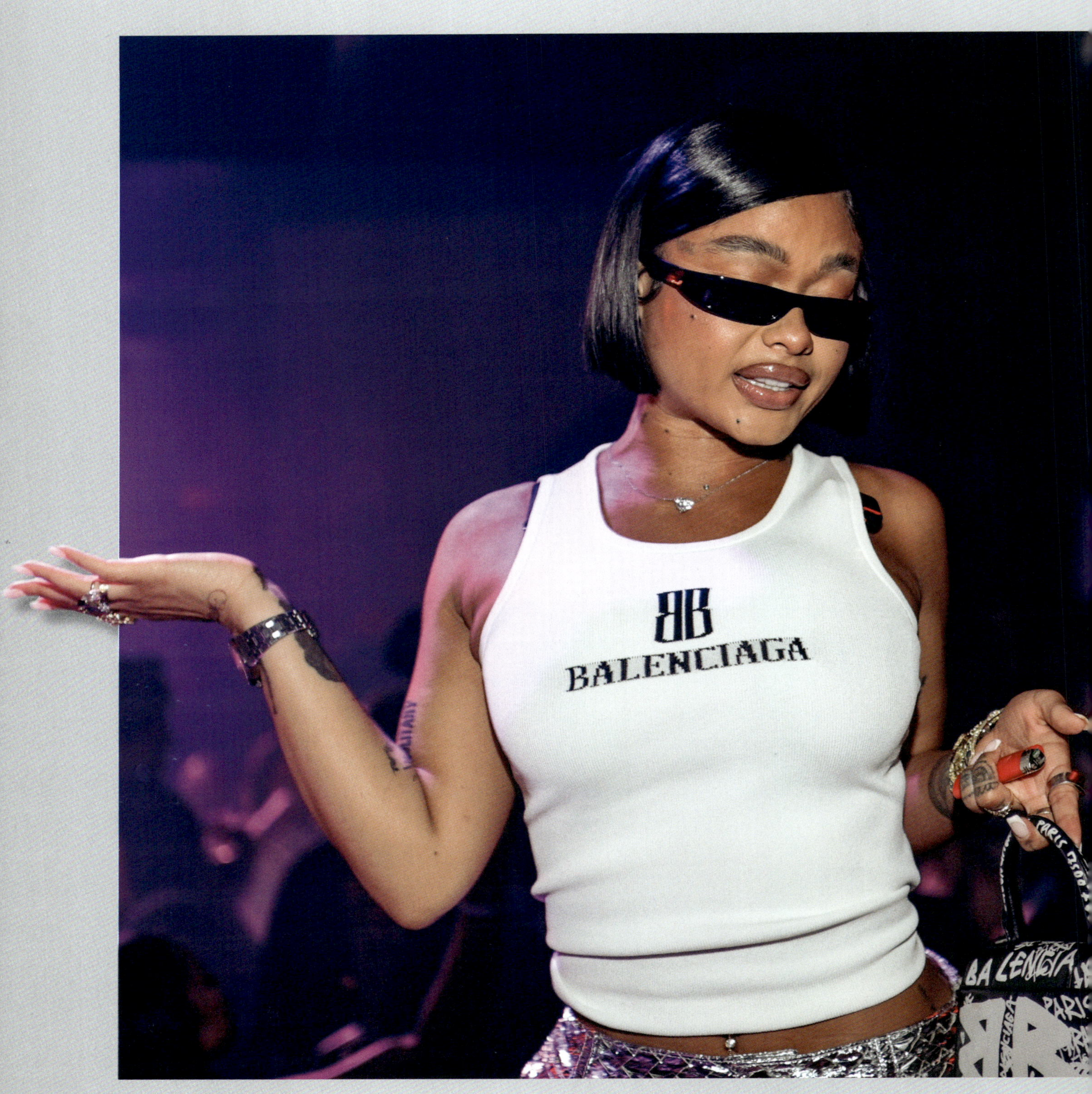

ABOVE: India Love attends Revel Nightclub wearing a Balenciaga top in Atlanta, Georgia, 2025
OPP PAGE: Suzanna Cruz wearing Balenciaga, 2025

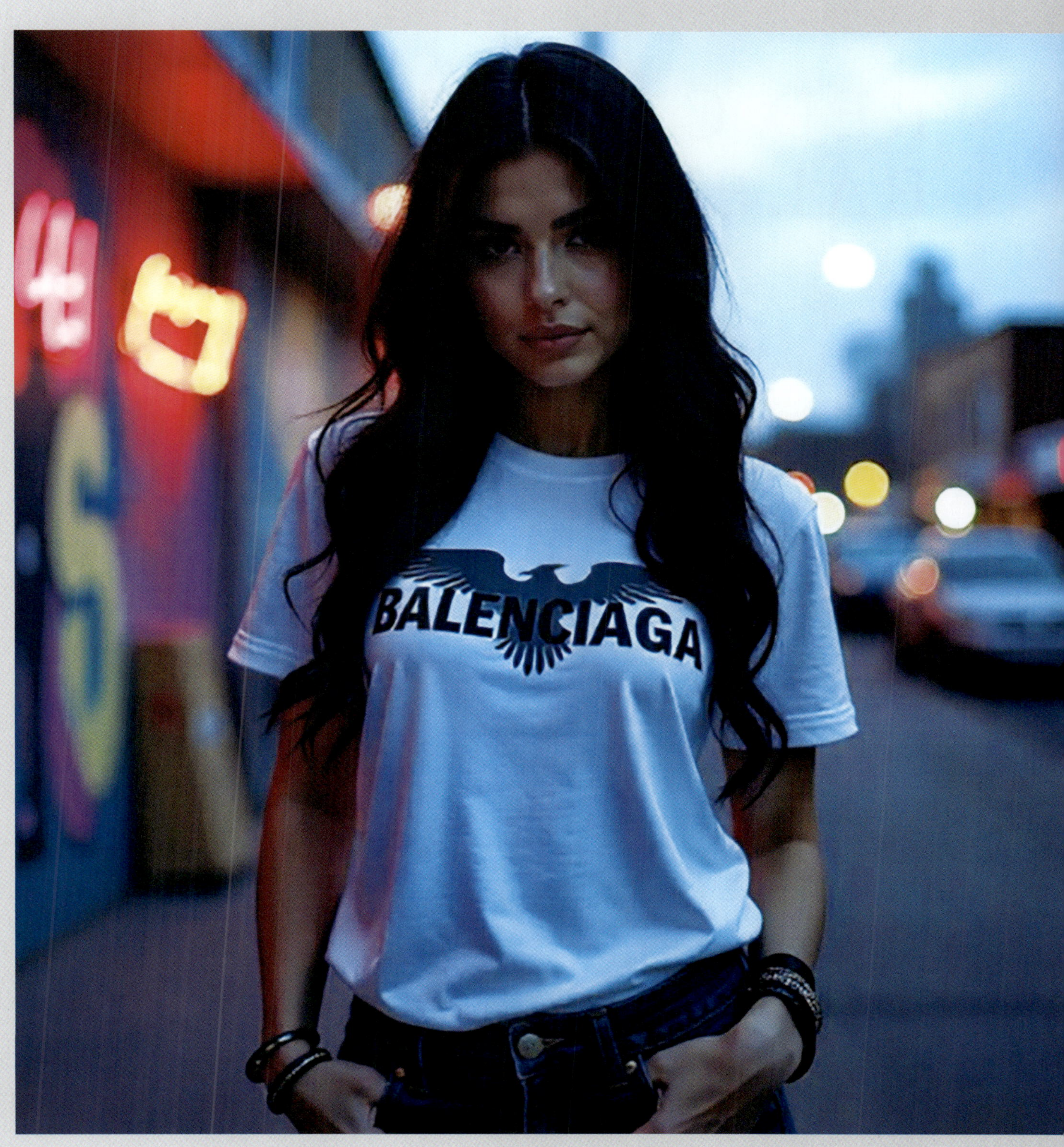
BALENCIAGA

RED CARPET BALENCIAGA

Balenciaga's presence on the red carpet is bold, boundary-pushing and uber-theatrical. Under Demna's direction, the brand redefined celebrity dressing with exaggerated silhouettes, dramatic trains and, at times, apocalyptic elegance. While Piccioli will bring his own vision to the brand, the red carpet will remain prime Balenciaga territory no matter who is at the helm.

KIM KARDASHIAN

Kim Kardashian has made a significant impact on the red carpet with her avant-garde Balenciaga ensembles, often pushing the boundaries of fashion and sparking widespread discussion. At the 2021 Met Gala, themed 'In America: A Lexicon of Fashion', KK wore a custom Balenciaga haute couture outfit in black that covered her from head to toe, including a face mask, gloves and a long train. The ensemble obscured her identity entirely, emphasizing her silhouette and challenging traditional notions of celebrity and fashion. At the 2022 LACMA Art + Film Gala, Kardashian appeared in a sleek, full-length black Balenciaga gown with a high neckline and long sleeves. The minimalist design highlighted her platinum blonde hair and emphasized the brand's signature silhouette. Embracing the Barbiecore trend, Kardashian attended the 2022 Baby2Baby Gala in a custom Balenciaga ensemble featuring a baby pink asymmetrical gown with bow details and a dramatic train. She completed the look with matching accessories and platinum hair, showcasing a playful side of Balenciaga's design. For the 2025 Vanity Fair Oscar Party, Kardashian donned a custom Balenciaga haute couture gown made from Tyvek, a material typically used in construction and medical packaging. The dress featured a voluminous skirt gathered at the front and a form-fitting back, creating a dramatic silhouette. The unconventional fabric choice drew mixed reactions, with some comparing it to household items like bedsheets or toilet paper. However, the publicity the ensemble garnered was priceless.

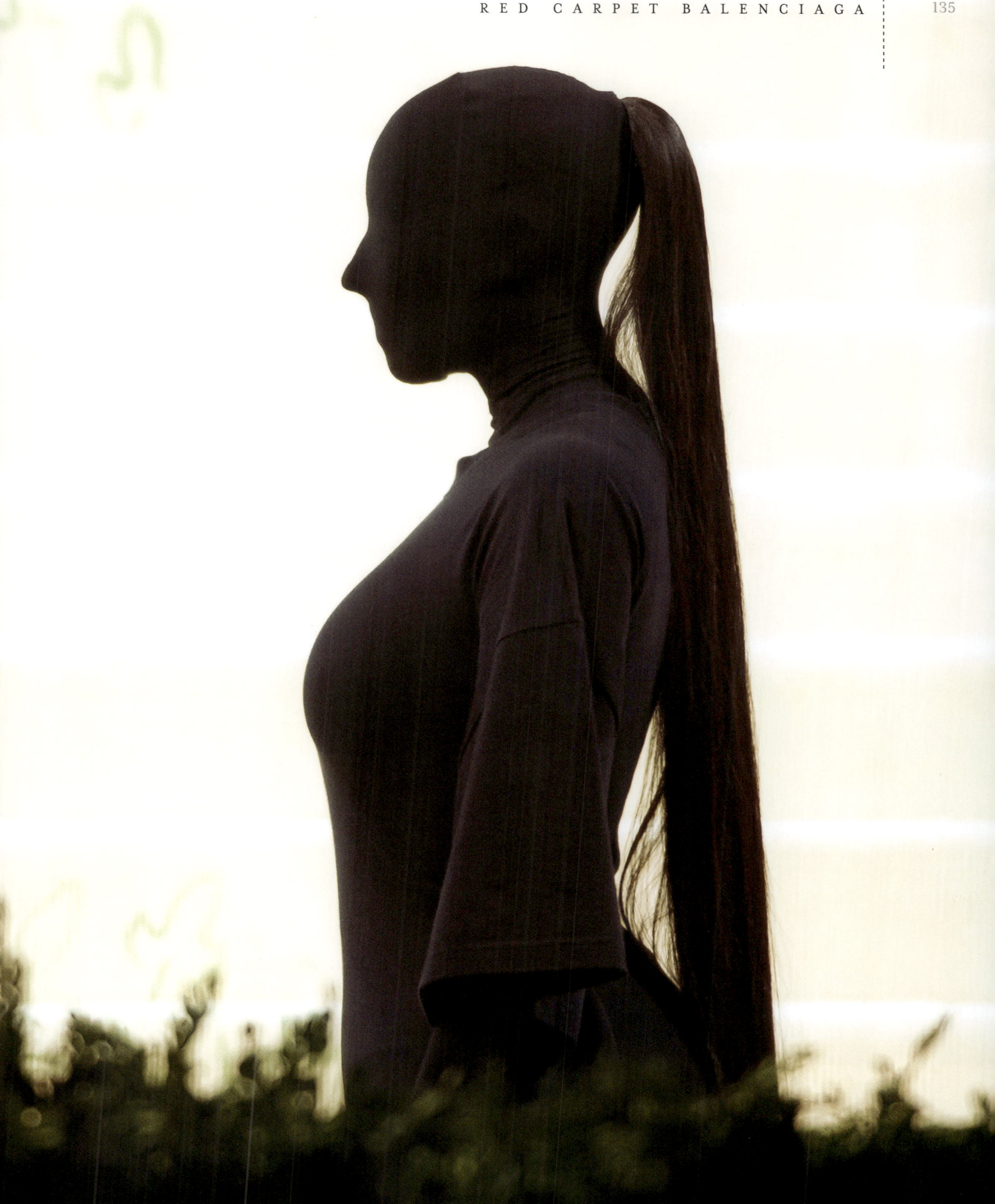

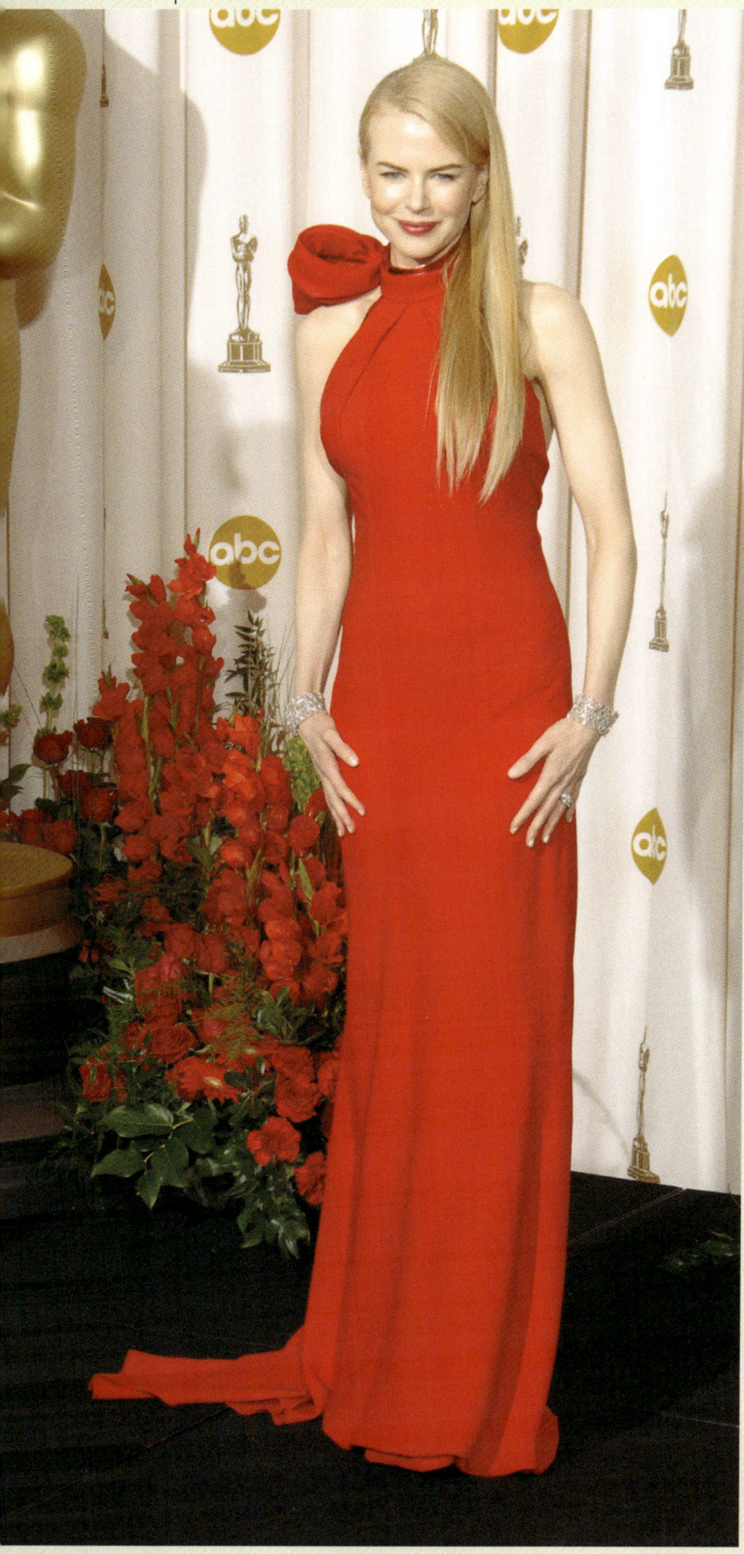

ABOVE: Nicole Kidman wows in a red Balenciaga gown at the 2007 Oscars
OPP PAGE: Isabelle Huppert at the 2024 'The Garden of Time' Met Gala in a Balenciaga silk satin dress

NICOLE KIDMAN

Balenciaga is regularly La Kidman's go-to designer for the red carpet appearances. At the 2007 Oscars, she wore a red Balenciaga gown complete with dramatic bow by Nicolas Ghesquière which is now regarded as iconic. She wore a custom Balenciaga Haute Couture gown to the 2022 Oscars afterparty – a dramatic, structured silver gown with a sweeping train and hyper-sculptural silhouette, evoking Old Hollywood glamour filtered through Demna's futuristic vision. At the 2024 GQ Men of the Year Awards in London, Kidman appeared in a striking red Balenciaga gown with long sleeves and a high neckline, embodying the brand's bold aesthetic. For the 82nd Annual Golden Globe Awards in January 2025 Kidman donned a sparkly silver Balenciaga gown with a flowy, one-shoulder neckline and a sleek, figure-skimming skirt. At the Met Gala 2025 themed 'Superfine: Tailoring Black Style', Kidman wore a custom Balenciaga Couture gown inspired by a 1952 Cristóbal Balenciaga design. The sculptural organza dress featured a Basque-style bodice, scalloped picot detailing, silk bow belts and an exaggerated silhouette supported by layers of tulle and petticoats. In May 2025, Nicole made a striking return to Cannes after eight years, attending the Kering Women in Motion Talk in a black leather corset-style jacket paired with baggy jeans from Balenciaga's Fall 2025 collection. Later on at the festival, she graced the Women in Motion Awards in a custom red guipure lace gown from Balenciaga's 52nd Couture collection,

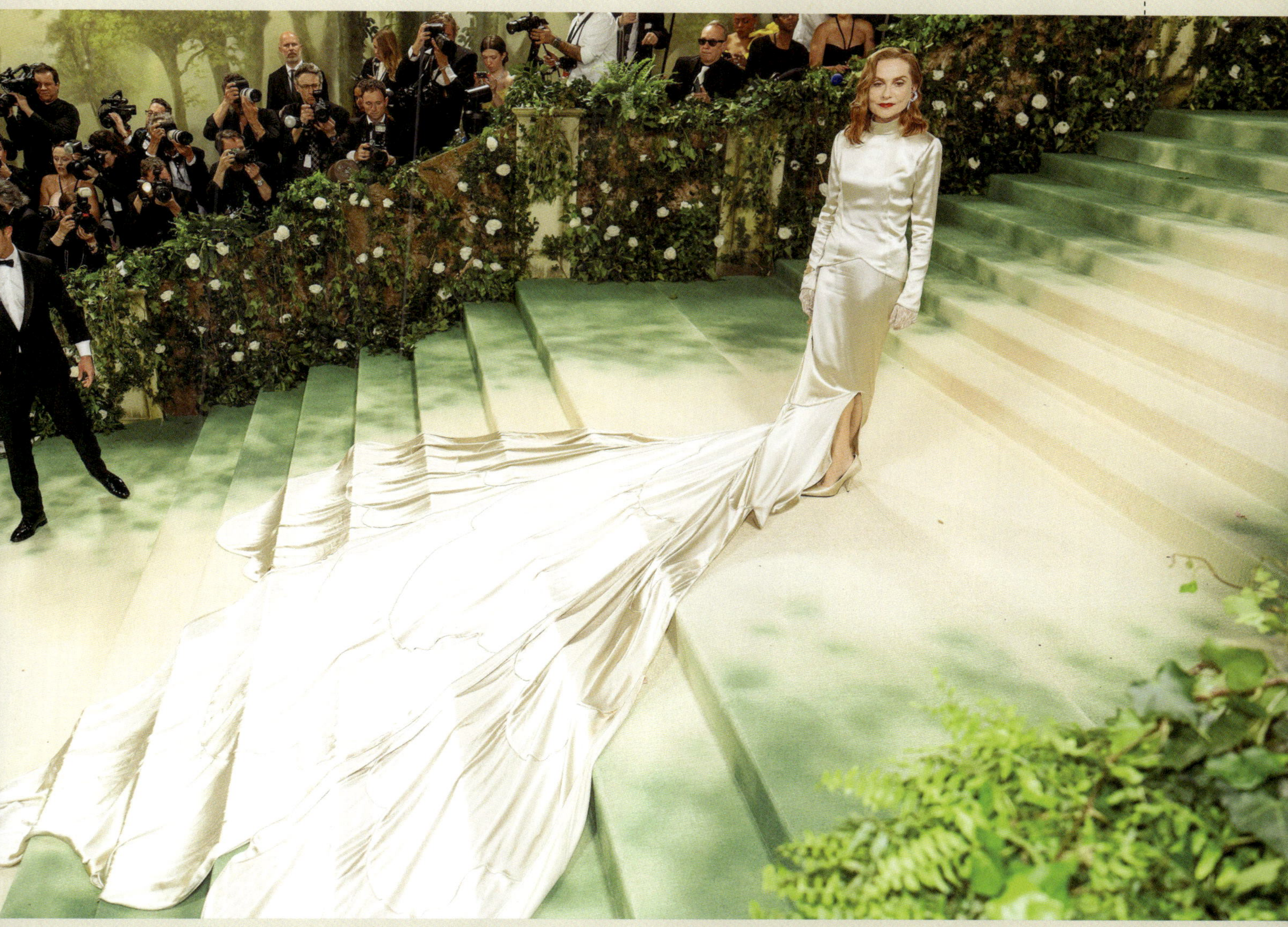

complemented by matching red spandex Knife pumps. Back in 2006, Nicole chose Balenciaga for the ultimate red carpet – her wedding to Keith Urban. Designed by Nicolas Ghesquière for Balenciaga in 2006, the garment is celebrated as one of the most iconic bridal gowns of the 21st century. Crafted from ivory silk chiffon and lace, the dress features a romantic silhouette with an empire waistline, delicate ruffles and a sweetheart neckline.

ISABELLE HUPPERT

French actress Isabelle Huppert has consistently showcased Balenciaga's avant-garde designs on the RC, blending classic elegance with contemporary edge. At the 2024 'The Garden of Time' Met Gala, Huppert wore a custom Balenciaga gown inspired by a 1930s Callot Sœurs wedding dress, originally crafted by her great-great-grandmothers. The champagne-coloured

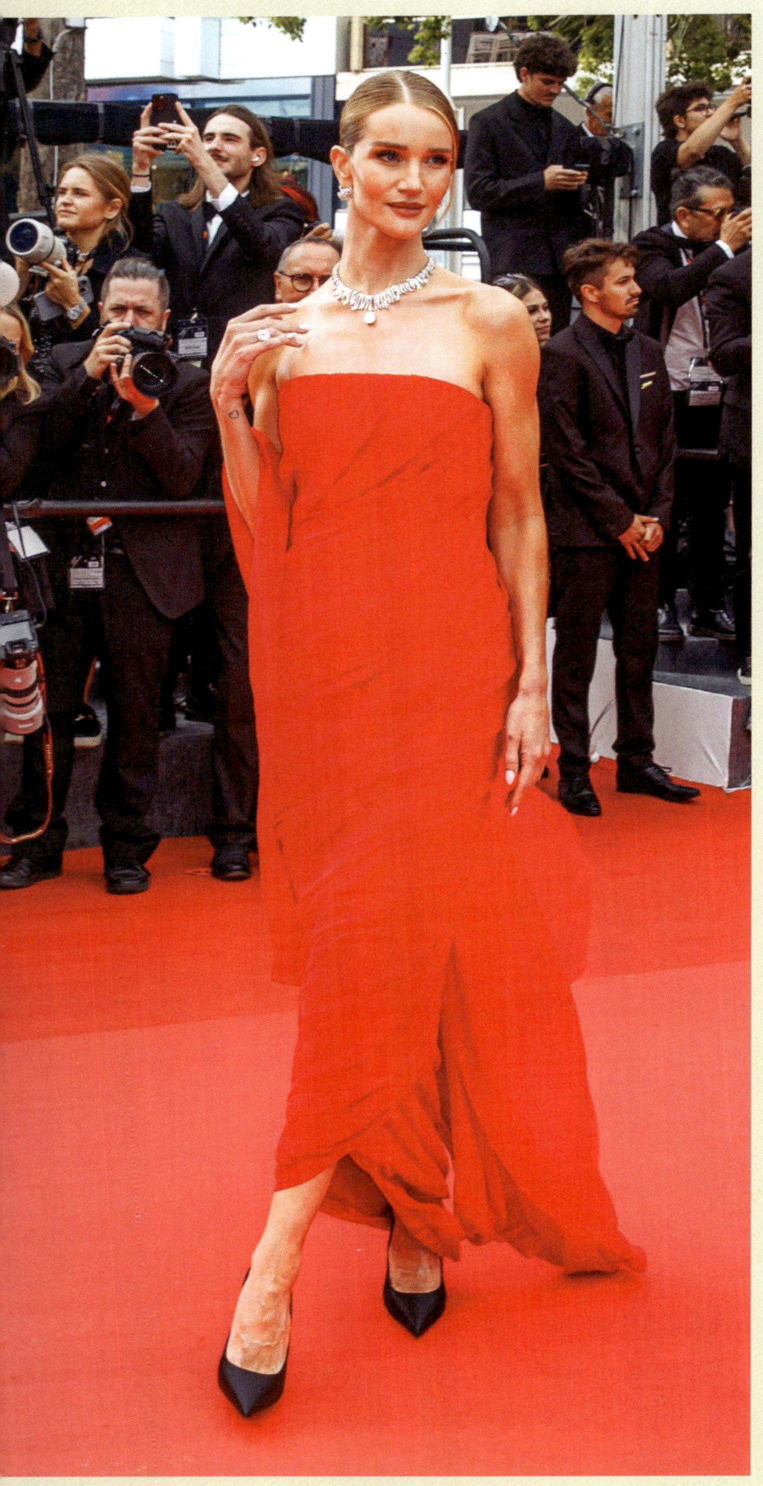

silk satin dress featured a dramatic four-metre-long train and intricate lace details, celebrating French haute couture heritage. At the closing ceremony of the 2024 Venice Film Festival, Huppert donned a minimalist yet striking white Balenciaga Pre-Fall 2024 gown. The design, evoking religious allusions, featured a structured silhouette that drew comparisons to a modern-day papal gown. Earlier at the festival, she wore a dark, textured Balenciaga gown with intricate animal print and a high neckline, exuding refined elegance with the long sleeves and flowing silhouette adding a timeless quality to the ensemble. At the 2024 Cannes Film Festival, Huppert turned heads in a custom white furry Balenciaga wrap dress, featuring a belted waist and a thigh-high slit. A year later, again in Cannes, she wore two distinct Balenciaga looks - a grungy denim ensemble for the photocall and a backward-worn denim jacket with a matching maxi skirt for the premiere. She accessorized with an oversized emerald brooch, showcasing her flair for making bold fashion statements.

Balenciaga was a runaway 'Red Carpet' success at Cannes 2025 with many high-profile personalities, in addition to Kidman and Huppert, wearing the brand.

ROSIE HUNTINGTON-WHITELEY

Breaking away from her usual neutral palette, model Rosie Huntington-Whiteley dazzled in a red chiffon strapless Balenciaga gown with asymmetrical ruching at the 'Nouvelle Vague' premiere.

NAOMI ACKIE

Actress Naomi Ackie opted for a black Balenciaga Fall 2024 Haute Couture gown at the 'Nouvelle Vague' premiere, a silhouette previously seen on Lindsay Lohan at the 2025 Vanity Fair Oscar Party.

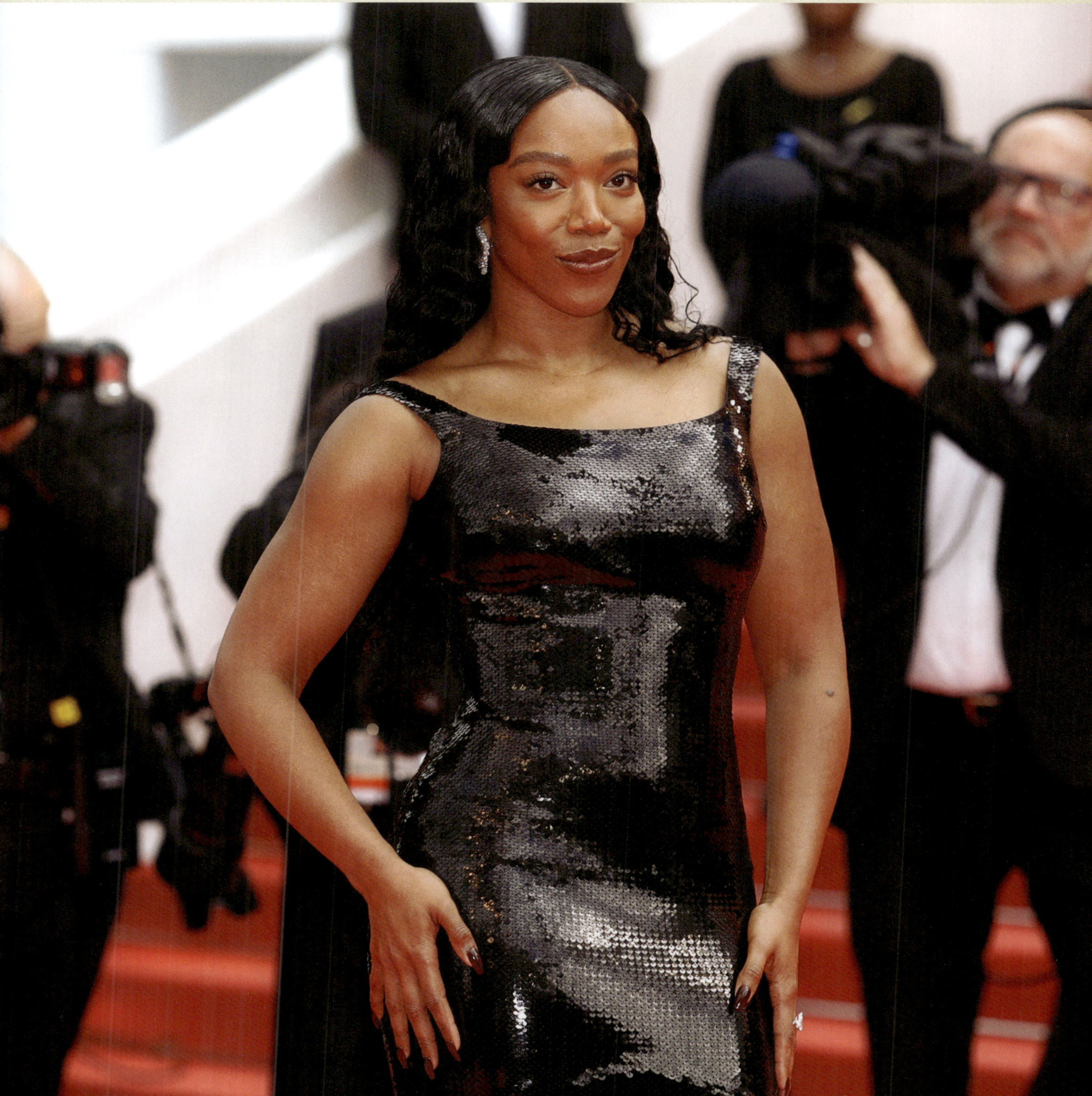

CHARLOTTE LE BON

Staying true to her minimalist style, Charlotte Le Bon wore a black beaded fringe-embroidered mini dress from Balenciaga's Fall 2022 Haute Couture collection at 'The Phoenician Scheme' premiere.

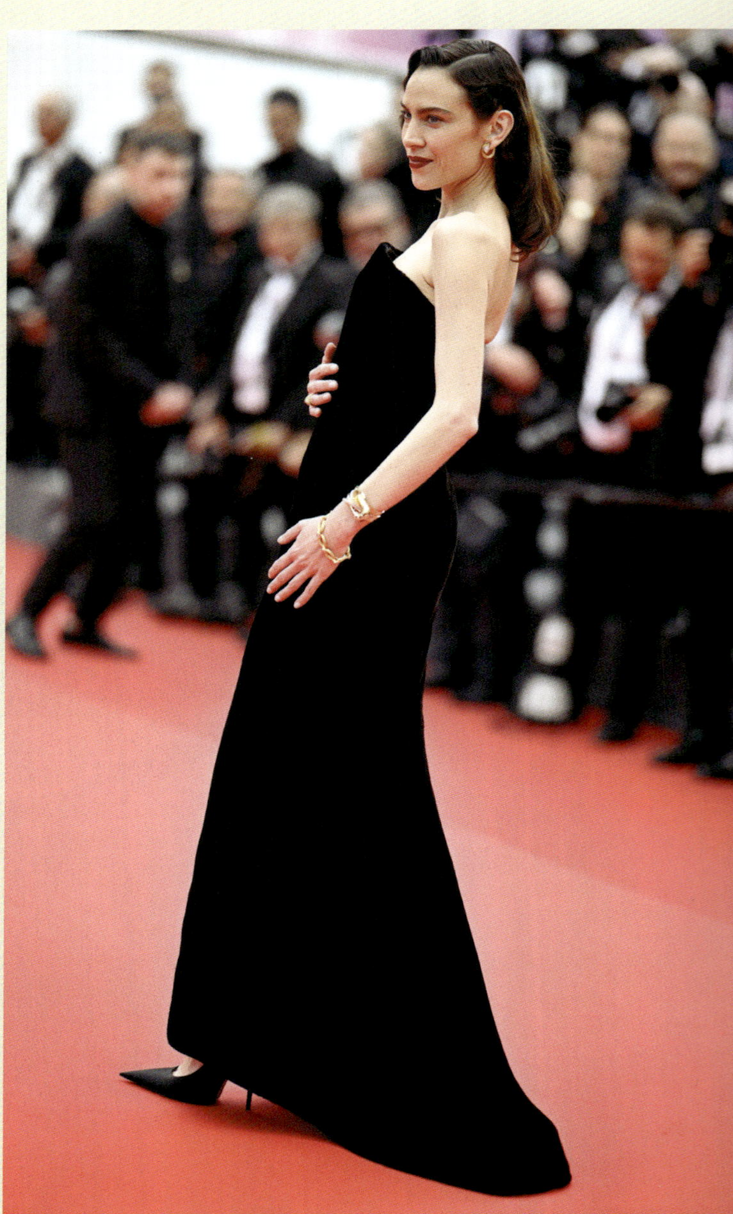

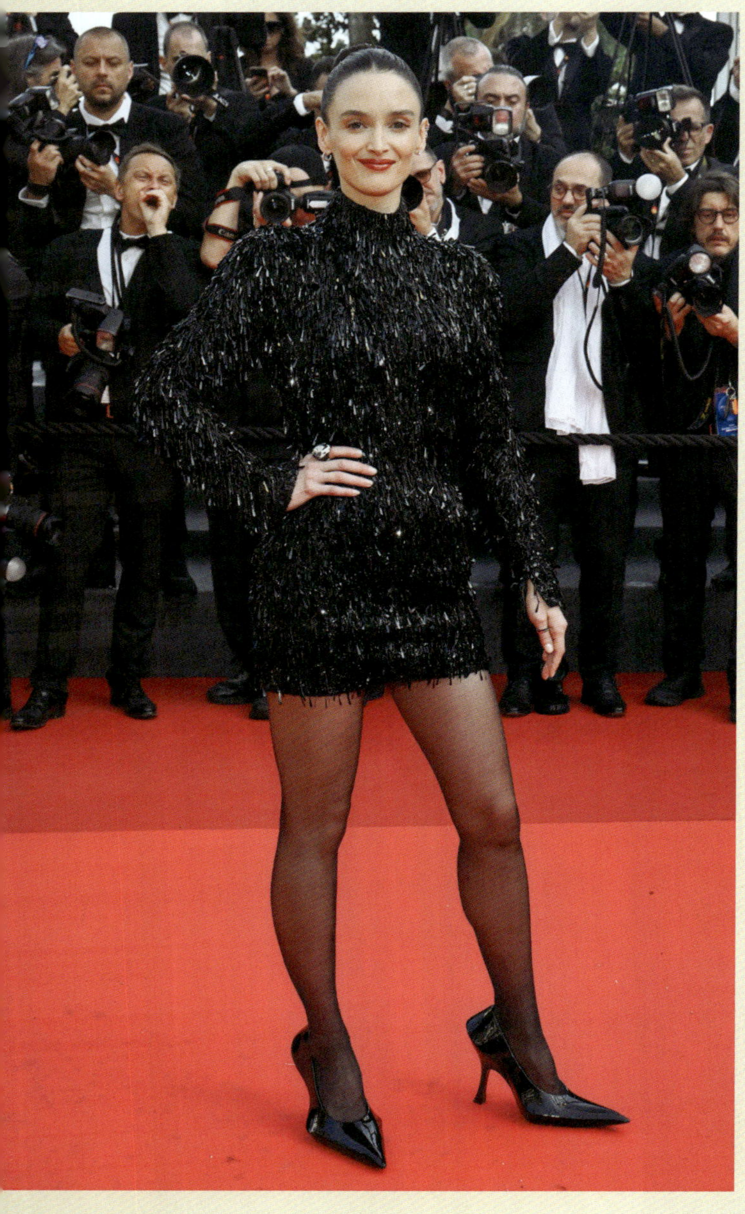

ALEXA CHUNG

Fashionista Alexa embraced a statuesque look in a strapless black Balenciaga gown with dramatic sculpted hips at the 'Nouvelle Vague' premiere.

MILENA SMIT

The Spanish actress wore a sculptural black gown from Balenciaga's Fall 2023 Haute Couture collection at the 'Highest 2 Lowest' premiere. The gown featured a dramatic off-the-shoulder neckline, reminiscent of a regal coat dress, and showcased Smit's signature affinity for bold, architectural silhouettes.

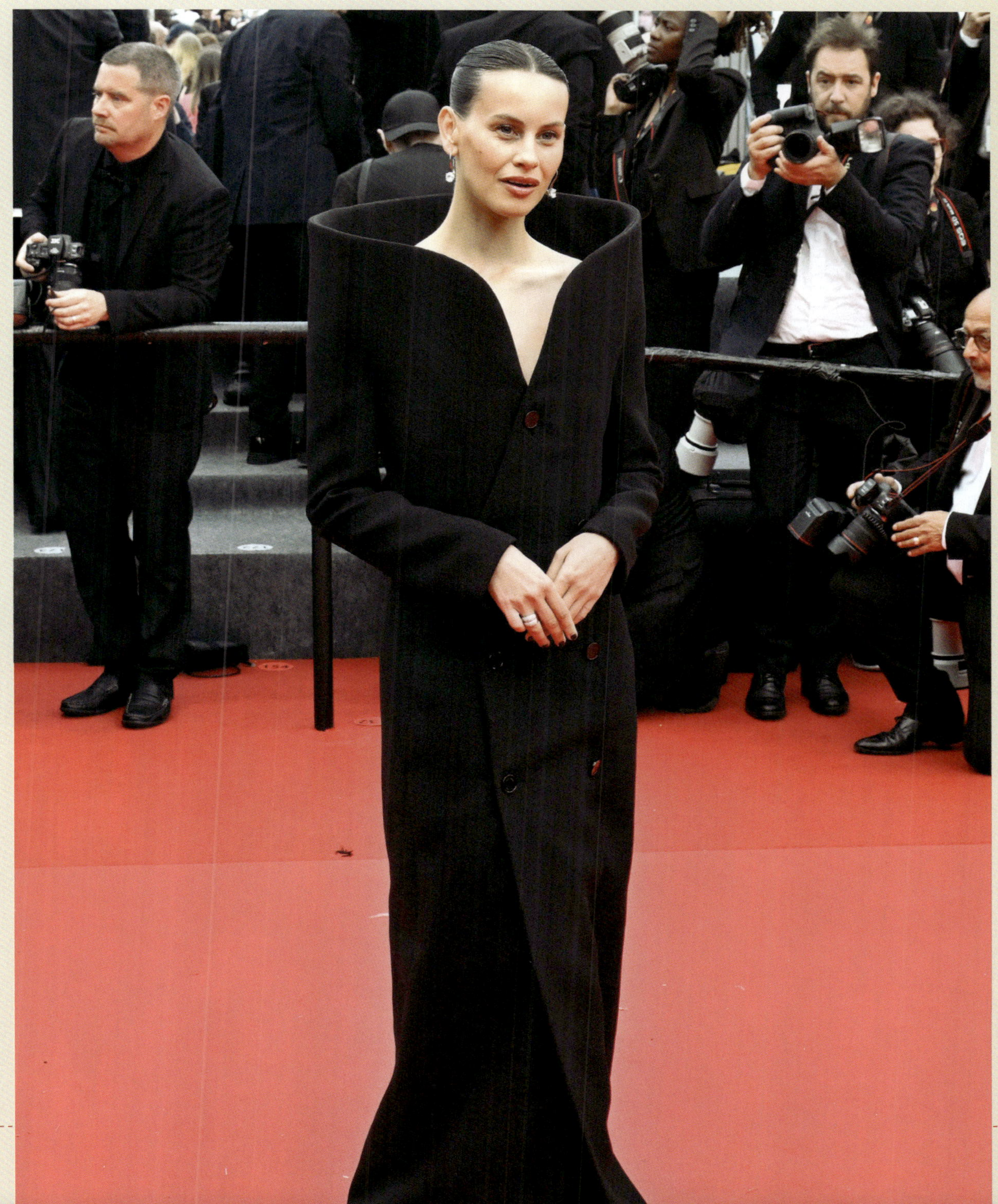

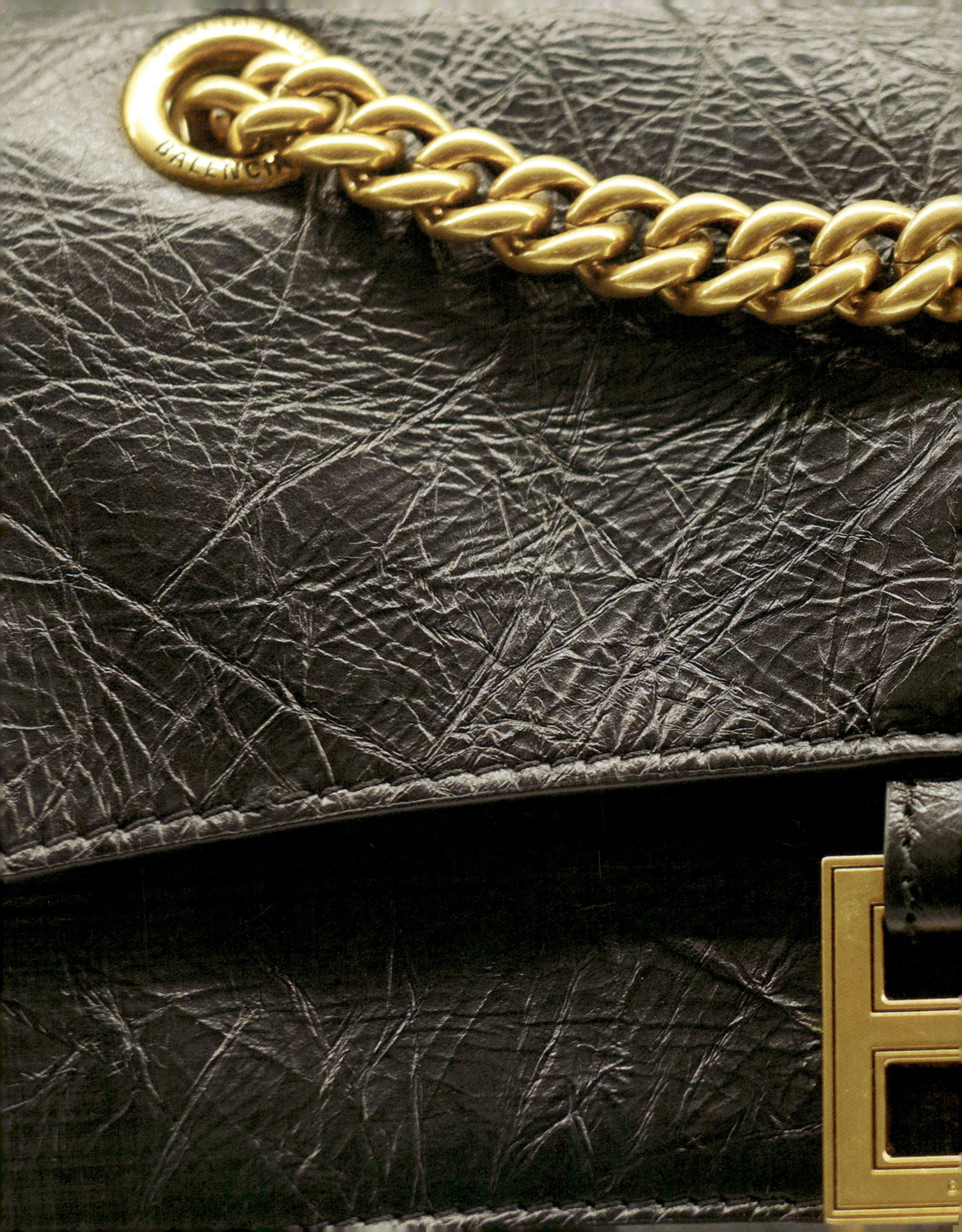